Excel

Revise in a Month

Year 2
NAPLAN*-style Tests

PASCAL
PRESS

* This is not an officially endorsed publication of the NAPLAN program and is produced by Pascal Press independently of Australian governments.

Lyn Baker & Tanya Dalgleish

© 2013 Lyn Baker, Tanya Dalgleish and Pascal Press
Reprinted 2015
Conventions of Language questions updated 2016
Reprinted 2019

Revised in 2020 for the NAPLAN Online tests

Reprinted 2021, 2022, 2023, 2024

ISBN 978 1 74125 419 8

Pascal Press
PO Box 250
Glebe NSW 2037
(02) 9198 1748
www.pascalpress.com.au

Publisher: Vivienne Joannou
Project editor: Rosemary Peers
Edited by Rosemary Peers
Answers checked by Peter Little and Dale Little
Cover and page design by DiZign Pty Ltd
Typeset by DiZign Pty Ltd and Grizzly Graphics (Leanne Richters)
Printed by Vivar Printing/Green Giant Press

Disclaimer
While information in this book is correct at the time of going to press, students should check the official NAPLAN website and ask their teachers about the exact requirements or content of the tests for which they are sitting, as this may change from year to year.

All efforts have been made to obtain permission for the copyright material reproduced in this book. In the event of any oversight, the publisher welcomes any information that will enable rectification of any reference or credit in subsequent editions.

The publisher thanks the Royal Australian Mint for granting permission to use Australian currency coin designs in this book.

Notice of liability
The information contained in this book is distributed without warranty. While precautions have been taken in the preparation of this material, neither the authors nor Pascal Press shall have any liability to any person or entity with respect to any liability, loss or damage caused or alleged to be caused directly or indirectly by the instructions and content contained in the book.

Contents

NAPLAN and NAPLAN Online

WHAT IS NAPLAN?

- NAPLAN stands for National Assessment Program—Literacy and Numeracy.
- It is conducted every year in March and the tests are taken by students in Years 3, 5, 7 and 9.
- The tests cover Literacy—Reading, Writing, Conventions of Language (spelling, grammar and punctuation)—and Numeracy.

WHAT IS NAPLAN ONLINE?

Introduction

- In the past all NAPLAN tests were paper tests.
- From 2022 all students have taken the NAPLAN tests online.
- This means students complete the NAPLAN tests on a computer or tablet.

Tailored test design

- With NAPLAN paper tests, all students in each year level took exactly the same tests.
- In the NAPLAN Online tests this isn't the case; instead, every student takes a tailor-made test based on their ability.
- Please visit the official ACARA site for a detailed explanation of the tailored test process used in NAPLAN Online and also for general information about the tests: https://nap.edu.au/online-assessment.
- These tailor-made tests mean broadly, therefore, that a student who is at a standard level of achievement takes a test mostly comprised of questions of a standard level; a student who is at an intermediate level of achievement takes a test mostly comprised of questions of an intermediate level; and a student who is at an advanced level of achievement takes a test mostly comprised of questions of an advanced level.

Different question types

- Because of the digital format, NAPLAN Online contains more question types than in the paper tests. In the paper tests there are only multiple-choice and short-answer question types. In NAPLAN Online, however, there are also other question types. For example, students might be asked to drag text across a screen, measure a figure with an online ruler or listen to an audio recording of a sentence and then spell a word they hear.
- Please refer to the next page to see some examples of these additional question types that are found in NAPLAN Online and how they compare to questions in this book. As you will see, the content tested is exactly the same but the questions are presented differently.

NAPLAN Online question types

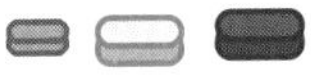

Additional NAPLAN Online question types	Equivalent questions in this book
Drag and drop Drag the correct word to fill the space. eating ate eaten eat Yuki does not _____ peanuts.	Choose the correct word to complete this sentence. Yuki does not ▨▨▨▨ peanuts. A eating B ate C eaten D eat
Text entry Be _____ with the kitten. Click on the play button to listen to the missing word. ❚❚ ◀)) ━━━━●━━━━ 0.08 / 0.09 Type the correct spelling of the word in the box.	Please ask your parent or teacher to read to you the spelling words on page 213. Write the correct spelling of each word in the box. <table><tr><td>Word</td><td>Example</td></tr><tr><td>1. careful</td><td>Be careful with the kitten.</td></tr></table>
Identifying/sorting Place the objects in order from lowest mass to highest mass. Put the lowest mass at the top.	 Which shows the objects in order from lowest mass to highest mass? A ▢ ▬ ▬ B ▬ ▬ ▢ C ▬ ▢ ▬ D ▬ ▢ ▬
Online ruler How long is this pencil in the picture below? Use the online ruler to measure the length of the pencil. ☐ 10 cm ☐ 11 cm ☐ 12 cm ☐ 13 cm	 Using this ruler, how long is this pencil? _____ cm

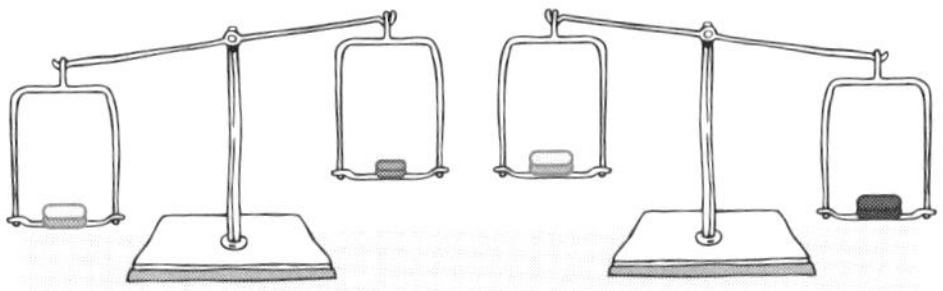

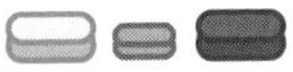

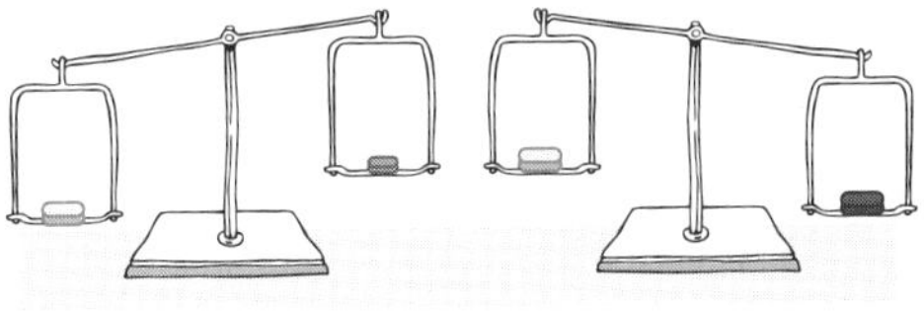

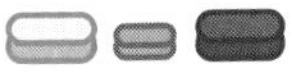

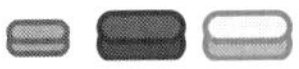

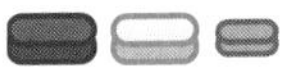

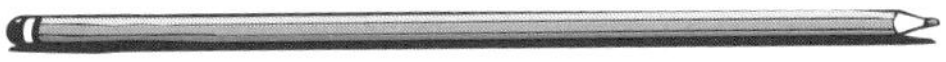

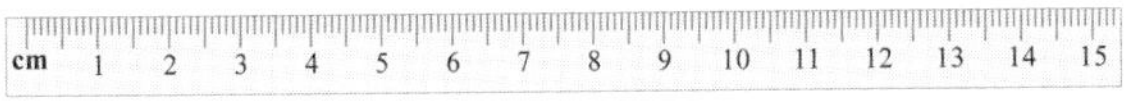

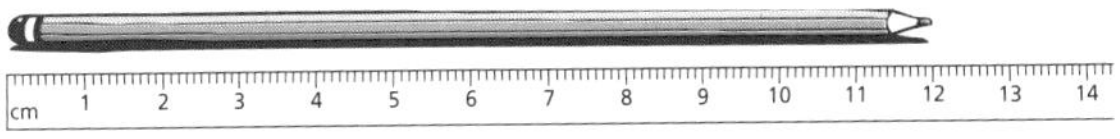

Maximise your results in NAPLAN Online

STEP 1: USE THIS BOOK

How *Excel* has updated this book to help you revise

Tailored test design

- We can't replicate the digital experience in book form and offer you tailored tests, but with this series we do provide Intermediate and Advanced NAPLAN Online–style Literacy and Numeracy tests
- This means that a student using these tests will be able to prepare with confidence for tests at different ability levels.
- This makes it excellent preparation for the tailored NAPLAN Online Literacy and Numeracy tests.

Remember the advantages of revising in book form

There are many benefits to a child revising using books for the online test:

- One of the most important benefits is that writing on paper will help your child retain information. It can be a very effective way to memorise. High-quality educational research shows that using a keyboard is not as good as note-taking for learning.
- Students will be able to prepare thoroughly for topic revision using books and then practise computer skills easily. They will only succeed with sound knowledge of topics; this requires study and focus. Students will not succeed in tests simply because they know how to answer questions digitally.
- Also, some students find it easier to concentrate when reading a page in a book than when reading on a screen.
- Furthermore it can be more convenient to use a book, especially when a child doesn't have ready access to a digital device.
- You can be confident that *Excel* books will help students acquire the topic knowledge they need, as we have over 30 years experience in helping students prepare for tests. All our writers are experienced educators.

STEP 2: PRACTISE ON *Excel Test Zone*

How *Excel Test Zone* can help you practise online

We recommend you go to www.exceltestzone.com.au and register for practice in NAPLAN Online–style tests once you have completed this book. The reasons include:

- for optimal performance in the NAPLAN Online tests we recommend students gain practice at completing online tests as well as completing revision in book form
- students should practise answering questions on a digital device to become confident with this process
- students will be able to practise tailored tests like those in NAPLAN Online, as well as other types of tests
- students will also be able to gain valuable practice in onscreen skills such as dragging and dropping answers, using an online ruler to measure figures and using an online protractor to measure angles.

Remember that *Excel Test Zone* has been helping students prepare for NAPLAN since 2009; in fact we had NAPLAN online questions even before NAPLAN tests went online!

We also have updated our website along with our book range to ensure your preparation for NAPLAN Online is 100% up to date.

About the NAPLAN tests and this book

ABOUT THE TESTS

Test results

- The test results are used by teachers as a diagnostic tool. The results provide students, parents and teachers with information that can be used to improve student learning.

- The student report provides information about what students know and can do in the areas of Reading, Writing, Conventions of Language (spelling, grammar and punctuation) and the various strands of Numeracy. It also provides information on how each student has performed in relation to other students in their year group and against the national average and the national minimum standard.

- NAPLAN tests are not aptitude or intelligence tests. They focus on what has been achieved, especially on the knowledge and skills taught in the syllabus. These are often called KLAs (key learning areas).

- Official tests are trialled on selected groups to test the reliability of the questions. The questions in this book are representative of questions that you can expect to find in an official test. They have been prepared by professionals who have an understanding of teaching and of testing procedures.

- The NAPLAN results present an objective view of student performance and form the basis from which schools can make informed educational decisions about further school learning programs.

- Because NAPLAN tests are national tests they provide authorities with sufficient information to track student educational development from primary to high school, or when transferring from one Australian school to another.

TYPES OF TESTS

- There are four different types of tests in Year 3 NAPLAN Online.
  1 The Numeracy test (45 minutes)
  2 The Conventions of Language test (45 minutes)
  3 The Reading test (45 minutes)
  4 The Writing test (40 minutes)
  Tests 2–4 form the Literacy component of the test.
  Note: The Writing test is a paper test for Year 3.

- The Writing test is held first, followed by the Reading test, the Conventions of Language test and finally the Numeracy test.

USING THIS BOOK

- This book is designed to be used over four weeks, with weekly exercises in various aspects of literacy and numeracy.

- Each session gives students an opportunity to Test their Skills, revise Key Points and practise a Real Test on a specific aspect of the curriculum.

- In a month the student will have covered much of the material that could be included in a NAPLAN Online test.

- Finally there are two Sample Test Papers based on the content used in past Year 3 NAPLAN test papers.

- Because NAPLAN tests are timed tests, times have been suggested for completing the various units in this book.

> Please note there are no Year 2 NAPLAN tests. This book will help you prepare for the Year 3 NAPLAN tests a year early.

Let's start to revise!

Week 1

This is what we cover this week:

Day 1   **Number and Algebra:**   ◎ Numbers and place value

Day 2   **Number and Algebra:**   ◎ Patterns and number sentences

Day 3   **Spelling:**   ◎ Hard and soft *c* and *g*, and consonant digraphs

   Grammar and Punctuation: ◎ Nouns and noun groups

Day 4   **Reading:**   ◎ Understanding reports

Day 5   **Writing:**   ◎ Descriptions

Test Your Skills 1

NUMBER AND ALGEBRA
Numbers and place value

20 MIN

---

1 Write down the next five numbers.

854, 855, 856, ☐ , ☐ ,

☐ , ☐ , ☐

☐ = 100   ☐ = 10   ☐ = 1

Write the numbers.

2 ☐

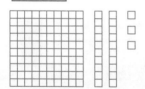

3 ☐

4 ☐

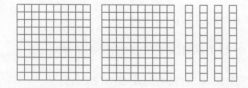

5 ☐

Write the numbers.

6 4 tens and 5 ones ☐

7 7 hundreds, 5 tens and 2 ones ☐

8 8 hundreds, 1 ten and 6 ones ☐

9 2 hundreds, 0 tens and 5 ones ☐

10 9 hundreds, 8 tens and 0 ones ☐

Fill in the blanks.

11 628 = 6 ☐ ,

2 ☐ and 8 ☐

12 573 = ☐ hundreds, ☐ tens and ☐ ones

13 402 = ☐ hundreds, ☐ tens and ☐ ones

14 360 = ☐ hundreds, ☐ tens and ☐ ones

Write the numbers.

15 forty-seven ☐

16 one hundred and sixty-four ☐

17 two hundred and seventeen ☐

18 eight hundred and seventy ☐

19 nine hundred and nine ☐

20 200 + 60 + 5 ☐

21 700 + 40 + 8 ☐

22 600 + 7 ☐

Excel Revise in a Month Year 2 NAPLAN*-style Tests

Test Your Skills 2

NUMBER AND ALGEBRA
Numbers and place value

20 MIN

Write in words.

1 76

2 128

3 315

4 490

Put these numbers in order from lowest to highest.

5 83, 87, 72, 79

6 127, 172, 165, 158, 136

7 504, 54, 450, 405

Fill in the three missing numbers on each number line.

8

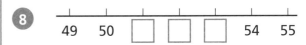

49   50   ☐   ☐   ☐   54   55

9

70   ☐   72   ☐   74   ☐   76

10

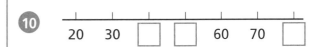

20   30   ☐   ☐   60   70   ☐

Fill in the missing numbers.

11 8 + ☐ = 10

12 32 = 2 + ☐

13 8 + 32 = 10 + ☐ = ☐

14 19 + 17 = 20 + ☐ = ☐

15 78 + 16 = 80 + ☐ = ☐

16 22 − 9 = ☐ − 10 = ☐

17 82 − 47 = ☐ − 50 = ☐

① **Learn to count from 1 to at least 1000.** Practise starting at any number less than 1000 and keep counting.

Example: 854, 855, 856, 857, 858, 859, 860, 861, and so on.

② **Numbers are made up of different digits**. 123 is a three-digit number. Its three digits are 1, 2 and 3. In this case 1 means hundreds, 2 means tens and 3 means ones. Other three-digit numbers using the same digits are 132, 213, 231, 312 and 321.

③ **Numbers can be represented by blocks.**
★ One block represents the number 1.

□ = 1

★ If you place ten of those blocks together you have a line of 10.

= 10

★ If you place ten of those lines together you have a square of 100.

= 100

★ So numbers up to 1000 can be represented by these diagrams.

Example:

This has 3 tens and 5 ones.
The number represented is **35**.

Example:

This has 1 hundred, 2 tens and 3 ones. It is the number **123**.

Example:

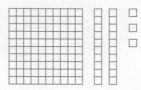

This has 2 hundreds, 4 tens and 0 ones. It is the number **240**.

Example:

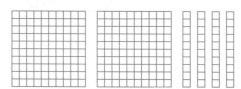

This has 3 hundreds, 0 tens and 4 ones. It is the number **304**.

④ **If you know how many hundreds, tens and ones are in a number you can write the number.**

Example:
■ 4 tens and 5 ones is 45.
■ 7 hundreds, 5 tens and 2 ones is 752.
■ 8 hundreds, 1 ten and 6 ones is 816.

⑤ **If there is a zero in a particular position, you must write 0 in the column for that position.** If the 0 is left out you would have a different number altogether.

Example:
■ 2 hundreds, 0 tens and 5 ones is 205.
■ 9 hundreds, 8 tens and 0 ones is 980.

Key Points

6 **When a number is written, the digits must be in the correct order or place value.** The last number on the right (if there is no decimal point) represents ones (or units). The second digit from the right represents tens and the third digit from the right represents hundreds.

Example: hundreds   tens   ones

628

628 = 6 **hundreds**, 2 **tens** and 8 **ones**.
573 = 5 hundreds, 7 tens and 3 ones
402 = 4 hundreds, 0 tens and 2 ones
360 = 3 hundreds, 6 tens and 0 ones

7 **Numbers written in words must be able to be written with numbers.**

Example:

- Forty-seven means 4 tens and 7 ones so forty-seven is written 47.
  Notice the spelling of 40. Although four has the letter *u* in it, forty does not.
- One hundred and sixty-four is 1 hundred, 6 tens and 4 ones or 164.

8 **Remember that numbers between 10 and 20 have names that use a different pattern to other numbers:**
11 eleven; 12 twelve; 13 thirteen; 14 fourteen; 15 fifteen; 16 sixteen 17 seventeen; 18 eighteen; 19 nineteen.

Example:

- Seventeen is one ten and 7 ones so two hundred and seventeen is 217.
- Eight hundred and seventy is 8 hundreds, 7 tens and no ones or 870.
- Nine hundred and nine is 9 hundreds, no tens and 9 ones or 909.

9 **When writing numbers in words, say the number to yourself.**

Example:

- 76 is seventy-six.
- 128 is one hundred and twenty-eight.
- 315 is three hundred and fifteen.
- 490 is four hundred and ninety.

10 **Numbers might also be broken into their separate parts and written as a sum.**

Example:

- 200 + 60 + 5 is 2 hundreds, 6 tens and 5 ones so 200 + 60 + 5 = 265.
- 700 + 40 + 8 = 748
- 600 + 7 = 607

11 **When arranging numbers in order, compare digits with the same place value.** Consider any thousands first, then hundreds, then tens and then ones.

Example:

- Look at the numbers 83, 87, 72 and 79.
- To write these numbers in order from lowest to highest, first look to see if they have the same number of digits.
- All these numbers have just two digits.
- Two have first digit 8 and two have first digit 7.
- Because 7 is less than 8, the two numbers that begin with 7 are both smaller than the two numbers that begin with 8.
- Now, considering 72 and 79, look at the second digits, 2 and 9.
- Because 2 is less than 9 you know that 72 is less than 79. Because 3 is less than 7 you know that 83 is less than 87.
- So, in order, the numbers are 72, 79, 83, 87.

Example: 127, 172, 165, 158, 136

All of these numbers have three digits, but the first digit is the same for all of them.

■ Next look at the second digits, 2, 7, 6, 5 and 3. When you put those in order you have 2, 3, 5, 6 and 7.

■ So, in order, the numbers are 127, 136, 158, 165 and 172.

Example: 504, 54, 450, 405

One of these numbers only has two digits so it is the smallest number.

■ Of the three three-digit numbers, two have first digit 4 and one has first digit 5. So 504 is the largest number.

■ Of the two three-digit numbers that begin with 4, look at the second digits. 0 is less than 5 so 405 is less than 450.

In order the numbers are 54, 405, 450 and 504.

12 **On a number line, numbers are evenly spaced along the line.** The numbers might go up by ones, twos, tens or some other number.

| 49 | 50 | 51 | 52 | 53 | 54 | 55 |

| 70 | 71 | 72 | 73 | 74 | 75 | 76 |

| 20 | 30 | 40 | 50 | 60 | 70 | 80 |

13 **Numbers can be partitioned into different parts to make adding and subtracting easier.**

Example: $8 + 2 = 10$
and $32 = 2 + 30$
So, $8 + 32 = 8 + 2 + 30$
$ = 10 + 30$
$ = 40$

Example: $19 + 1 = 20$
and $17 = 1 + 16$
So $19 + 17 = 19 + 1 + 16$
$ = 20 + 16$
$ = 36$

Example: $78 + 16 = 78 + 2 + 14$
$ = 80 + 14$
$ = 94$

Example: $9 + 1 = 10$
and $22 + 1 = 23$
So $22 - 9 = 23 - 10$
$ = 13$

Example: $47 + 3 = 50$
and $82 + 3 = 85$
So $82 - 47 = 85 - 50$
$ = 35$

Real Test

NUMBER AND ALGEBRA
Numbers and place value

20 MIN

For some of the questions you will need to write the answer in the box (or boxes). For other questions you need to circle the correct answer.

1 Write five hundred and ninety-four as a number.

2 Which shows the number 56?

A   B   C   D

3 Which is the number 408?
A four hundred and eighty   B four hundred and eight
C forty-eight   D eight hundred and four

4

```
  |  |  |  |  |  |  |  |  |  |  |  |  |  |
 50       55       60
```

What number is the arrow pointing to on the number line?

5 Which equals 831?
A 8 + 3 + 1   B 100 + 30 + 8   C 800 + 3 + 10   D 800 + 30 + 1

6 Which numbers are in order from lowest to highest?
A 219, 135, 372, 348   B 135, 219, 372, 348   C 135, 219, 348, 372   D 135, 372, 348, 219

7 400 + 50 + 7 =
A 400 507   B 40 057   C 40 507   D 457

8 Which is the same as 98 + 8?
A 100 + 6   B 100 + 7   C 100 + 8   D 100 + 10

9

How many stars are shown?

☞ Answers and explanations on page 170

Excel Revise in a Month Year 2 NAPLAN*-style Tests

10

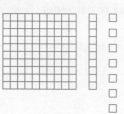

What is this number? ☐

11 Which number is closest to 30?

A 25   B 28   C 34   D 39

12 Calves on a farm are given a number when they are born.

What number will be given to the calf that is born next after this one? ☐

13 Which is **not** the same as 9 + 7?

A 10 + 8   B 6 + 10   C 7 + 9   D 8 + 8

14

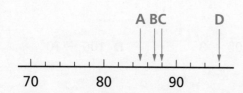

Which arrow points to 87 on the number line?

A A   B B   C C   D D

15 Write the numbers 603, 360, 630 and 306 in order from largest to smallest.

largest   smallest

☐   ☐   ☐   ☐

☞ **Answers and explanations on page 170**

Test Your Skills 1

NUMBER AND ALGEBRA
Patterns and number sentences

20 MIN

Here is a pattern of shapes.

□○△○◆□○△○◆□○△○◆□○...

1 How many different shapes are used in the pattern? ☐

2 Which shape will come next in the pattern? ☐

3 How many shapes altogether are being repeated each time? ☐

4 How many ○ are used for each △? ☐

Here is a pattern of diamond shapes made with sticks.

Shape 1   Shape 2   Shape 3

5 How many sticks are used used in Shape 1? ☐

6 How many sticks are used in Shape 2? ☐

7 How many sticks are used in Shape 3? ☐

8 How many **extra** sticks are needed each time? ☐

9 How many sticks will be needed for Shape 4? ☐

Here is a pattern made with straws.

Shape 1   Shape 2   Shape 3   Shape 4

10 How many straws are used for Shape 1? ☐

11 How many straws are used for Shape 2? ☐

12 How many straws are used for Shape 3? ☐

13 How many straws are used for Shape 4? ☐

14 How many **extra** straws are used for each shape? ☐

15 How many straws will be needed for Shape 5? ☐

16 How many straws will be needed for Shape 6? ☐

Answers: 1 4 2 △ 3 5 4 2 5 4 6 8
7 12 8 4 9 16 10 5 11 9 12 13 13 17
14 4 15 21 16 25

Excel Revise in a Month Year 2 NAPLAN*-style Tests

9

Test Your Skills 2

NUMBER AND ALGEBRA
Patterns and number sentences

20 MIN

These patterns are made by adding 4 each time. Write down the next number in each pattern.

1 2, 6, 10, 14, ☐

2 3, 7, 11, 15, 19, ☐

3 44, 48, 52, 56, ☐

These patterns are formed by taking away 3 each time. Write down the next number in each pattern.

4 32, 29, 26, 23, ☐

5 98, 95, 92, 89, ☐

A pattern is formed by adding 3 each time. The first number is 4.

6 What is the second number? ☐

7 What is the third number? ☐

8 What is the **fifth** number? ☐

What number is being added each time in these patterns?

9 5, 7, 9, 11, 13 ☐

10 2, 7, 12, 17, 22, 27 ☐

11 35, 45, 55, 65 ☐

What number is being subtracted each time in these patterns?

12 176, 174, 172, 170, 168 ☐

13 35, 31, 27, 23, 19, 15 ☐

Write down the next number in each pattern.

14 12, 14, 16, 18, ☐

15 5, 10, 15, 20, 25, ☐

16 90, 80, 70, 60, ☐

Fill in the missing number in each pattern.

17 3, 6, 9, 12, ☐ , 18, 21, 24

18 ☐ , 8, 15, 22, 29, 36

19 32, 28, ☐ , 20, 16, 12

Fill in the numbers to make these number sentences true.

20 5 + ☐ = 12

21 ☐ + 8 = 10

22 6 + ☐ = 4 + 6

23 9 − ☐ = 4

24 ☐ − 3 = 7

Key Points

NUMBER AND ALGEBRA
Patterns and number sentences

1. **Patterns can be made with shapes or objects.** In these patterns the shapes or objects are repeated, often over and over again.

   Example: In this pattern there are four different shapes: the square, circle, triangle and diamond.

   □○△○♦□○△○♦□○△○♦□○…

   - The last two shapes shown in the pattern are a square and a circle.
   - Looking at the pattern you can see that when a circle follows a square the next shape is a triangle. So the next shape in the pattern is △
   - There are five shapes in the pattern that repeat: □○△○♦
   - When you look at the five repeating shapes you can see that there is 1 square, 1 triangle and 1 diamond but there are 2 circles.
   - So there are 2 ○ for every △

2. **Sometimes there can be a pattern of shapes and also a pattern of the number of objects that make the shapes.**

   Example: In this pattern there is a pattern of shapes, a pattern of diamonds in each shape and a pattern of sticks that make each shape.

   Shape 1   Shape 2   Shape 3

   - First you can see that the number of diamonds in each shape is the same as the shape number. So there will be 4 diamonds in Shape 4 and 5 diamonds in Shape 5, and so on.

   - By counting, you can see that there are 4 sticks in Shape 1, 8 sticks in Shape 2 and 12 sticks in Shape 3.
   - There are 4 extra sticks for each shape.
   - So for Shape 4 the number of sticks needed will be 4 more than for Shape 3. $12 + 4 = 16$
   - So 16 sticks will be needed for Shape 4.

   Example: By counting, you can see that 5 straws are needed for Shape 1 in this pattern.

   Shape 1   Shape 2   Shape 3   Shape 4

   - Again by counting, you can see that 9 straws are needed for Shape 2 and 13 straws are needed for Shape 3. 17 straws are needed for Shape 4.
   - To find the number of extra straws needed for each shape you can look at the pattern formed: 5, 9, 13, 17.
   - Now $5 + 4 = 9$
     and $9 + 4 = 13$
     and $13 + 4 = 17$
     So 4 extra straws are needed for each shape.
   - You could also look at the shapes and see where the extra straws are placed each time.

   Shape 1   Shape 2   Shape 3   Shape 4

   - So you need 5 straws for the first shape and then 4 more each time.
     You can continue the pattern by adding 4 each time.
     $17 + 4 = 21$
     So 21 straws will be needed for Shape 5.
     $21 + 4 = 25$
     And 25 straws will be needed for Shape 6.

Key Points

NUMBER AND ALGEBRA
Patterns and number sentences

(continued)

3 **Patterns with numbers are often made by adding the same number over and over again.**

Example: If a pattern is made by adding 4 each time, you need to add 4 again to find the next number.

2, 6, 10, 14, ?

■ Now 14 + 4 = 18

So the next number in the pattern will be 18.

■ 3, 7, 11, 15, 19, **23** because 19 + 4 = 23

■ 44, 48, 52, 56, **60** because 56 + 4 = 60

4 **A pattern can also be made by subtracting the same number every time.**

Example: So if a pattern is made by taking away 3 each time, you need to subtract 3 again to find the next number.

■ 32, 29, 26, 23, **20** because 23 − 3 = 20

■ 98, 95, 92, 89, **86** because 89 − 3 = 86

5 **A pattern of numbers is sometimes called a sequence.**

6 **Each number in a pattern is often called a term of the pattern.**

If you know the number that is being added or subtracted each time in a pattern then you only need one number in the pattern to find the other terms.

Example: You can have a pattern where 3 is being added each time.

■ If the first number is 4 then the second number is 4 + 3 or 7.

■ If the second number is 7 then the third number is 7 + 3 or 10.

■ If the third number is 10, the fourth number is 10 + 3 or 13 and the fifth number is 13 + 3 or 16.

7 Sometimes you can just look at a pattern and see straight away what number is being added each time. But **you can always find the number that is being added each time in a pattern if you find the difference between terms.**

Example: Look at the pattern 5, 7, 9, 11, 13.

■ You might be able to see that you are counting forward by 2 each time.

■ Or you can find the differences between the terms.

7 − 5 = 2

9 − 7 = 2

11 − 9 = 2

13 − 9 = 2

■ The number being added each time is 2.

Example: For 2, 7, 12, 17, 22, 27

7 − 2 = 5

12 − 7 = 5

17 − 12 = 5

22 − 17 = 5

27 − 22 = 5

The number being added each time is 5.

8 If you find the difference between the first two terms in a sequence you can then **check whether that number is the number being added each time.**

Example: 35, 45, 55, 65

45 − 35 = 10

■ So check if adding 10 each time will give the pattern.

45 + 10 = 55

55 + 10 = 65

■ So you have the correct pattern. The number being added each time is 10.

Key Points

NUMBER AND ALGEBRA
Patterns and number sentences

(continued)

9 If the numbers go down instead of up in a pattern then **a number might be being subtracted each time rather than added**.

Example: 176, 174, 172, 170, 168

$176 - 174 = 2$
$174 - 172 = 2$
$172 - 170 = 2$
$170 - 168 = 2$

The number being subtracted each time is 2.

Example: 35, 31, 27, 23, 19, 15

$35 - 31 = 4$

So check if 4 is being taken away each time.

$31 - 4 = 27$
$27 - 4 = 23$
$23 - 4 = 19$
$19 - 4 = 15$

So the number being subtracted each time is 4.

10 **To find the next number in a pattern you first need to find if the same number is being added** each time, **or** if the same number is being **subtracted** each time.

Example: 12, 14, 16, 18, ☐

2 is being added each time.
Now $18 + 2 = 20$.
So, the next number is 20.

Example: 5, 10, 15, 20, 25, ☐

The number being added each time is 5.
Now $25 + 5 = 30$ so the next number is 30.

Example: 90, 80, 70, 60, ☐

The numbers are going down by 10 each time. The next number is 50.

11 **To find the missing number in a pattern you again find the rule for the pattern.**

Example: 3, 6, 9, 12, ☐, 18, 21, 24

The numbers are going up by 3 each time.
Now $12 + 3 = 15$ and $15 + 3 = 18$.
So, the missing number is 15.

Example: ☐, 8, 15, 22, 29, 36

These numbers are going up by 7 each time.
Now $8 - 7 = 1$ so the missing number is 1.

Example: 32, 28, ☐, 20, 16, 12

These numbers are going down by 4 each time. The missing number is 24.

12 **To find the missing number in a number sentence use the words 'what number' in the sentence.**

Example: 5 plus what number is 12?

$5 + \mathbf{7} = 12$
$\mathbf{2} + 8 = 10$
$6 + \mathbf{4} = 4 + 6$
$9 - \mathbf{5} = 4$
$\mathbf{10} - 3 = 7$

10, 9, 8, 7, 6
5, 4, 3, 2, 1,
LIFT OFF!

Real Test

NUMBER AND ALGEBRA
Patterns and number sentences

20 MIN

1 17 + 8 = ☐

2 25, 30, 35, 40, 45, ?
What number comes next in this pattern? ☐

3 Write a number in the box to make this number sentence correct.

32 + ☐ = 48

4 Alice puts beads on a string. The beads make a pattern.
Which bead comes next in the pattern?

A   B ◇

C   D ◆

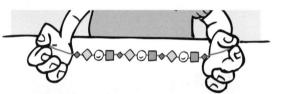

5 A pattern is made by adding 7 each time.
1, 8, ?, 22, 29
What is the missing number? ☐

6 Write a number in the box to make this number sentence correct.

42 − ☐ = 37

7 27 + 25 = ☐

8 68, 60, 52, ?
What is the next number in this pattern?
A 42   B 44   C 46   D 48

9 56 − 34 = ☐

10 Dan is making a pattern with cards. The first
shape has 5 cards, the second shape has
8 cards and the third shape has 11 cards.
How many cards will the next shape have?
A 12   B 13
C 14   D 15

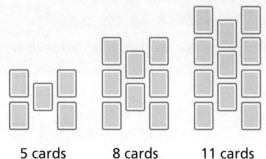

5 cards   8 cards   11 cards

☞ **Answers and explanations on pages 170-171**

Real Test

NUMBER AND ALGEBRA
Patterns and number sentences

(continued)

11 The first number is missing in this pattern.

?, 31, 35, 39, 43

What is the first number?

A 27   B 28   C 29   D 30

12 Add 100 to find the next number in this pattern.

742, 842, 942, ☐

13 Here is a pattern.

✳ ☐ ☐ ◆ ☐ ☐ ☐ ✳ ☐ ☐ ◆ ☐ ☐ ☐ ✳ ...

How many ☐ are needed for each ◆ ?

A 1   B 2   C 3   D 5

14 Write a number in the box to make the number sentence correct.

38 + ☐ = 70

15 43 − 18 = ☐

16 Zane uses sticks to make a pattern.

The first shape uses 3 sticks. The second shape uses 9 sticks. The third shape uses 18 sticks and the fourth shape uses 30 sticks.

How many sticks will Zane need for the fifth shape?

A 36   B 39   C 42   D 45

17 43, 49, 55, 61, ?

What number comes next in this pattern?

A 67   B 69   C 65   D 68

18 Place numbers in each box to make a pattern. Begin with 6 and add 4 each time.

☐ ☐ ☐ ☐

☞ Answers and explanations on pages 170–171

- There are 26 letters in the English alphabet. The consonants are ***b c d f g h j k l m n p q r s t v w x y z***. The vowels are ***a e i o u***. Every word in English needs a vowel sound. Sometimes ***y*** acts as a vowel.

  Example: gym

- The letters of the alphabet combine to spell the sounds in English words. There are around 40 sounds in English. These sounds are spelt using around 600 letter combinations.

- There are patterns and rules for spelling the sounds in English words. Sometimes there are exceptions to the rules. Exceptions are words that don't follow typical patterns. In English there are lots of exceptions.

1 The letters ***c*** and ***g*** can make hard or soft sounds depending on which other letters come after them in a word.
Hard sounds are in *cat* and *get*.
Soft sounds are in *cent* (***c*** sounds like an ***s***) and *gel* (***g*** sounds like a ***j***).

2 When ***g*** is in front of the vowels ***e***, ***i*** or ***y*** it <u>often</u> makes a soft sound like ***j***.

Examples: 'ge'—gentle, 'gi'—imagine, 'gy'—energy
Exceptions: get, girl, tiger

3 When ***c*** is in front of ***e***, ***i*** or ***y*** it <u>often</u> makes a soft sound like an ***s***.

Examples:
'ce'—dance, 'ci'—city,
'cy'—fancy

Will the tiger get the girl?

4 Note: There are also words with a silent ***d*** where 'dge' says a ***j*** sound.

Examples: judge, hedge, fudge, smudge, sludge

5 Some consonants work together to make a single sound. These are called consonant digraphs.

Examples: 'sh'—ship, shape, bush, push, shaggy
'ch'—chip, bench, chair, couch, chin
soft 'th'—thin, think, throw, three, thank
hard 'th'—this, that, there, their, they
'ph'—elephant, phone, photo, alphabet, graph
'wh'—whip, where, when, what, why
'ck'—tick, clock, deck, back, bucket

Test Your Skills

15 min

Learn to spell the words in the columns below. These strategies will help:

- **LOOK SAY COVER WRITE SAY CHECK**: <u>Look</u> at the word carefully and try to remember the way it looks. <u>Say</u> the word out loud and think about the sounds you hear. <u>Cover</u> the word and <u>write</u> it from memory. Focus on how it feels to write the sequence of letters. Look at the word you have written and <u>say</u> it out loud again. Think: is it correct? Revise it, if necessary, then <u>check</u> it.
- Break the word into **syllables**: gi–raffe.
- Break the word into parts using **prefixes, word roots** and **suffixes**: dis–cover.

1 Add extra examples of your own to each column.

hard *c*		soft *c*		hard *g*		soft *g*	
cake	crunch	cell	excel	goat	going	danger	emergency
carrot	camel	dance	pencil	grape	dragon	germ	giraffe

2 Write words that use the pairs of letters below.

'sh'   'ch'   'ck'

_____   _____   _____

_____   _____   _____

'th'   'ph'   'wh'

_____   _____   _____

_____   _____   _____

Real Test

20 MIN

Please ask your parent or teacher to read to you the spelling words on page 213. Write the correct spelling of each word in the box.

1   Be _____ with the kitten.

2   The emu's egg is _____.

3   It's _____ to ride a bike without a helmet.

4   The _____ Tree Frog lives in treetops.

5   We need to _____ the trip.

6   Make some carrot _____.

7   Regular _____ is important.

8   This curry is too _____.

9   Male _____ sing.

10 Jack and Jill carried the _____.

11 The _____ was bigger than me.

12 Pick up the dirty _____.

13 Do you like your _____ dinner?

14 My story is about a fire-breathing _____.

15 Mum will drive me _____ to school after soccer.

16 I asked Dad to make chocolate _____.

17 I am _____ to see the dentist tomorrow.

18 There are twenty-six letters in the _____.

☞ **Answers and explanations on pages 171–172**

Excel Revise in a Month Year 2 NAPLAN*-style Tests

Read the text *The school concert.*

Each line has one word that is incorrect. Write the correct spelling of the underlined word in the box.

The school concert

19 Our <u>klass</u> is performing in the

20 school <u>consert</u>. We are going to sing and

21 play <u>musikal</u> instruments. Our teacher

22 is <u>hapy</u> with our singing.

23 She <u>sed</u> that

24 this is our <u>chans</u> to shine.

25 Zac will use a <u>microfone</u>

26 to <u>introdus</u> our performance.

27 I hope we are <u>fantastik</u>.

Each sentence has one word that is incorrect. Write the correct spelling of the word in the box.

28 Eric is talking on the telefone.

29 Frow the ball to the dog.

30 The ball rolled under a busch.

31 Were is the key?

32 The clok has stopped.

33 We had to wip the cream for the cake.

34 Tim had a foto of his puppy.

35 The pen cost free dollars.

☞ **Answers and explanations on pages 171–172**

Key Points

GRAMMAR AND PUNCTUATION
Nouns and noun groups

1 A **noun** is a naming word. Nouns name people, animals, places and things.

  a The names of everyday things are **common nouns.**

    Examples: children, tigers, home, pencils

  b The names of specific people, animals, places and things are **proper nouns**. Proper nouns start with capital letters.

    Examples: James and Leyla, Greater Bilby, Australia, Sydney Harbour Bridge

  c Nouns can be **concrete.** You can see or touch them.

    Examples: city, worm, pencil

  d Nouns can be **abstract.** You can't see or touch them.

    Examples: love, peace, memories

2 A **noun group** is a group of words built around a noun.

  a Noun groups give extra information about the noun such as **number** (e.g. three, some, many) and **quality** (e.g. tiny, huge, red, black, round, spiky, strong, delicious).

  b Noun groups help readers build a mental picture of the person, animal, place or thing.

    Examples: tired old dog, two frisky little dogs, filthy wet dog

  The descriptive words tell readers exactly what kind of dog to imagine.

3 A noun can be used to classify the main noun in a noun group.

  Examples: <u>male</u> cicada, <u>tennis</u> match, <u>sand</u> crab.

4 Words in a noun group that describe the noun are called **adjectives**.

  Examples: <u>noisy</u> cicada, <u>yellow</u> cicada, <u>huge</u> cicada, <u>beautiful</u>, <u>shiny</u> cicada

How to build a noun group about cicadas

Add number information	*two*
Add size information	*large*
Add colour information	*green*
Add classifying information	*male*
Noun	*cicadas*

Adjectives do not have to be part of the noun group.

Examples: The cicada was <u>beautiful</u> and <u>yellow</u>.

5 A noun group can include words that show **possession** or **ownership**.

  Examples: <u>our</u> Banksia tree, <u>my</u> old school bag, <u>your</u> dog

6 A noun group can include words that **point out**.

  Examples: <u>this</u> cicada, <u>that</u> apple, <u>those</u> bananas

7 A noun group can include **question words**.

  Examples: <u>Which</u> cicada …? <u>What</u> time is it? <u>Whose</u> footprint …?

8 A noun group can start with *a*, *an* or *the*. *A* is used before words starting with a consonant sound. *An* is used before words starting with a vowel sound. *A* and *an* are indefinite. They refer to any nouns. *The* is a definite article. *The* is used to refer to particular nouns.

  Examples: I'll have <u>an</u> egg for breakfast. (meaning 'any egg')

  I'll eat <u>the</u> egg for lunch. (meaning 'the particular egg')

GRAMMAR AND PUNCTUATION
Nouns and noun groups

Circle the common noun in each row.

1 happy sad lonely dog

2 creepy crocodile silly hungry

3 dull yellow beach slow

4 muddy road icy slippery

5 Write these proper nouns with the correct punctuation.

australia

_____

harry

_____

tasmania

_____

new zealand

_____

isobelle

_____

glen street state school

_____

roald dahl

_____

jeannie baker

_____

Circle an appropriate adjective to fill the gap in each sentence.

6 Fleas are _____ insects.

colourful   tiny   delicious   gigantic

7 Adult cicadas have _____ lives.

short   hairy   green   angry

8 Male cicadas are _____ singers.

dangerous   yellow   loud   creamy

9 Cicadas have _____ antennae.

horrid   childish   short   naughty

Circle the noun group in each sentence.

10 The red apples taste best.

11 I saw a frog.

12 I read an exciting book.

13 The tiny creature crawled slowly past.

Write a word from the box in each sentence to show possession.

my	your	their	her	his

14 Jo and Tim washed _____ dog.

15 I finished _____ homework.

16 "Tidy _____ room," said Dad.

17 Matilda left _____ hat at school.

18 Dad brushed _____ teeth.

Real Test

GRAMMAR AND PUNCTUATION
Nouns and noun groups

20 MIN

1 Which word correctly completes this sentence?

Cicadas are _____ .

A insects   B books   C home   D trees

2 Which word correctly completes this sentence?

We played _____ at lunchtime.

A games   B sandwiches   C books   D library

3 Which word correctly completes this sentence?

The children ate _____ for afternoon tea.

A pretty   B ugly   C fruit   D my

4 Which word correctly completes this sentence?

I have spelling _____ .

A funny   B homework   C sad   D angry

5 Which word correctly completes this sentence?

The dog jumped onto the old _____ chair.

A my   B your   C wooden   D new

6 Which word correctly completes this sentence?

The bats flew into their _____ cave.

A car   B table   C hungry   D dark

7 Which sentence is written correctly?

A Michael lives in sydney.   B Michael lives in Sydney

C Michael lives in Sydney.   D michael lives in Sydney.

8 Which sentence is written correctly?

A Suri saw animals at Taronga Zoo   B suri saw animals at taronga Zoo.

C Suri saw animals at Taronga Zoo.   D Suri saw animals. at Taronga Zoo.

Read the text *Cicada summer*. Choose the best word to fill each gap.

Cicada summer

I found a large Black Prince _____ .

9 | pencil | hair | backyard | cicada |
|--------|------|----------|--------|
| A | B | C | D |

It had a beautiful, black and brown _____ .

10 | backyard | flower | shell | foot |
|----------|--------|-------|------|
| A | B | C | D |

Cicadas suck _____ from plants.

11 | potatoes | apples | trees | juice |
|----------|--------|-------|------|
| A | B | C | D |

They have two pairs of _____ for flying.

12 | legs | heads | eggs | wings |
|------|-------|------|-------|
| A | B | C | D |

☞ **Answers and explanations on pages 172–173**

Real Test

GRAMMAR AND PUNCTUATION
Nouns and noun groups

(continued)

13 Choose a word to describe taste.

Nanna cooks ▨▨▨▨ cakes.

A yellow   B delicious   C red   D blue

14 Which of the following correctly completes this sentence?

The dog chewed on an ▨▨▨▨ bone.

A huge   B enormous   C big   D large

15 Which word correctly completes this sentence?

▨▨▨▨ kind of cicada do you like best?

A This   B That   C Those   D Which

16 Which word correctly completes this sentence?

Kathy said, "This is ▨▨▨▨ book."

A which   B she's   C she   D my

17 Which word correctly completes this sentence?

Year 2 children have ▨▨▨▨ spelling test tomorrow.

A their   B you're   C my   D his

Choose the correct word for each sentence.

18 Henry has ▨▨▨▨ swimming lesson tomorrow.

A a   B an   C her   D them

19 ▨▨▨▨ children have a reading test now.

A A   B An   C The   D This

20 A cicada is ▨▨▨▨ interesting insect.

A a   B an   C these   D him

The writing below has gaps. Choose the best noun for each gap.

A ▨▨▨▨ of magpies lives

in the ▨▨▨▨ near my

home. The baby ▨▨▨▨ are

always hungry. The ▨▨▨▨ bring

the babies ▨▨▨▨ all day long.

	A	B	C	D
21	family	birds	trees	street
22	river	caves	ocean	trees
23	trees	eggs	birds	nest
24	babies	parents	trees	fish
25	nest	food	lollies	flowers

☞ Answers and explanations on pages 172–173

Key Points

1 A **report** is an informative text. Reports give information.

2 Reports can have illustrations, maps, photos, graphs or tables.

3 Some reports have headings and subheadings to help you find specific information.

4 Reports usually have the following structure:

a a **title** or **heading**

b an **opening statement** to define the topic

c a **sequence of paragraphs** about different aspects of the topic with each paragraph built around a main idea with supporting detail (Reports can also be written in bullet points.)

d a **summing-up paragraph** or **concluding statement**. (This is optional.)

5 Reports often use descriptions and technical terms. Reports use noun groups with adjectives to give detailed information about the topic.

Magpies on page 25 is a factual report. It is written in paragraphs. Paragraph 1 is the introduction. Paragraphs 2 and 3 give information about magpie families and magpie behaviour. Paragraph 4 is a concluding statement. There are no personal comments because *Magpies* is a factual report.

Important sites on page 26 is a factual report. It is written in paragraphs. Paragraph 1 is the introduction. Paragraph 2 gives information about sacred sites. Paragraph 3 gives information about non-sacred sites such as Birrigai rock shelter. This report includes technical terms: *sacred site*, *The Dreaming*, *ancestor*.

School champion on page 27 is a biography. A biography is a type of report. A biography gives information about a person and some events in the person's life. A biography can tell about the person's whole life or just part of the person's life. Biographies can give the writer's opinions about the subject. *School champion* tells readers that the swimmer, Judy, is the writer's hero. *School champion* is written in paragraphs.

Read the report *Magpies*. Circle the correct answers to the questions below.

1 **Magpies**

2 Magpies are very common in Australia. They live in bushland
3 and towns and cities. All magpies have black and white feathers.

4 Magpies are known as songbirds. They love to sing. Magpies are
5 also good mimics. They are able to copy the sounds they hear.
6 Magpies can sound like other birds and even barking dogs.

7 Magpies live in family groups. A family group can be parents,
8 children and grandchildren. Older children help to feed younger
9 brothers and sisters and teach them how to find their own food. Magpies protect their
10 nests from intruders. In nesting season male magpies might swoop at people to protect
11 their nests. Magpies nest in trees. The female lays two to five eggs at a time. Baby
12 magpies beg loudly and constantly for food. Magpies eat worms, snails, lizards, frogs,
13 spiders and insects. Magpies mostly peck for food on the ground. They also eat grains.

14 Magpies are protected in Australia. It is against the law to hurt magpies in any way.

1 Which sentence is true?
  A Magpies only live in the bush.   B Magpies are white.
  C Magpies are common in Australia.   D Magpies only live in cities.

2 Where do magpies mostly find their food?
  A on the ground   B in the water   C in the trees   D in cities

3 Magpie nests can be found
  A in trees.   B in caves.   C on the ground.   D in roofs.

4 Which of the following will a magpie eat?
  A apples   B fish   C snails   D grass

5 What do baby magpies do to get food?
  A swoop at people   B beg loudly   C sing   D find it themselves

6 Why do magpies swoop at people?
  A because they are hungry   B because they don't like people
  C because they are protecting their nests   D because they are songbirds

7 Another good title for this text could be
  A All about baby magpies.   B Travelling in Australia.
  C Australian animals.   D An interesting Australian bird.

Answers: 1 C 2 A 3 A 4 C 5 B 6 C 7 D

☞ **Explanations on page 173**

Real Test

Read *Important sites*. Circle the correct answers to the questions below.

Important sites

1

There are Aboriginal sites all over Australia. These are
special places.

2
3

Some Aboriginal sites are sacred. They might be
sacred because important traditional ceremonies were
held there. They might be burial sites. Sacred sites are
often connected to stories of The Dreaming. Many
Aboriginals believe that sacred sites are protected by
ancestor spirits. Some Aboriginals think that visitors
should not be allowed to enter any sacred sites.

4
5
6
7
8
9
10

Other important Aboriginal sites are not sacred. Local Aboriginal elders allow visitors
onto these sites. One such site is Birrigai rock shelter. Birrigai is a large rock ledge. Up
to twelve people can stand under it. Many experts think Birrigai rock shelter is the
oldest Aboriginal site in Canberra. Aboriginal people used the rock shelter long, long
ago. Many tourists visit the Birrigai rock shelter site. Schoolchildren visit on school
excursions.

11
12
13
14
15
16

---

1 Aboriginal sites are found
   A all around Australia.
   C in traditional places.
   B only in Canberra.
   D in watercourses.

2 Another word for *site* is
   A seeing.   B place.   C sight.   D home.

3 Many Aboriginals believe that sacred sites are protected by
   A ancestor spirits.   B experts.   C tourists.   D schoolchildren.

4 Where is Birrigai rock shelter?
   A a rock shelter   B Canberra   C The Dreaming   D an Aboriginal site

5 Who allows visitors onto sacred sites?
   A a school
   C the local Aboriginal elders
   B their parents
   D the government

6 This report was most likely written for
   A girls.   B teachers.   C boys.   D children.

7 Another good title for this text could be
   A Holiday places.   B Aboriginal sites.   C The Dreaming.   D School excursions.

☞ **Answers and explanations on page 173**

Real Test

15 min

Read *School champion*. Circle the correct answers to the questions below.

1   **School champion**

2   Judy Chen is in Year 6 at our school. She is a champion swimmer. She is my hero.

3   Judy was born in a coastal town in Queensland. She started swimming in races when
4   she was four. She joined her local Nippers when she was six. She loves competing in
5   swimming events. She also loves just having fun in the pool or in the surf.

6   Judy's favourite swimming stroke is butterfly, which
7   she calls 'fly'. Judy has won all the butterfly events
8   at our school swimming carnival for the last four
9   years. She also swims for a local swimming club called
10 'Little Dolphins'. The name of the club suits the way
11 Judy swims. In the butterfly kick you keep your feet
12 together and move them up and down just like a
13 dolphin. Judy streaks through the water with her
14 butterfly kick.

15 Judy hopes to compete in the Olympics when she is
16 older. I think she will make it. I hope she does.

1   Judy started swimming in races when she was

A six.
B four.
C born.
D in Year 6.

2   How is Judy like a dolphin?

A She wins swimming races.
B She can fly through the water.
C She loves playing in the water.
D She kicks her feet up and down for the butterfly kick.

3   Little Dolphins is the name of

A a dolphin species.
B a racing club.
C a swimming club.
D a surf carnival.

4   Judy has been winning school swimming events

A for six years.
B for three years.
C for four years.
D this year.

5   Judy is best described as a person who is

A energetic.
B timid.
C lazy.
D lonely.

6   Which idea best matches this text?

A If you love something, you will most likely be good at it.
B Winning is everything.
C Dolphins are great swimmers.
D Nippers helps you win swimming races.

7   Write the numbers 1 to 4 in the boxes to show the order of events in Judy's life.

☐ Judy is now in Year 6

☐ Judy was born.

☐ Judy joined Nippers.

☐ Judy started swimming in races.

☞ Answers and explanations on pages 173-174

GENERAL WRITING TIPS

Each weekly writing plan provides three exercises. This allows for two forty-minute writing sessions each week, with any extra exercises to be used for practice at a later time.

Writing Tests are designed to test your ability to express ideas, feelings and points of view.

You will be assessed on:

- the thought and content of your writing
- the structure and organisation of your ideas
- the expression, style and appropriate use of language of your writing
- the amount you write in the given time.

To get the best results, follow these steps.

Step 1—Before you start writing

- **Read the question.** Do you understand the type of writing you are being asked to do? If the question wants you to write an explanation, you should write an explanation—not a story or any other type of writing. Read the instructions carefully. Ask yourself if you should be describing, explaining, entertaining, telling a story, expressing a point of view, expressing an emotion or persuading the reader.
- **Check the stimulus material carefully.** *Stimulus material* means the topic, title, picture, words, phrases or extract of writing you are given to base your writing on. Your writing must be based on this material.
- **What writing style?** If you are given a choice of writing styles (text types), pick the style you are most comfortable with.
- **Warning:** don't try to make a pre-planned piece of writing (that is, something you have already written) fit the stimulus material you are given.

Step 2—Jot down points

Give yourself a few minutes before you start to get your thoughts in order and jot down points. You won't have time to write a draft. Depending on the writing style required, jot down points on:

- who (characters), why (reasons for action), where (setting), when (time)
- sequences of events/arguments/points
- any good ideas you suddenly have
- how to include the senses and your feelings.

Remember: you can choose not to use any ideas that don't fit into your final approach.

Step 3—Make a brief outline

List the points or events in order. This will become your framework. It can be changed as you write.

GENERAL WRITING TIPS

Step 4—Start writing

- Make your **paragraphing** work for you. New paragraphs are usually needed for:
  - o new incidents in stories
  - o changes in time or place
  - o descriptions that move from one sense to another (e.g. from sight to sound)
  - o a change in the character using direct speech.
- Don't forget that your **vocabulary** is being tested. Don't use unusual words or big words just to impress the assessor. A mistake here will show that you might not understand the words properly.
- It is important that you **complete your piece of writing**. Unfinished work may lose you marks, as will extremely short pieces of writing.
- Get as much of the **punctuation, spelling and grammar** right as you can, but allow yourself a couple of minutes after you finish to proofread your work. You won't have time to go over it in detail, but a quick check at the end will help.
- If you are writing a story, know the **ending** before you start. Try to make the ending unusual and well-written—not just *I woke up and found it was only a dream!*
- If you are asked to give a **point of view**, think through the evidence you can use to support your 'argument' so that you can build to a strong conclusion.
- If you are including **descriptions** in your writing, think about all the senses—sights, smells, tastes, sounds and physical feelings. You may also include an **emotional response**.
- Have a **concluding sentence** that 'rounds off' your work.
- Keep your **handwriting** reasonably neat (i.e. readable).

Step 5—When you finish

When you finish, **re-read** your work and do a quick check for spelling, punctuation, capital letters and grammar.

 Check the Writing section (www.nap.edu.au/naplan/writing) **of the official NAPLAN website for up-to-date and important information on the Writing Test**. Sample Writing Tests and marking guidelines that outline the criteria markers use when assessing your writing are also provided. Please note that, to date in NAPLAN, the types of texts that students have been tested on have been narrative and persuasive writing.

The Australian Curriculum for English requires students to be taught three main types of texts:
- imaginative writing (including narratives and descriptions)
- informative writing (including procedures and reports)
- persuasive writing (expositions).

Informative writing has not yet been tested by NAPLAN. The best preparation for writing is for students to read a range of texts and to get lots of practice in writing different types of texts. We have included information on all types of texts in this book.

TIPS FOR WRITING DESCRIPTIONS

Text structure and organisation

Descriptions can:

- give information about a person, place, animal or thing
- be factual or imaginative
- be part of other texts such as persuasive texts, reports, recounts, poems or narratives
- be written in a number of paragraphs, a single paragraph, or a sentence
- include photographs and illustrations.

Before you start to write a description, think about:

- the **purpose** and **audience** for your text
- the **opening statement** (This introduces the topic and tells readers what the description is about.)
- the **information** you will include (Group your ideas into paragraphs. Plan to write a paragraph for each idea.)
- a **summing-up** or **concluding statement**; you can also add a personal comment.

Expressing and developing ideas

When you write a description, remember to:

- use noun groups

Example 1: A description in a persuasive text uses adjectives.
LAPTOP FOR SALE: *lightweight, sleek, super-fast*

Example 2: A description in a science report uses technical terms.
Cicadas have a special, sharp proboscis.

Example 3: A description of a character in a narrative helps readers to get to know the character.
Megan felt shivery tingles up her spine and her hair stood on end.

Example 4: A description of a setting in a narrative helps readers to imagine a place.
It was a dark and spooky night.

Example 5: Some descriptions use words that give the writer's point of view.
This is a positive point of view of a rainforest:
*It's dark and cool under the forest canopy,
safe from the burning sun.*
This is a negative point of view of a rainforest:
Rainforests are full of spider webs and creepy-crawly things that scurry around behind your back. I think about snakes slithering close and vines growing down to strangle me.

Example 6: Descriptions in factual reports do not give the writer's point of view.
The rainforest canopy protects the rest of the rainforest from the sun.

- proofread your text and check that it makes sense
- check spelling and punctuation.

When you have finished your writing, give it to an adult to read and check.

Excel Revise in a Month Year 2 NAPLAN*-style Tests

My dog

My family has a dog. His name is Rufus. Rufus is a gentle giant. We've had Rufus since he was one year old. We rescued him from the animal shelter. His previous owners had given him up because they said he grew too big.

Rufus has shaggy cream-coloured fur, floppy ears, alert and watchful eyes, and a lolling tongue. He weighs 30 kg. He is big and bouncy.

Rufus is not very obedient but he is learning to follow commands. I take him for a walk each day after school. He loves all other dogs. He looks as if he could eat them but he really just wants to play. He is a little bit afraid of cats. I know this because he starts to whimper when he sees one and he'll just freeze on the spot. It's hard to get him moving again past a cat.

Sometimes Rufus gets so excited that he forgets how strong he is. Then he pulls me along on the end of his leash and almost pulls me over. It takes all my strength to hold him back.

I love Rufus. He is the best dog in the world.

This text is beyond what would be expected of a typical Year 2 student. It is provided here as a model. The assessment comments are based on the marking criteria used to assess the NAPLAN Writing Test.

Vocabulary
- Noun groups provide descriptive detail.
- Verbs are used accurately. They include being and having verbs (e.g. has, is, gets) past-tense verbs (e.g. rescued) and verb groups (e.g. starts to whimper, wants to play).

Sentence structure
A variety of sentence structures are used:
- simple sentences
- compound sentences
- complex sentences.

Ideas
- Ideas all relate to the purpose of describing a pet. Ideas have supporting detail.

Punctuation
- The writer uses correct sentence punctuation. Capital letters are used for sentence beginnings and proper nouns. Commas and full stops are used correctly.

Spelling
- Difficult and challenging words are spelt correctly (e.g. obedient, weighs) and words which include blends (e.g. creamy), digraphs (e.g. whimper) and silent letters (e.g. tongue).

Audience
- The text meets the needs of an audience. It includes background information to help the reader relate to the topic. The writer describes a subject that is very familiar to them.

Text structure
- The text has an appropriate structure. It starts with an introduction. Ideas are grouped in a logical sequence. It ends with a summing-up statement and personal opinion.

Paragraphing
- Ideas are grouped in paragraphs.
- Paragraph 1 provides introduction and background.
- Paragraph 2 describes the dog's appearance.
- Paragraph 3 describes one aspect of the dog's behaviour.
- Paragraph 4 describes a different aspect of the dog's behaviour.
- Paragraph 5 is the concluding statement.

Cohesion
- Ideas are linked using conjunctions (e.g. and, but, because).
- Ideas are linked through time (e.g. then).
- Noun-pronoun reference is accurate (e.g. Rufus—he).

Character and setting
- Rufus is described in detail so readers can build a mental picture. The writer's point of view about the subject is apparent: *I love Rufus.*

Real Test and Tips

WRITING
Descriptive text 1

40 MIN

Before you start, read the **Tips for writing descriptions** on page 30.

Today you are going to write a description. Your purpose is to **describe an animal** to readers of your own age.

You can describe any animal you choose. It can be an animal that you like or are interested in. It can be an animal that you dislike or are frightened of. It can be a pet animal, farm animal, zoo animal, animal in the wild, imaginary animal or animal that you have seen on television.

Make sure your description helps readers to build a picture of the animal in their own minds.

Before you start to write, think about the animal and picture it in your mind.
- What does it look like?
- How does it move?
- What does it do?
- How does it behave?
- What sounds does it make?

Remember to:
- plan your writing
- write in paragraphs—each paragraph should describe one aspect of the animal
- use noun groups and adjectives to describe the animal
- write in sentences
- check spelling and punctuation
- write as neatly as you can so that readers can understand your writing
- ask a parent or teacher to read and check your finished work.

Use your own paper to write your description.

☞**Marking Guide on pages 174-175**

Real Test and Tips

WRITING
Descriptive text 2

40 MIN

Before you start, read the **Tips for writing descriptions** on page 30.

Today you are going to write a description. Your purpose is to **describe a place** to readers of your own age.

You can describe any type of place you choose. It can be real or imaginary. It can be a place you have visited. It can be a place you would never want to visit. This place could be the setting for a scary story or a story set in outer space. It could be somewhere in your own home or neighbourhood. It's up to you.

Make sure your description tells your readers all about this place. Describe the place using your senses (sight, sound, smell, touch). Help your readers imagine what this place is like.

Before you start to write, think about the place and picture it in your mind.
- What can you see?
- How does it make you feel (e.g. safe, happy, scared, worried, excited)?
- What sounds can you hear?
- What can you smell?

Remember to:
- plan your writing
- write in paragraphs—each paragraph should be about one main idea
- use words to describe the place
- write in sentences—use capital letters and full stops
- check spelling and punctuation
- write as neatly as you can so that readers can understand your writing
- ask a parent or teacher to read and check your finished work.

Use your own paper to write your description.

☞Marking Guide on page 175

WRITING
Descriptive text 3

40 MIN

Before you start, read the **Tips for writing descriptions** on page 30.

Today you are going to write **a letter or email to a new penfriend**. The penfriend might live in Australia or in another country. Your purpose is to tell your new penfriend about yourself and your life. You can describe your family and where you live. You should describe things your penfriend might find interesting about you.

Before you start to write, think about:
- the introduction
- how to describe yourself, your family and your home
- the concluding statement.

Remember to:
- plan your writing
- write in paragraphs—each paragraph should be about one aspect of your life
- use noun groups
- write in sentences—use capital letters and full stops
- check spelling and punctuation
- write as neatly as you can so that readers can understand your writing
- ask a parent or teacher to read and check your finished work.

Use your own paper to write your description.

☞ **Marking Guide on pages 175-176**

What's next ?

Week 2

This is what we cover this week:

Day 1   **Number and Algebra:** ◎ Adding, subtracting, multiplying and dividing

Day 2   **Number and Algebra:** ◎ Fractions and money

Day 3   **Spelling:** ◎ Two- and three-letter consonant blends, silent consonants and vowel digraphs

            Grammar and Punctuation: ◎ Verbs, commas in lists and commas in direct speech

Day 4   **Reading:** ◎ Understanding procedures

Day 5   **Writing:** ◎ Procedures; recounts

Test Your Skills 1

NUMBER AND ALGEBRA
Adding, subtracting, multiplying and dividing

20 min

Fill in the blanks.

1 $5 + \boxed{} = 7$

2 $7 - \boxed{} = 5$

3 $7 - 5 = \boxed{}$

4 $6 + \boxed{} = 9$

5 $9 - 6 = \boxed{}$

6 $9 - \boxed{} = 6$

7 $\boxed{} + 3 = 8$

8 $8 - \boxed{} = 3$

9 $8 - 3 = \boxed{}$

Here are some nails.

10 How many nails are there? $\boxed{}$

11 If 6 more nails are added, how many nails will there be? $\boxed{}$

Here are some paperclips.

12 How many paperclips are there? $\boxed{}$

13 If 5 paperclips are taken away, how many paperclips will be left? $\boxed{}$

Jill has 5 stickers and Selma has 8 stickers.

Jill   Selma

14 How many stickers do they have altogether? $\boxed{}$

15 How many more stickers does Selma have than Jill? $\boxed{}$

Selma gives 2 of her stickers to Jill.

16 How many stickers does Jill have now? $\boxed{}$

17 How many stickers does Selma have now? $\boxed{}$

Fill in the blanks.

18 $32 + 18 = 30 + \boxed{}$

19 $67 + 47 = 70 + \boxed{}$

20 $82 - 19 = \boxed{} - 20$

21 $55 - 38 = \boxed{} - 40$

NUMBER AND ALGEBRA
Adding, subtracting, multiplying and dividing

Fill in the blanks.

1 $3 + 3 + 3 + 3 + 3 = \boxed{} \times 3$

2 $7 + 7 + 7 + 7 = \boxed{} \times 7$

3 $2 + 2 + 2 + 2 + 2 + 2 + 2$

$= \boxed{} \times \boxed{}$

Here is a pack of drinks.

4 How many drinks are in the pack? $\boxed{}$

5 How many drinks would be in 2 packs? $\boxed{}$

6 The number of drinks in 5 packs would be $5 \times \boxed{} = \boxed{}$

Here are some pencils.

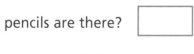

7 How many pencils are there? $\boxed{}$

8 If 2 boys share the pencils, how many will they each have? $\boxed{}$

9 If 3 girls share the pencils, how many will they each have? $\boxed{}$

10 If 4 children share the pencils, how many will they each have? $\boxed{}$

Which one of these would be used to work out the answer to each problem below?
A $6 + 2$ **B** $6 - 2$ **C** 6×2 **D** $6 \div 2$

11 Suzy has 6 books. She gives 2 books to Max. How many books does Suzy have now?

$\boxed{}$

12 Pat and Kim share 6 books equally. How many books does Pat get?

$\boxed{}$

13 Zac has 2 piles of books. There are 6 books in each pile. How many books does Zac have?

$\boxed{}$

14 Mia has 6 books. Jon has 2 books. How many more books does Mia have than Jon?

$\boxed{}$

15 Sam has 6 books. Billy has 2 books. How many books do they have altogether?

$\boxed{}$

Answers: 1 5 **2** 4 **3** 7, 2 **4** 6 **5** 12 **6** 6, 30 **7** 12 **8** 6 **9** 4 **10** 3 **11** B **12** D **13** C **14** B **15** A

1 **Adding and subtracting are related.**

Examples:

■ $5 + 2 = 7$ and $7 - 2 = 5$.

■ If you add 2 to 5 you get 7 and if you then take away that 2 you get back to 5. So subtracting undoes what you did when you added.

■ If you want to find what number to add to 5 to get 7 you can work that out by subtracting. $7 - 5 = 2$.

■ $6 + 3 = 9$ and $9 - 6 = 3$ and $9 - 3 = 6$ are all related number sentences.

■ $5 + 3 = 8$ and $8 - 5 = 3$ and $8 - 3 = 5$ are also all related.

2 **You can solve problems using addition, subtraction, multiplication or division.** Sometimes you can work out the answers to problems by looking and counting. But if you know some rules for addition and subtraction, for example, you will be able to use those rules to find the answers to harder problems.

Example: Here are 9 nails.

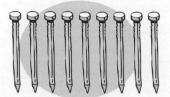

If 6 more nails are added then the number of nails is $9 + 6 = 15$.

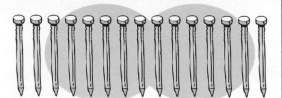

Example:
Here are 13 paperclips.

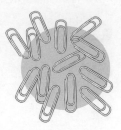

If 5 paperclips are taken away then the number of paperclips that are left is $13 - 5 = 8$.

Example:

Jill   Selma

■ By counting, you can see that Jill has 5 stickers and Selma has 8 stickers.

■ Together, Jill and Selma have $5 + 8 = 13$ stickers.

■ Now $8 - 5 = 3$.
So Selma has 3 more stickers than Jill.

■ Selma gives 2 of her stickers to Jill.

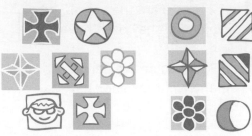

Jill   Selma

Now Jill has 7 stickers. $5 + 2 = 7$.
Now Selma has 6 stickers. $8 - 2 = 6$.

Key Points

NUMBER AND ALGEBRA
Adding, subtracting, multiplying and dividing

(continued)

3 **You can partition numbers to make large numbers easier to add or subtract.**

Example: To add 32 and 18 you can take 2 away from 32 and add it to 18.
$32 + 18 = 30 + 2 + 18 = 30 + 20 = 50$

Example:

Suppose you need to add $67 + 47$.
You could add 3 to 67 to make 70, and take 3 away from 47.
$67 + 47 = 67 + 3 + 44 = 70 + 44 = 114$

Example:

■ Suppose you need to subtract $82 - 19$. It is easier to subtract 20 than to subtract 19 so add 1 to 19 to make 20.

■ Then you also need to add 1 to 82 so that the question is still the same.
$82 - 19 = 83 - 20 = 53$
$55 - 38 = 57 - 40 = 17$

4 **Multiplication is a way of adding lots of the same number.**

Examples: $3 + 3 + 3 + 3 + 3$ means you are adding 5 lots of 3 together. But 5 lots of 3 is 5×3.
$3 + 3 + 3 + 3 + 3 = \mathbf{5} \times \mathbf{3}$
$7 + 7 + 7 + 7 = \mathbf{4} \times \mathbf{7}$
$2 + 2 + 2 + 2 + 2 + 2 + 2 = \mathbf{7} \times \mathbf{2}$

Example:

■ By counting, you can see that there are 6 cans of drink in one pack.

■ In 2 packs there will be $6 + 6$ or 2×6 or 12 cans of drink.

■ The number of drinks in 5 packs will be $6 + 6 + 6 + 6 + 6$ or $5 \times 6 = 30$ cans.

5 **Division is a way of breaking up a number of things in equal parts.**

Example:

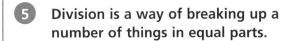

■ By counting, you can see that there are 12 pencils.

■ If you divide those 12 pencils into 2 parts, you can see that there are 6 pencils in each part. $12 \div 2 = 6$

So if 2 boys share the pencils, they will have 6 pencils each.

■ If you divide the 12 pencils into 3 parts, you can see that there are 4 pencils in each part. $12 \div 3 = 4$

So if 3 girls share the pencils, they will have 4 pencils each.

■ If you divide the 12 pencils into 4 parts, you can see that there are 3 pencils in each part. $12 \div 4 = 3$

So if 4 children share the pencils, they will have 3 pencils each.

Key Points

NUMBER AND ALGEBRA
Adding, subtracting, multiplying and dividing

(continued)

6 **Addition, subtraction, multiplication and division are sometimes referred to as operations.**

It is very important that you understand which operation to use when solving a problem.

There are some **key words** that help you understand what is required.

★ If you are asked to add, or plus, or find the total, or find the sum, or find how many altogether you need to add the numbers together.

★ If you are asked to subtract, take away, minus, or find the difference you need to subtract the numbers. If you are asked how many more one is than another, you subtract the smaller number from the larger one.

★ If you are asked to multiply, times, or find the product you need to multiply. If you have 2 lots of 8 then altogether you have 2×8.

★ If you are asked to divide, split, or share you need to divide one number by another. If you need to know how many lots of 2 there are in 8 then you need to divide 8 by 2.

___

Example:
■ Suzy has 6 books. She gives 2 books to Max. How many books does Suzy have now?
■ You will need to take 2 away from 6 to find the answer. The operation you need is $6 - 2$.

___

Example:

■ Pat and Kim share 6 books equally. How many books does Pat get?
■ You need to divide 6 by 2 because the 6 books are being divided into 2 shares. The operation you need is $6 \div 2$.

___

Example:
■ Zac has 2 piles of books. There are 6 books in each pile. How many books does Zac have?
■ There are 2 piles of books and 6 books in each pile. You need to multiply 6×2 to find the number of books.

___

Example:
■ Mia has 6 books. Jon has 2 books. How many more books does Mia have than Jon?
■ You want to find the difference between the number of books that Mia has and the number that Jon has, so you need to subtract. The operation you need is $6 - 2$.

___

Example:
■ Sam has 6 books. Billy has 2 books. How many books do they have altogether?
■ You need to add the numbers together. The operation you need is $6 + 2$.

Real Test

NUMBER AND ALGEBRA
Adding, subtracting, multiplying and dividing

20 min

1 Molly had these pencils.

She gave 3 to Ken. How many pencils did Molly have left?

A 3   B 4   C 5   D 6

2 Will put all his blocks into 3 equal stacks. Each stack has 6 blocks.

How can Will find the total number of blocks?

A 6 ÷ 3

B 6 + 3

C 6 × 3

D 6 − 3

3 Rose has 37 books. Mary has 56 books. How many books do Rose and Mary have altogether?

A 91   B 93   C 81   D 83

4 Tennis balls are sold in packs of 4.

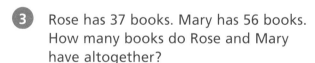

Sam needs 11 tennis balls. What is the least number of packs Sam needs?

A 2   B 3   C 4   D 5

5 Jay has 30 toy trucks. He puts the trucks into rows. There are 5 trucks in each row.

Which of these shows how to work out the total number of rows needed for the trucks?

A 30 + 5

B 30 − 5

C 30 × 5

D 30 ÷ 5

6 Tim is putting pies in boxes. Each box holds 4 pies.

How many boxes will Tim need for 20 pies?

7 18 + 37 has the same value as

20 +

8 $30 is shared equally among 6 boys. How much will each boy get?

$

☞ Answers and explanations on pages 176-177

Real Test

NUMBER AND ALGEBRA
Adding, subtracting, multiplying and dividing

(continued)

9 What numbers go in the boxes to show the number of candles in the picture?

| | × 5 candles = | | candles

10 Here are 3 rows of 8 books.

This is the same as 6 rows of how many books?

A 4   B 6
C 8   D 16

11 Bill has 83 spanners. Jed has 27 spanners.
How many **more** spanners does Bill have than Jed?

12 Each plate has 4 cakes.

Which of these shows one way to work out the total number of cakes?

A 4 + 3
B 4 + 4 + 4 + 4
C 4 × 3
D 3 + 3 + 3

13 Which gives the same answer as 9 + 7?

A 7 + 9
B 10 + 8
C 8 + 6
D 12 + 10

14 Some boys share these 18 marbles.

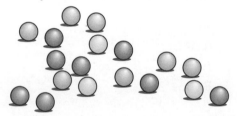

Each boy gets 3 marbles.
How many boys share
the marbles?

15 Two girls each play with 3 toy cars.
Which shows the number of cars the girls play with?

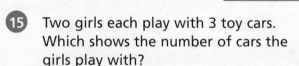

A
B
C
D

☞**Answers and explanations on pages 176-177**

Test Your Skills 1

NUMBER AND ALGEBRA
Fractions and money

20 MIN

Here are some toy cars.

1 Jack owns half of the cars. How many of the cars does Jack own?

2 Will owns one-quarter of the cars. How many of the cars does Will own?

3 Ed owns one-eighth of the cars. How many of the cars does Ed own?

What fraction is shaded?

4

5

6

7

8

9

10

Here are some oranges.

11 How many halves can each orange be cut into?

12 If all the oranges are cut into halves, how many halves will there be?

13 How many quarters can each orange be cut into?

14 If all the oranges are cut into quarters, how many quarters will there be?

Test Your Skills 2

NUMBER AND ALGEBRA
Fractions and money

20 MIN

Here are some coins.

1 Which coin has the largest value?

2 Which coin has the smallest value?

3 What is the value of the coin between the 20-cent and the 5-cent coins?

4 Which coin is worth more than the first coin but less than the last coin?

Look at these two coins.

5 Which coin is worth more?

6 What is the value of the two coins together?

Look at these three coins.

7 Which coin is worth the most?

8 Which coin is worth the least?

9 What is the value of the three coins altogether?

Look at this money.

10 Which note is worth the most?

11 Which note is worth the least?

12 What is the total value of this money?

Excel Revise in a Month Year 2 NAPLAN*-style Tests

1 A fraction is part of a whole.

2 If you take a collection and divide it into two equal parts then each of those parts is one-half of the collection.

Example:

■ If you divide these 8 cars into 2 groups, there will be 4 cars in each group.

■ Each group of 4 cars is one-half of the collection.

■ If Jack owns half of the cars, he owns 4 cars.

3 If you take a collection and divide it into four equal parts, then each part will be one-quarter of the collection.

(One-fourth means the same thing as one-quarter, but you usually say one-quarter not one-fourth.)

Example:

■ If you divide the collection of 8 cars into 4 groups, there will be 2 cars in each group.

■ So if Will owns one-quarter of the cars, he owns 2 cars.

4 If you take a collection and divide it into 8 equal parts, then each part is one-eighth of the collection.

Example: If you divide the collection of 8 cars into 8 equal groups there will be just one car in each group.

So if Ed owns one-eighth of the cars, he owns 1 car.

5 To work out what fraction you have of a set of things or an object, you first need to know how many parts the set of things or object has been divided into.

Example:

This diagram has been divided into 2 equal parts. 1 of those 2 parts has been shaded. The fraction that is shaded is one-half or $\frac{1}{2}$.

Example:

This diagram has been divided into 4 equal parts. 1 of the 4 equal parts has been shaded so the fraction that is shaded is one-quarter or $\frac{1}{4}$.

NUMBER AND ALGEBRA
Fractions and money

(continued)

Example:

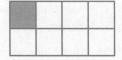

This diagram has been divided into 8 equal parts. 1 of the 8 equal parts has been shaded. The fraction that is shaded is one-eighth or $\frac{1}{8}$.

Example:

In this diagram 1 of 2 equal parts is shaded.

The fraction that is shaded is one-half or $\frac{1}{2}$.

Example:

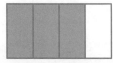

In this diagram 3 of 4 equal parts have been shaded. The fraction that is shaded is three-quarters or $\frac{3}{4}$.

Example:

In this diagram the same number of squares are shaded as are not shaded. So you can see that one-half of the diagram is shaded. Or 4 of 8 equal parts are shaded. As 4 is half of 8 the shaded part is one-half or $\frac{1}{2}$.

Example:

In this diagram 3 of 8 equal parts are shaded. The fraction that is shaded is three-eighths or $\frac{3}{8}$.

6 **One whole can be divided into smaller parts.** There are two halves in one whole. There are four quarters in one whole.

Example:

■ If an orange is cut into 2 equal pieces, each piece is one-half. So an orange can be cut into 2 halves.

■ To find the total number of halves when 4 oranges are cut, you can count by twos or you can multiply: $4 \times 2 = 8$.

■ If 4 oranges are cut into halves, there will be 8 halves altogether.

■ If an orange is cut into 4 equal pieces, each piece is one-quarter. So an orange can be cut into 4 quarters.

■ To find the total number of quarters when 4 oranges are cut you can multiply: $4 \times 4 = 16$.

■ If 4 oranges are cut into quarters, there will be 16 quarters altogether.

Key Points

NUMBER AND ALGEBRA
Fractions and money

(continued)

7 With money, the value of the different coins should be known.

$2
two dollars

$1
one dollar

50c
fifty cents

20c
twenty cents

10c
ten cents

5c
five cents

Remember that one dollar is equal to 100 cents.

Example:

- In this line of coins the coin with the largest value is the $2 coin.
  The coin with the least value is the 5c coin.

- The coin between the 20c coin and the 5c coin is the third coin. Its value is 10c. The first coin is worth 50c. The last coin is worth $2. The coin with a value between 50c and $2 is the $1 coin.

Example:

- These coins are worth 50c and 20c. The larger value is 50c.
- Because 50 + 20 = 70 the total value is 70c.

Example:

- These three coins have values of 5c, 10c and $1.
- The largest value is $1 and the smallest value is 5c.
- Now 10c + 5c = 15c.
  So the total value is $1 + 15c or $1.15.

8 The value of the different notes should also be known.

$100
one hundred dollars

$50
fifty dollars

$20
twenty dollars

$10
ten dollars

$5
five dollars

Example:

- Of the notes below, the first note is worth $50 and has the greatest value. The second note is worth $5 and has the least value.

- Now 50 + 5 + 10 + 20 = 85.
  So the total value is $85.

Real Test

NUMBER AND ALGEBRA
Fractions and money

20 MIN

1 Ed has these pencils.

He gives half of the pencils to Nick.

How many pencils does Ed give to Nick?
A 4 **B** 6 **C** 12 **D** 24

2 Kylie has only these coins.

How much money does she have?
A 40 cents **B** $4.35
C $5.35 **D** $40

3 Max cut some oranges into quarters. He has 8 quarters.

How many oranges did Max cut?
A 2 **B** 4 **C** 8 **D** 32

4 Which shape has one-eighth shaded?

A

B

C

D

5 Which coins are in order from highest value to lowest? Choose all possible answers.

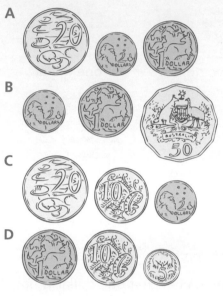

A

B

C

D

6 Jake cut these apples into quarters.

How many quarters did Jake have?

7 Kevin has only these coins.

He buys a ruler for 75 cents. How much money does Kevin have left?
A $1.35 **B** $1.30
C $1.25 **D** 36 cents

☞ **Answers and explanations on pages 177-178**

Real Test

NUMBER AND ALGEBRA
Fractions and money

(continued)

8 Which shape has one-half shaded?

A

B

C

D

9 Toby makes a cake. He needs one and a half cups of sugar.

This scoop holds half a cup.

How many scoops of sugar does Toby need?

A 1   B $1\frac{1}{2}$.   C 2   D 3

10 Sue has this money in her purse.

How much money is this?

A $85   B $95   C $105   D $115

11 Jill has these balloons.

She gives half the balloons to Luke. Then Jill gives half of the balloons that are left to Alice. How many balloons will Jill have after she has given the balloons to Luke and Alice?

A 2   B 3   C 4   D 6

12 Ellen has these coins.

She buys a banana.

Now she has these coins left.

How much was the banana?

☐ cents

☞ **Answers and explanations on pages 177-178**

Key Points

SPELLING
*Two- and three-letter consonant blends,
silent consonants and vowel digraphs*

When learning to spell a new word:
- listen for the individual sounds in the word
- look at the letter combinations that make the sounds
- use the strategy **LOOK, SAY, COVER, WRITE, SAY, CHECK** to practise spelling any word you find challenging.

Consonant blends

1 **Some consonants regularly go together** in words, with no vowel between them. The consonants *l*, *r* and *s* are used with other consonants at the beginning of words. Each letter in these two or three consonant blends makes its own distinct sound.

Examples:

- blends with *l*— 'bl' black, 'cl' clip, 'fl' flop, 'gl' glow, 'pl' plop, 'sl' slow, 'spl' splash
- blends with *r* —'br' brick, 'cr' crack, 'dr' drip, 'fr' fry, 'gr' grow, 'pr' pry, 'scr' scratch, 'spr' spring, 'str' string, 'tr' tree, 'wr' wreck
- blends with *s*—'sc' scar, 'scr' scratch, 'sk' sky, 'sm' small, 'sn' snow, 'sp' spot, 'spl' splash, 'spr' spring, 'str' string, 'st' stop, 'sw' swim
- blends with *t*—'tr' tree, 'tw' twice

2 Some consonants are often found together at the **end of words**. Each consonant makes its own sound.

Examples: 'ct' fact, 'ft' lift, 'lt' built, 'st' post, 'mp' lump, 'nd' sand, 'ng' song, 'nk' sink, 'nt' print, 'pt' kept, 'sk' task, 'sp' wasp, 'st' last

3 Sometimes **three consonants together** only make two sounds. Two of the consonants make a single sound to blend with the third consonant in the cluster of letters.

Examples: 'sph' sphere, 'shr' shrink, 'thr' three, 'nth' ninth

Silent letters

4 Sometimes words have a number of consonants in a row but the letters do not make distinct sounds because one of the consonants is a **silent letter**.

Examples: thum**b**, **s**cent, ya**ch**t, We**d**nesday, rei**g**n, fli**gh**t, din**gh**y, **k**nee, woul**d**, **m**nemonic, autum**n**, recei**p**t, govern**m**ent, is**l**and, lis**t**en, **w**ho

Vowel digraphs

5 Sometimes **two vowels together** make only one sound.

Examples:

- 'ue'—blue, glue
- 'oo'—boot, shoot, boom, room, zoo, hoop, loop (long 'oo')
  'oo'—stood, good, hook, took, foot (short 'oo')
- 'ea'—eat, beat, cheat, heat, squeal, heal
- 'ee'—meet, sheet, steel, sleet
- 'ai'—rain, mail, again, pain

Excel Revise in a Month Year 2 NAPLAN*-style Tests

Test Your Skills

15 min

Answer the questions below. Use a dictionary to check your spelling.

1 Choose letters from the box to make words that end with the letters below.

ma	ha	cla	sti
pe	so	sta	be

_____ -st

_____ -mp

_____ -nd

_____ -nk

_____ -ng

_____ -sk

_____ -lt

_____ -ft

2 Write words that start with the following letters.

bl- _____ _____

cr- _____ _____

fr- _____ _____

sl- _____ _____

tr- _____ _____

scr- _____ _____

shr- _____ _____

thr- _____ _____

3 Write rhyming words for the words with silent letters.

(silent **b**) thumb cr _____

(silent 'gh') flight n _____

(silent **l**) would c _____

4 Add the missing silent letters from the box to finish each word.

d	n	s	k
k	gh	t	l

We ____nesday   i____land

shou ____d   lis____en

autum ____   ____nock

____nuckle   si ____t

5 Write words with the same pairs of vowels and the same vowel sounds as each word below.

school _____

eat   _____

blue   _____

boot   _____

rain   _____

meet   _____

Answers: **1** pest, stamp, hand, stink, clang, mask, belt, soft   **2** Answers will vary. Suggestions include: (bl) black, blue; (cr) crab, cream; (fr) Friday, fright; (sl) slip, slop; (tr) tree, try; (scr) scrap, scream; (shr) shrink, shred; (thr) three, throw.   **3** Suggestions include crumb, night, could.   **4** Wednesday, island, should, listen, autumn, knock, knuckle, sight   **5** Examples include pool, fool, drool; cheat, heat, beat; glue, flue; shoot, hoot, loot; strain, pain, again, remain; sleet, sheet, steel.

Real Test

SPELLING
*Two- and three-letter consonant blends,
silent consonants and vowel digraphs*

20 MIN

Please ask your parent or teacher to read to you the spelling words on page 213. Write the correct spelling of each word in the box.

1 "_____ down from the tree," called Dad.

2 The gorilla's _____ scraped on the ground.

3 The dog followed the _____ of the cat.

4 _____ wants to play chess?

5 I get my new reading glasses on _____.

6 I wish I _____ go to Jenna's after school.

7 Some trees lose their leaves in _____.

8 I borrowed a book about Kangaroo _____.

9 Ya-ya is _____ the baby a jumper.

10 Grandpa said his _____ is sore.

11 I dressed up as a _____ for Halloween.

12 Please use a _____ to tidy your hair.

13 King Arthur is said to have pulled a _____ from a stone.

14 Do you _____ what time the movie starts?

15 I heard the brakes on the car _____.

16 You must _____ to the instructions.

17 Be gentle or the cat will _____ you.

18 Recycle _____ cans.

☞ **Answers and explanations on pages 178-179**

Real Test

SPELLING
*Two- and three-letter consonant blends,
silent consonants and vowel digraphs*

(continued)

Each sentence has one word that is incorrect. Write the correct spelling of the underlined word in the box.

19 We ate <u>samon</u> sandwiches.

20 "Our boat <u>sangk</u>," said Luis.

21 Ben <u>whent</u> to the library at lunchtime.

22 "I ate the <u>hole</u> mango," said Petra.

23 <u>Lissen</u> to the teacher.

24 The children played on the <u>beech</u>.

25 The story was about <u>nights</u> who fought battles.

26 My shoes are too <u>tite</u>.

27 It takes one <u>our</u> to drive to Grandpa's.

Each sentence has one word that is incorrect. Write the correct spelling of the word in the box.

28 The jumper might shringk in the wash.

29 Rose sprained her rist.

30 Henry stomped through the puddle in his boowts.

31 We had swimming races in the pule.

32 I used gloo to stick the foil onto my collage.

33 You shoud walk your dog every day.

34 I mite go to the park later.

35 Thinck about your spelling.

☞ **Answers and explanations on pages 178-179**

Key Points

GRAMMAR AND PUNCTUATION
Verbs, commas in lists and commas in direct speech

1 A **verb** is essential in every clause or sentence. Verbs tell what's going on with the nouns.

★ Verbs can be a single word or a group of words.

Examples: ran, was running, won't run
There are different kinds of verbs.

★ **Doing verbs** are the action verbs. These verbs tell what actions happen, are happening or have happened,

Examples: swim → swimming → swam, jump → jumping → jumped, eat → eating → ate

★ **Being and having verbs** are the verbs that tell that something exists. They also tell that something belongs to, or relates to, something else.

Examples: is, are, were, has, have, belong, became
Being verbs: I <u>am</u> Ali. You <u>are</u> my friend. They <u>were</u> out. It <u>is</u> cold. It <u>was</u> cold yesterday.
Having verbs: Whales <u>have</u> blowholes. Harry <u>had</u> a cold last week.

★ **Thinking verbs** are the verbs that tell what goes on in the mind. You can't see these verbs taking place in the same way that you can see the doing verbs taking place.

Examples: believe, like, hate, love, want → wanted, hope → hoped → am hoping, was thinking

★ **Saying verbs** tell how something is being said.

Examples: <u>said</u> Jon, <u>yelled</u> the coach, <u>giggled</u> Tamara, <u>whispered</u> Sebastian, <u>croaked</u> the frog, <u>cried</u> the sad child

2 Verbs are often used at the start of **commands**.

Examples: <u>Clean</u> your feet. <u>Eat</u> your peas. <u>Stir</u> the soup. <u>Stop</u>!

3 **Verbs** have **tense.** Verb tense tells whether something has already happened (past tense), is happening now (present tense) or will happen in the future (future tense). Sometimes **helper verbs** are needed to show tense (e.g. will, can, has, have, had, do, does, did).

Examples:

■ Past tense: I <u>ran</u> to school. I <u>ate</u> strawberries for breakfast this morning.

■ Present tense: I <u>run</u> to school every day. I <u>am running</u> as fast as I can. I <u>eat</u> strawberries all the time.

■ Future tense: I <u>will run</u> to school tomorrow.
I <u>want to eat</u> the strawberries later.

4 **Commas** are used to separate items in a list.

Examples: Add the chopped carrots, potatoes, pumpkin, parsnips and turnip.
Note: You don't need a comma before 'and'.

YEH PEAS!

5 **Commas** are also used before and after direct speech,

Examples: "I love peas," declared William.
Luca said, "Let's all eat peas."

GRAMMAR AND PUNCTUATION
Verbs, commas in lists and commas in direct speech

15 MIN

Write the correct doing verb in each space.

1 Tran _____ his horse to school today.
(ride, rode, riding)

2 Denni _____ an apple every day.
(eats, eaten, eating)

3 Angus can _____ fifty metres.
(swam, swimming, swim)

4 The children have _____ their homework.
(finish, finishing, finished)

Choose a helper verb from the box for each sentence.

must	has	can	did
A	B	C	D

5 My clever dog _____ count to three.

6 We _____ learn our spelling for the test.

7 Dad _____ try to fix my bike yesterday.

8 Mum _____ eaten all the strawberries.

Choose a thinking verb from the box to complete each sentence.

believes	worried	like	loves
A	B	C	D

9 Mum is _____ about Grandma.

10 I _____ walking our dog.

11 Grandpa _____ to watch tennis.

12 David _____ the tooth fairy will visit tonight.

Choose a saying verb from the box to complete each sentence.

barked	called	quacked	grunted
A	B	C	D

13 "Jump in the pond!" _____ the mother duck.

14 "It's so much fun!" _____ the children from the Ferris wheel.

15 "Stay out of my cave!" _____ the Troll.

16 "Woof woof!" _____ the dog.

17 Which sentence is punctuated correctly?
A Tina bought eggs flour sugar oats and walnuts
B Tina bought eggs flour sugar oats and walnuts.
C Tina bought eggs, flour, sugar, oats and walnuts.
D Tina bought eggs, flour, sugar, oats, and, walnuts.

18 Number the sentences in time order, 1–3, starting with what happens first (1).

☐ Then I cleaned my teeth.

☐ I had dinner.

☐ After that I went to bed.

Real Test

GRAMMAR AND PUNCTUATION
Verbs, commas in lists and commas in direct speech

20 MIN

1 Which sentence is correct?

A The frog jump over the lily pad.

B The frog jumping over the lily pad.

C The frog jumper over the lily pad.

D The frog jumped over the lily pad.

Choose a word from the box to complete each sentence.

were	was	are	is
A	B	C	D

2 The ducks _____ swimming in the pond yesterday.

3 The duck _____ swimming in the pond yesterday.

4 A duck _____ swimming in the pond, right now.

5 Ducks _____ swimming in the pond, right now.

6 Which of the following correctly completes this sentence?

Tomorrow we ▮▮▮▮ to the library.

A will go   **B** be going   **C** went   **D** had gone

7 Which sentence is correct?

A The children is collecting autumn leaves.

B The children were collecting autumn leaves.

C The children was collecting autumn leaves.

D The children will collecting autumn leaves.

8 A comma (**,**) has been left out of this sentence. Where should the comma go?

Dad bought　rice, cashews, chicken　broccoli　and　onions for the stir fry.
　　　　　　　Ⓐ　　　　　　　　　　　Ⓑ　Ⓒ　Ⓓ

9 Which word correctly completes this sentence?

Billy counted his pencils and ▮▮▮▮ that some were missing.

A seen   **B** saw   **C** sawn   **D** see

10 Which word correctly completes this sentence?

"Let's read a book," ▮▮▮▮ Mum.

A talk   **B** suggested   **C** asked   **D** speaking

11 Which word correctly completes this sentence?

Helen ▮▮▮▮ she is tired.

A sayed   **B** saying   **C** say   **D** said

12 Which word or word group correctly completes this sentence?

Pets quickly become sick if ▮▮▮▮ in a hot car.

A lefted   **B** left   **C** being left   **D** leaved

☞ **Answers and explanations on page 179**

Real Test

13 Which of these is a complete sentence?

   A Go to the library.   **B** Five fat frogs.

   C My friends's house.   **D** Mum and Dad.

Choose a word from the box to complete each sentence.

are	is	has	am
A	B	C	D

14 My name _____ Petra.

15 I _____ eight years old.

16 Children in Dunedoo _____ lucky.

17 Dunedoo _____ great schools.

18 Which of these is a complete sentence?

   A Fabien and Tina.   **B** Yesterday, at midnight.

   C Wendy ran in the race.   **D** Bread and honey.

19 Which sentence tells about the past?

   A I went to the park.   **B** I want to go to the park.

   C I will go to the park.   **D** I am going to the park.

Choose a doing verb from the box to start each command.

Beat	Add	Bake	Pour
A	B	C	D

20 _____ the flour to the mixture.

21 _____ the eggs until smooth.

22 _____ the juice into a glass.

23 _____ in a hot oven for 30 minutes.

24 Which sentence has the correct punctuation?

   A "I love stories about aliens said Frankie."

   B "I love stories, about aliens" said Frankie.

   C "I love stories about aliens," said Frankie.

   D "I love stories about aliens," said, Frankie

25 Choose the correct word to complete this sentence.

Yuki does not ▅▅▅▅ peanuts.

   A eating   **B** ate   **C** eaten   **D** eat

☞ Answers and explanations on page 179

Key Points

1 **A procedure** is an informative text. Procedures tell how to do something.

Examples: play a game, use equipment, make something, cook something, cross the road, play safely, find your way somewhere

2 Recipes, directions and instructions are procedures.

3 Procedures often have the following structure:

a a **heading** or **goal**

b a list of things needed such as **ingredients** or **equipment**

c a **sequence of steps** which are sometimes numbered and sometimes listed as bullet points (The steps are often written as commands.)

d a **conclusion** or **final statement** (e.g. suitable for freezing; store in an airtight container). A conclusion is not essential.

4 Procedures use doing verbs to tell what needs to be done. Doing verbs are used to start commands.

Example: Shake well before each use.

Hair-growth Tonic on page 59 is a recipe. The heading tells what the recipe is for. There is a list of ingredients. The method is written as a series of steps in numbered sequence. Each step is a command that starts with a verb. A concluding statement gives instructions for using the tonic and a warning about its use.

How to train a pet mouse on page 60 is a set of instructions. The heading gives the goal of the instructions. After the goal there is a statement of advice: *Mice are timid so training will take time and patience.* Each instruction tells what to do. Each instruction begins with a verb. The instructions are listed in number order, 1 to 5. There is a concluding statement.

Rules for young chimpanzees on page 61 is a set of rules. Bullet points are used rather than numbers because the rules are of equal value. Each rule is a command. The commands tell what to do. Each command starts with a verb.

READING
Procedures: recipes

Read *Hair-growth Tonic*. Circle the correct answers to the questions below.

1 This kind of text is a

A story.

B recount.

C report.

D recipe.

2 Which word from the text means 'throw away'?

A massage

B discard

C pour

D avoid

3 What sort of oil is used to make the tonic?

A tomato

B olive

C coconut

D hair-growth oil

4 How should the tonic be used?

A Massage onto head.

B Massage onto any hairless skin.

C Massage over legs.

D Store Hair-growth Tonic in fridge.

5 A strainer

A collects lumpy bits.

B pulls your muscles.

C separates coconut from the shell.

D is used for storing liquids.

6 Where should the tonic be stored?

A overnight

B in the fridge

C daily

D until signs of hair growth

7 Who would use the tonic?

A babies

B people with hairy feet

C bald people

D hungry people

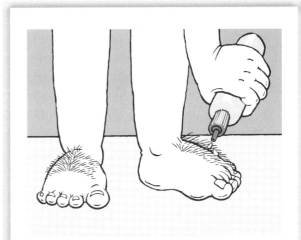

1 **Hair-growth Tonic**

2 Tonic makes hair grow thick and fast.

3 Not suitable for babies.

4 **Ingredients**

5 1 tablespoon tomato sauce

6 1 cup coconut oil

7 1 teaspoon grated ginger

8 1 teaspoon grated garlic

9 **Method**

10 1 Mix together all ingredients.

11 2 Pour mixture through a strainer.

12 3 Discard any lumpy bits.

13 4 Pour tonic into a clean bottle.

14 5 Shake well before each use.

15 6 Store Hair-growth Tonic in fridge.

16 **Instructions for use**: Massage into

17 affected area (bald spots) daily until

18 signs of hair growth. Only for use on

19 heads. Especially avoid getting tonic

20 on soles of feet.

Answers: **1** D **2** B **3** C **4** A **5** A **6** B **7** C

☞ **Explanations on pages 179-180**

Real Test

15 min

1 **How to train a pet mouse**

2 Mice are timid so training will take time and patience.

3 **1** Make sure your mouse is happy to be handled. The more
4 you handle your mouse the more easily it will learn tricks.
5 You can rub your hands on the mouse bedding so that you
6 smell more mouse-like until the mouse gets used to you.

7 **2** Reward your mouse with its favourite food treat each time
8 you handle it. Try treats such as millet, oats or sunflower seeds.

9 **3** Make a clicking noise with your tongue each time you
10 give the mouse a treat. It will learn that the clicking sound
11 means a treat. Eventually it will come straight to you
12 whenever you make the sound.

13 **4** Reward all good behaviour with food treats.

14 **5** Keep training sessions short.

15 *Note*: Mice are sociable and like to live with other mice. Single mice get bored and lonely.

Read *How to train a pet mouse.* Circle the correct answers to the questions below.

1 These instructions are for
   A people with pet mice.
   B vets.
   C Teachers.
   D children.

2 Which treats do mice prefer?
   A toys.   **B** chips
   C oats   **D** rewards

3 What does *sociable* mean in the text?
   A friendly   **B** bored
   C active   **D** lonely

3 Trained mice learn that a clicking sound means
   A stand up.
   B here's a food treat.
   C the mouse needs a reward.
   D a mouse is in training.

5 Why does training a mouse take time?
   A Mice are timid.
   B Mice can't stand up and beg.
   C Mice are sociable.
   D Mice like to eat all the time.

6 Why do pet mice sometimes get lonely?
   A Their home is too big for them.
   B They aren't taught enough tricks.
   C Their owner doesn't handle them enough.
   D They don't have other mice to live with.

7 Why would you rub your hands on the mouse bedding?
   A to get mouse germs
   B to warm the bedding
   C to make you smell like a mouse
   D to feel if the bedding is wet

☞ **Answers and explanations on page 180**

Real Test

READING
Procedures: rules

15 min

Read *Rules for young chimpanzees*. Circle the correct answers to the question below.

1 **Rules for young chimpanzees**
2 ● Stay out of the way of the alpha male.
3 ● Greet other chimps with a kiss and a hug.
4 ● Listen out for happy, barking sounds in
5 the morning. These sounds mean that
6 food has been found.
7 ● Eat fruit, leaves, termites, vegetables,
8 eggs, nuts, honey and wild pig when you
9 can catch one.
10 ● Use grass and leaves to build ground
11 nests, for afternoon naps.
12 ● Rest during the hottest part of the day.
13 ● Build nests high in trees for night
14 sleeping, safe from hungry leopards.
15 ● Help your friends and family with grooming; remove dirt and ticks.
16 ● Stay close to your mother until you are at least four years old.

1 Chimps make this sound when they find food.

A growling   B barking
C grunting   D hissing

2 Chimpanzees are eaten by

A alpha males.   B leopards.
C termites.   D ticks.

3 At night chimpanzees sleep

A in nests on the ground.
B in grass and leaves.
C in nests high in trees.
D with friends.

4 Young chimps need to *stay out of the way of*

A missing a meal.
B friends who play tricks.
C hot days.
D the alpha male.

5 Why do chimps build nests on the ground?

A for afternoon naps
B to catch pigs
C for sleeping at night
D to hide from dangers

6 Young chimpanzees should follow the rules so that

A they have food.
B they make friends.
C they learn how to be safe and happy.
D they will be clean.

7 Chimps eat

A plants only.
B leopards.
C eggs and plants.
D a variety of plant and animal foods.

☞ **Answers and explanations on pages 180–181**

Before you start, read **Understanding procedures** on page 58.

Today you are going to write a **recipe.** Your purpose is to write an imaginative recipe for readers of your own age. You can create a recipe for anything you like. It could be for something you would like to eat. It could be a magical recipe for a story idea. Include any warnings, special advice or instructions for users of your recipe.

Before you start to write, think about:
- the goal of the recipe
- how it will be used
- the ingredients needed
- the steps needed to make the recipe (method).

Remember to:
- plan your writing
- write the steps as commands
- be specific with ingredients and amounts
- use action verbs
- write in sentences
- check spelling and punctuation
- write as neatly as you can so that readers can understand your writing
- ask a parent or teacher to read and check your finished work.

Use your own paper to write your recipe.

☞**Marking Guide on page 181**

Real Test and Tips

Before you start, read **Understanding procedures** on page 58.

Today you are going to write a set of **instructions**. The instructions can be for anything you choose. They could be for how to play a game, how to make or build something, how to use a piece of equipment, or how to care for a pet.

Write about something you are very familiar with. Imagine you are writing the instructions for children of your own age who have never done this before. Your readers will need very clear instructions to tell them what to do.

Before you start to write, think about:
- the activity you will write the instructions for
- the heading or goal of the instructions
- the equipment needed
- the steps needed.

Remember to:
- plan your writing
- write the steps as commands using action verbs
- write the steps in sequence—use numbering
- check your punctuation and spelling
- write neatly so that readers can understand your writing
- ask a parent or teacher to read and check your finished work.

Use your own paper to write your instructions.

☞ **Marking Guide on pages 181-182**

TIPS FOR WRITING RECOUNTS

Text structure and organisation

A **recount** tells about events that have happened. Recounts can be found in diaries, journals, letters, newspaper articles, biographies, autobiographies and conversations. Recounts can make use of illustrations, photos, film and time lines.

Recounts can be factual. A recount of a science experiment is one example of a factual recount.

Recounts can give opinions. In diaries and letters, writers give opinions about events they are recounting.

Before you start to write a recount, think about:

- the **purpose** and **audience** for your text
- the **orientation** or **introduction**—this tells readers who was involved in the events, and when and where events took place
- the **sequence of events** (These need to be told in time order. Start with what happened first, then what happened next, what happened after, and what happened at the end.)
- a **conclusion**. You can sum up the events or write a concluding statement. This is optional in a recount.

You can include personal comments and judgements in a recount.

Expressing and developing ideas

When you write a personal recount remember to:

- use past-tense verbs because the events have already happened
- use thinking and feeling verbs to describe what you think and feel about events
- use words that tell <u>where</u> (e.g. at the park) and <u>when</u> (e.g. last Sunday, during the summer, firstly, then)
- use noun groups (e.g. my family) and pronouns (e.g. us, I, they, he, she, them) to label the people involved in the events
- use first-person pronouns consistently (e.g. I went to the museum last Thursday. I had a great day.)
- proofread your text and check that it makes sense
- check spelling and punctuation.

When you have finished your writing give it to an adult to read and check.

(a sample answer to the question on page 66)

Harmony Day

Our school held a multicultural feast day, last Thursday, to celebrate Harmony Day. Students invited their families to join in.

In the morning each class made a different kind of food. There was Vietnamese food, Indian food, Korean food, Greek food, Malaysian food, Indonesian food, Lebanese food and Fijian food. We ate lunch in the assembly hall. All the food was delicious. My favourite food was the Vietnamese spring rolls. They were made by Thanh in Year 1 with the help of his grandmother. There was a tasty dipping sauce for the spring rolls. It was made with lime juice, fish sauce, chilli, garlic and sugar.

In the afternoon we played different sports and games. We had to work in teams. We had relays, scavenger hunts, ball games, tag and hopscotch. I liked the ball games best. My team worked together well in captain ball.

I am looking forward to our Harmony Day celebrations next year. I hope we can invite family members again and have another multicultural feast.

This text is beyond what would be expected of a typical Year 2 student. It is provided here as a model. The assessment comments are based on the marking criteria used to assess the NAPLAN Writing Test.

Vocabulary
- Foods are classified according to country of origin. Ingredients for the dipping sauce are listed.
- Past-tense verbs are used appropriately.

Sentence structure
- A variety of sentence structures is used.

Ideas
- The purpose of the writing is to recount events that have taken place. Food items and activities are listed and grouped logically.

Punctuation
- Appropriate sentence punctuation is used.
- Commas are used accurately to separate items in lists.
- Proper nouns have capital letters.

Spelling
- Challenging words are spelt correctly, e.g. *delicious, favourite.*

Audience
- The text is for a school and local community audience. The context is established in the introduction which tells who, where and when.

Text structure
- The text follows the usual structure of a personal recount. It has an introduction. Events are sequenced through time over one day. There is a summing-up or concluding statement. Personal opinions are included.

Paragraphing
- Ideas are grouped in paragraphs. Each paragraph is built around one idea or one aspect of the topic.
- Paragraph 1 establishes the context for events.
- Paragraph 2 describes food.
- Paragraph 3 describes activities.
- Paragraph 4 gives a conclusion.

Cohesion
- The text is a first-person recount. Pronouns are consistent.
- Events are linked in time order.

Character and setting
- The writer's point of view is established: *I hope, my favourite, delicious.*

© Pascal Press ISBN 978 1 74125 419 8

Real Test and Tips

WRITING
Recount text

`40 MIN`

Before you start, read the **Tips for writing recounts** on page 64.

Today you are going to write a **recount**. Your purpose is to tell readers of your own age about something that happened to you or something that you did. It might be about a classroom experiment that you did, a school excursion that you went on, a game you played, or something you did at school with your friends. Make sure you recount events in time order.

Before you start to write, think about the event or activity.
- What happened first?
- What happened next?
- What happened last?
- How did you feel about events?

Remember to:
- plan your writing
- make sure ideas are grouped in paragraphs
- use past-tense verbs
- use pronouns to refer to yourself and others
- write in sentences
- check spelling and punctuation
- write neatly so that readers can understand your writing
- ask a parent or teacher to read and check your finished work.

Use your own paper to write your recount.

☞ Marking Guide on page 182

We're halfway there!

Week 3

This is what we cover this week:

Day 1   **Measurement and Geometry:** ◎ Measurement and shape

Day 2   **Measurement and Geometry:** ◎ Time and mass

Day 3   **Spelling:** ◎ Long vowels, 'qu', common contractions and vowel/consonant blends

   Grammar and Punctuation: ◎ Types of sentences, joining sentences and sentence punctuation

Day 4   **Reading:** ◎ Understanding narratives

Day 5   **Writing:** ◎ Narratives

Test Your Skills 1

MEASUREMENT AND GEOMETRY
Measurement and shape

20 MIN

Write down the letter beside the instrument you would use to measure

1 how long a cake tin is.

2 the mass of flour to put in a cake.

3 the amount of milk to put in a cake.

4 how long the cake is in the oven.

5 how hot it is in the kitchen.

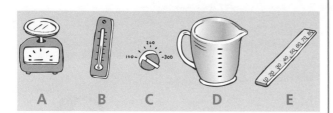

A   B   C   D   E

Here are some ribbons.

Red

Yellow

Blue

Pink

Green

What colour is

6 the longest ribbon?

7 the shortest ribbon?

8 the ribbon that is longer than the pink ribbon but shorter than the red ribbon?

These jugs all hold different amounts when full. The number of litres can be seen.

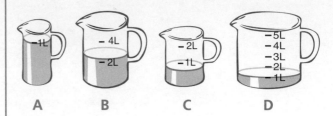

A   B   C   D

9 Which jug has the most juice in it?

10 Which jug has the least amount of juice in it?

11 Which two jugs have the same amount of juice?

[   ] and [   ]

Look at these shapes.

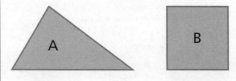
A
B

C
D

12 Which shape is a circle?

13 Which shape is a triangle?

14 Which shape is a square?

MEASUREMENT AND GEOMETRY
Measurement and shape

 20 MIN

Look at these shapes.

How many of the shapes are

1 triangles?

2 circles?

3 rectangles?

This is a rectangular prism.

4 How many faces does it have?

5 What shape are its faces?

6 How many corners does it have?

7 How many edges does it have?

This is a triangular prism.

8 How many faces does it have?

9 How many faces are triangles?

10 How many faces are rectangles?

11 How many corners does it have?

12 How many edges does it have?

Choose the object that matches each name.

13 cube   14 cone

15 cylinder   16 pyramid

 A   B   C   D

Three pavers have been put on this space.

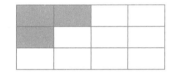

17 How many pavers altogether will fit on the space?

18 How many more pavers will fit on the space?

These rectangular prisms were built with blocks like this.

How many blocks were needed?

19   20

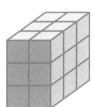   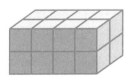

Answers: 1 4 2 2 3 3 4 6 5 rectangles
6 8 7 12 8 5 9 2 10 3 11 6 12 9
13 D 14 B 15 A 16 C 17 12 18 9
19 18 20 16

Excel Revise in a Month Year 2 NAPLAN*-style Tests   69

Key Points

MEASUREMENT AND GEOMETRY
Measurement and shape

1 **Instruments can be used to measure things like length, mass and time.**

2 **To measure the length of something you can use a ruler or tape measure.** Length can be measured in millimetres, centimetres, metres or kilometres.

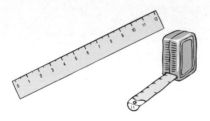

Example: You might use a ruler to find how long a cake tin is.

3 **To find the mass or weight of an object you can use scales.** These might be kitchen scales, bathroom scales or balance scales. Mass can be measured in milligrams, grams, kilograms or tonnes.

Example: You would use kitchen scales to measure the mass of flour needed in a cake.

4 **To find the amount of liquid you could use a cup or a measuring jug.** The capacity of a cup or jug could be measured in millilitres or litres.

Example: To find the amount of milk to put in a cake you could use a measuring jug.

5 **To measure a length of time, you might use a clock, a stopwatch, an oven timer or an hourglass (egg-timer).** Time can be measured in seconds, minutes or hours, or in days, weeks, months or years.

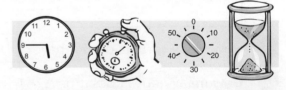

Example: You would use an oven timer to find how long a cake is in the oven.

6 **To measure temperature, you would use a thermometer.** Temperature is measured in degrees.

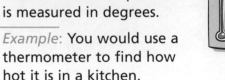

Example: You would use a thermometer to find how hot it is in a kitchen.

MEASUREMENT AND GEOMETRY
Measurement and shape

(continued)

7 **You can often find the longest or tallest of a group without needing to measure. You just need to compare.** Often arranging objects in order can help you compare.

Example: These ribbons have been placed in order from longest to shortest.

Blue
Red
Green
Pink
Yellow

The longest ribbon is blue.
The shortest ribbon is yellow.
The ribbon that is longer than the pink ribbon but shorter than the red ribbon is the green ribbon.

8 **A scale on an instrument helps you to measure.**

Example: Each of these jugs has a scale showing the number of litres.

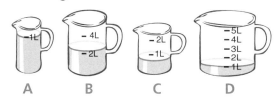

- Jug B has the most juice because it is the only jug holding more than 2 litres.
- Jug C has the least amount of juice because it is the only one holding less than 1 litre.
- Jug A and Jug D have the same amount because they both hold 1 litre.

9 **Any flat shape that has exactly 3 sides is a triangle.** Triangles might look different from one another, but if they have 3 sides they are all the same type of shape.

So there are 4 triangles in this group of shapes.

10 **A shape that is round like a ring is called a circle.** There are 2 circles in this group of shapes.

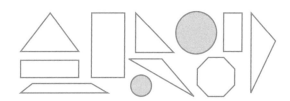

11 **A rectangle is a shape that has 4 sides. All the corners of a rectangle must be right angles.** In this group of shapes there are 3 rectangles.

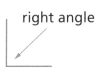

right angle

12 **A square is a special rectangle where all the sides are the same length.**

MEASUREMENT AND GEOMETRY
Measurement and shape

(continued)

13 **A rectangular prism is a 3D shape like a box.** 3D shapes are not flat but take up space. A rectangular prism has 6 faces. The faces are all rectangles.

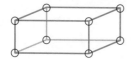

14 **A rectangular prism has 8 corners.**

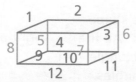

These corners are often called **vertices**.

15 **A rectangular prism has 12 edges.**

The edges are the lines where the faces meet.

16 A **cube** is a special rectangular prism. All of the edges of a cube are the same length.

17 **A triangular prism is another 3D object.** It has 5 faces.

2 of the faces are triangles and the other 3 faces are rectangles.

A triangular prism has 6 corners and 9 edges.

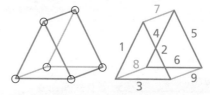

18 A **cylinder** is a special 3D object. Each end is a circle and there is a curved surface between the ends.

Example: A can of drink and a water pipe are examples of cylinders.

19 A **cone** is another special 3D object. One end is a circle and a curved surface comes to a point (vertex) at the other end.

Example: An ice-cream cone and a witch's hat are examples of cones.

MEASUREMENT AND GEOMETRY
Measurement and shape

(continued)

20 A **sphere** is a 3D object shaped like a ball.

Example: **An orange and the Earth are examples of spheres.**

21 A **pyramid** is a 3D object with a base and triangular sides that meet at a point. Pyramids are named after the base.

square-based pyramid   triangular pyramid   rectangular pyramid

22 **Area is a measure of flat space.** You can divide an area into squares of the same size. Then, by counting the number of squares, you can compare the size of areas.

Example:

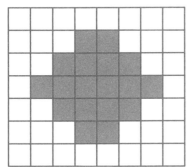

The shaded area is 18 square units.

Example:

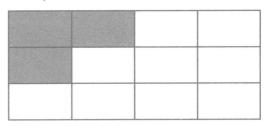

■ You can see that 3 pavers have been placed on this space. By counting, you can see that 12 pavers could fit on the space altogether.

■ You could also get this answer of 12 by seeing that there are 3 rows with 4 pavers able to fit in each row, so 3 × 4 = 12.

■ By counting you can also see that 9 more pavers will fit on the space. 12 − 3 = 9

23 **Volume is a measure of the space in a 3D object.** You can find volume by counting cubes.

Examples:

 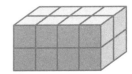

■ The first object has 18 blocks because there are 6 blocks in the top layer and 3 layers.
6 + 6 + 6 = 18 or 3 × 6 = 18

■ The second object has 16 blocks because there are 8 blocks in the top layer and 2 layers. 2 × 8 = 16

MEASUREMENT AND GEOMETRY
Measurement and shape

1 Which dog is the tallest?

A   B   C   D

2 What is this 3D shape?

A   pyramid
B   cone
C   cube
D   cylinder

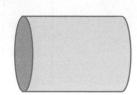

3 Choose all the shapes that are triangles.

A   B   C   D   E   F

4 This is a square pyramid.

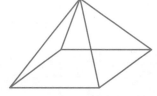

How many faces does it have?
A 4   B 5   C 6   D 8

5 Which would you use to measure length?

A   B   C   D

6 Cass is putting stamps on a card.

How many stamps like these
will fit on the card altogether?

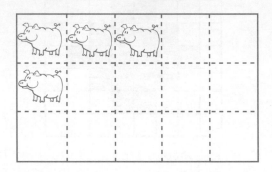

☞ **Answers and explanations on page 183**

Real Test

MEASUREMENT AND GEOMETRY
Measurement and shape

(continued)

7 Which number is in the circle and in the triangle, but not in the square?

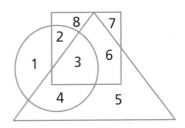

8 Luke built this cube from blocks like this.

How many blocks did Luke need?

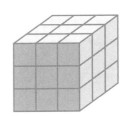

9

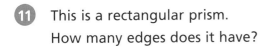

How many of these shapes are rectangles?

A 2   B 3   C 4   D more than 4

10 This bucket holds 20 litres when full. There is some milk in the bucket.

About how much milk is in the bucket?

A 16 litres   B 11 litres
C 6 litres   D 1 litre

11 This is a rectangular prism.
How many edges does it have?

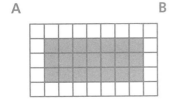

A 6   B 8   C 10   D 12

12 Which shape has the most squares coloured?

A   B   C   D

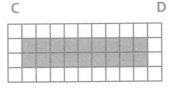
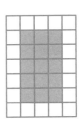

📝 Answers and explanations on page 183

Excel Revise in a Month Year 2 NAPLAN*-style Tests

Test Your Skills 1

MEASUREMENT AND GEOMETRY
Time and mass

20 MIN

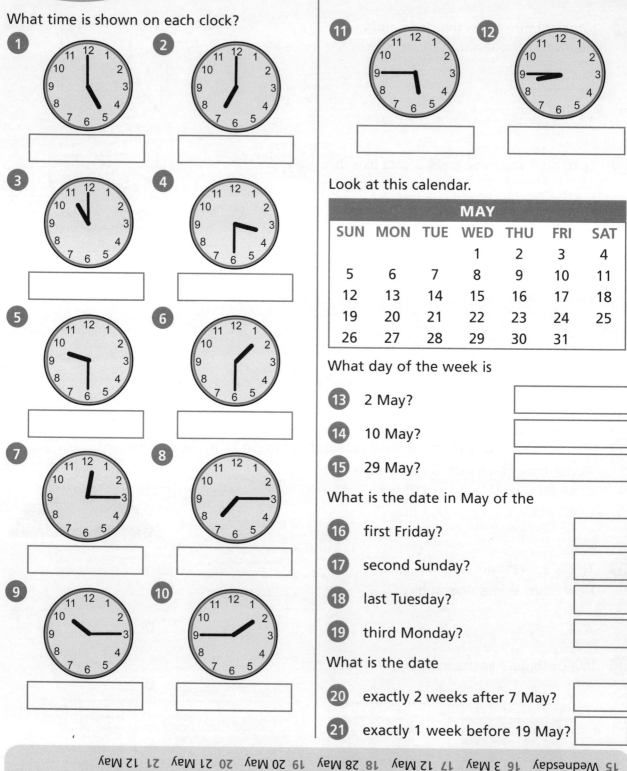

What time is shown on each clock?

1 [ ]

2 [ ]

3 [ ]

4 [ ]

5 [ ]

6 [ ]

7 [ ]

8 [ ]

9 [ ]

10 [ ]

11 [ ]

12 [ ]

Look at this calendar.

MAY						
SUN	MON	TUE	WED	THU	FRI	SAT
			1	2	3	4
5	6	7	8	9	10	11
12	13	14	15	16	17	18
19	20	21	22	23	24	25
26	27	28	29	30	31	

What day of the week is

13 2 May? [ ]

14 10 May? [ ]

15 29 May? [ ]

What is the date in May of the

16 first Friday? [ ]

17 second Sunday? [ ]

18 last Tuesday? [ ]

19 third Monday? [ ]

What is the date

20 exactly 2 weeks after 7 May? [ ]

21 exactly 1 week before 19 May? [ ]

MEASUREMENT AND GEOMETRY
Time and mass

1 List in order the 12 months of the year.

How many days are in

2 April?

3 June?

4 August?

5 October?

Answer true or false.

6 The three summer months are November, December and January.

What season (spring, summer, autumn or winter) is it in

7 January?

8 July?

9 October?

10 March?

How long is it

11 from 9 o'clock in the morning until 3 o'clock in the afternoon?

12 from quarter to seven until quarter past seven?

Circle the letter on the object that has the greater mass.

13

14

A or B   C or D

Answers: 1 January, February, March, April, May, June, July, August, September, October, November, December 2 30 3 30 4 31 5 31 6 false 7 summer 8 winter 9 spring 10 autumn 11 6 hours 12 half an hour (or 30 minutes) 13 A 14 D

Excel Revise in a Month Year 2 NAPLAN*-style Tests

77

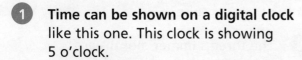

1 **Time can be shown on a digital clock** like this one. This clock is showing 5 o'clock.

Other clocks have a face and hands.
The longer hand is the minute hand and travels once around the clock in one hour. The shorter hand is the hour hand and points to the hour.

Examples:

■ This clock is also showing 5 o'clock. The longer hand points to 12 and the shorter hand points to 5.

■ When the minute hand points to 12 and the hour hand points to 7, it is 7 o'clock.

■ When the minute hand points to 12 and the hour hand points to 11, it is 11 o'clock.

Examples:

■ When the minute (longer) hand points to 6, it is **half past the hour**. The hour (shorter) hand should be halfway past the hour.

■ So if the minute hand points to 6 and the hour hand is halfway past 3 (halfway between 3 and 4) then the time is half past three.

■ When the minute hand points to 6 and the hour hand is halfway past 9, the time is half past nine.

■ When the minute hand points to 6 and the hour hand is halfway past 1, the time is half past one.

Examples:

When the minute hand points to 3, it is **quarter past the hour**. The hour hand should be quarter of the way past the hour.

■ So if the minute hand points to 3 and the hour hand is a quarter of the way past 12, then the time is quarter past twelve.

■ When the minute hand points to 3 and the hour hand is a quarter of the way past 7, the time is quarter past seven.

■ When the minute hand points to 3 and the hour hand is a quarter of the way past 10, the time is quarter past ten.

Examples:

When the minute hand points to 9, it is **quarter to the hour**. The hour hand will have moved three-quarters of the way to the next hour, or a quarter before the hour.

Key Points

MEASUREMENT AND GEOMETRY
Time and mass

(continued)

- So if the minute hand points to 9 and the hour hand points to a quarter of the way before 2, then the time is quarter to two.
- When the minute hand points to 9 and the hour hand is a quarter before 6, the time is quarter to six.
- When the minute hand points to 9 and the hour hand is a quarter before 9, the time is quarter to nine.

2 The minute hand makes it easy to see the time and is needed when you want the accurate time, **but you can still tell the time by looking at the position of the hour hand alone**.

3 **A calendar is a table that shows all the dates for a month or a year.**

Example:

MAY						
SUN	MON	TUE	WED	THU	FRI	SAT
			1	2	3	4
5	6	7	8	9	10	11
12	13	14	15	16	17	18
19	20	21	22	23	24	25
26	27	28	29	30	31	

From this calendar you can see that 2 May is a Thursday.

MAY						
SUN	MON	TUE	WED	THU	FRI	SAT
			1	2	3	4
5	6	7	8	9	10	11
12	13	14	15	16	17	18
19	20	21	22	23	24	25
26	27	28	29	30	31	

10 May is a Friday and 29 May is a Wednesday.
3, 10, 17, 24 and 31 May are all Fridays.
So the first Friday is 3 May.
The second Sunday is 12 May and the last Tuesday is 28 May.
The third Monday is 20 May.

4 **To find the date of a day one week after another you just need to look at the next date in that column.**

Example: The date one week after 7 May is 14 May and another week after that is 21 May. The day one week before 19 May is 12 May.

5 **There are 12 months in a year.**

The months are January, February, March, April, May, June, July, August, September, October, November and December.

6 **February has 28 days in a normal year and 29 days in a leap year** when there is one extra day.

7 **April, June, September and November all have 30 days.**

8 **All of the other months have 31 days.**

9 You might remember the number of days in each month by learning this poem:

30 days has September,
April, June and November.
All the rest have thirty-one,
except for February alone,
which has 28 days clear
and 29 in each leap year.

Key Points

MEASUREMENT AND GEOMETRY
Time and mass

(continued)

10 **There are four seasons in a year.**
These are spring, summer, autumn and winter.

In Australia, the months of spring are September, October and November.
The summer months are December, January and February.
Autumn is March, April and May.
Winter is June, July and August.
So in January it is summer, in July it is winter and in October it is spring. In March it is autumn.

11 **There are 24 hours in a day.**
To find the length of time from 9 o'clock in the morning until 3 o'clock in the afternoon you count the hours. It is 3 hours until 12 noon and another 3 hours until 3 o'clock. So it is 6 hours from 9 o'clock in the morning until 3 o'clock in the afternoon.

12 **There are 60 minutes in an hour.**
From a quarter to 7 until 7 o'clock is a quarter of an hour or 15 minutes. From 7 o'clock to a quarter past 7 is another 15 minutes so it is 30 minutes or half an hour from a quarter to 7 until a quarter past 7.

The minute hand moves halfway around the clock so the time taken is half an hour.

13 **A set of scales is an instrument used to measure mass.**

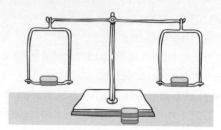

If the set of scales is in **balance** then the masses of the two objects are the same.
If one side of the scales is lower than the other, then the mass of the object on the side that is lower is greater than that of the object on the higher side.

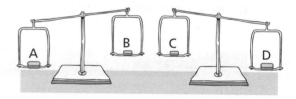

So, in the first diagram, Object A has a greater mass than Object B. You might say A is heavier than B.
In the second diagram, Object D has a greater mass than Object C.

Real Test

MEASUREMENT AND GEOMETRY
Time and mass

1 What time is shown on this clock?

A quarter past five   B quarter to five   C quarter past four   D quarter to four

2 Oliver was born on 18 July 2012.

On what day of the week was Oliver born?
A Saturday
B Tuesday
C Wednesday
D Sunday

July 2012						
SUN	MON	TUE	WED	THU	FRI	SAT
1	2	3	4	5	6	7
8	9	10	11	12	13	14
15	16	17	18	19	20	21
22	23	24	25	26	27	28
29	30	31				

3 Which of these is used to measure mass?

A   B    C    D

4 The minute hand is missing from this clock.

What time is it?
A 8 o'clock   B half past eight   C quarter to eight   D 9 o'clock

5 Write the correct time below each clock. Choose from these times:
3:25, 5:15, 9:35, 5:03, 9:25, 6:45, 6:15, 3:30, 5:45, 6:30

☞ **Answers and explanations on page 184**

Real Test

MEASUREMENT AND GEOMETRY
Time and mass

(continued)

6 Jo is getting married in Sydney next September. What season will it be?

A spring   B summer   C autumn   D winter

7 How long is a quarter of an hour?

A 15 minutes   B 15 seconds   C 25 minutes   D 25 seconds

8 This is a calendar for September.
What is the date of the third Saturday?

A 13
B 20
C 21
D 27

September						
SUN	MON	TUE	WED	THU	FRI	SAT
	1	2	3	4	5	6
7	8	9	10	11	12	13
14	15	16	17	18	19	20
21	22	23	24	25	26	27
28	29	30				

9 Which of these months has 31 days?

A February   B April   C October   D November

10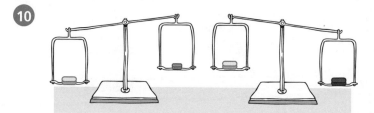

Which shows the objects in order from lowest mass to highest mass?

A   B   C   D

11 Ben gets to work at 9 o'clock in the morning and leaves work at 4 o'clock in the afternoon. How many hours is Ben at work?

A 5   B 6   C 7   D 8

12 25 December is Christmas Day.
What is the date exactly three weeks before Christmas?

A 4 December
B 10 December
C 22 December
D 11 December

December						
SUN	MON	TUE	WED	THU	FRI	SAT
				1	2	3
4	5	6	7	8	9	10
11	12	13	14	15	16	17
18	19	20	21	22	23	24
25	26	27	28	29	30	31

☞ **Answers and explanations on page 184**

Key Points

SPELLING
*Long vowels, 'qu', common contractions
and vowel/consonant blends*

When learning to spell a new word:
- listen for the individual sounds in the word
- look at the letter combinations that make the sounds
- use the strategy **LOOK, SAY, COVER, WRITE, SAY, CHECK** to practise spelling any words you find challenging.

Long vowels

1 Sometimes vowels (*a e i o u*) say their own names inside words. These sounds are called long vowel sounds.

2 The letter *e* often makes other vowels take on these long vowel sounds. In words where there is a consonant and an *e*, the vowel before the consonant often says its own name. The *e* is silent at the end of these words.

Examples: hate, ape, make, these, theme, five, bite, hope, home, tube, use

'qu'

3 The letter *q* is usually followed by *u* and then 'qu' says 'kw'.

4 Some words start with 'qu'.

Examples: queen, quote, quick, quack, quite, quit, quiet, quest, quiz, question

5 Other words have 'qu' in the middle.

Examples: earthquake, equal, squelch, squid, squeeze, squeal

6 Occasionally there is an exception and 'qu' does not say the 'kw' sound.

Example: plaque

Common contractions

7 Contractions are formed when letters are left out of words to shorten them. Apostrophes (') are used to mark the place of the letters that have been left out.

Examples: The **o** is left out of the word *not* in the following: do not → don't, does not → doesn't, cannot → can't, was not → wasn't, is not → isn't, are not → aren't, did not → didn't

8 Some verbs can be contracted after a pronoun.

Examples: I am → I'm, you are → you're, they are → they're, we are → we're, he is → he's, she is → she's, it is → it's

Vowel/consonant blends

9 Sometimes vowels blend with consonants.

Examples:
- 'ar'—far, farm, alarm, hard, garden
- 'or'—for, short, store, bore, before
- 'ow'—cow, how, power, shower, owl
- 'ay'—Monday, delay, stay, pay, play

squeeze

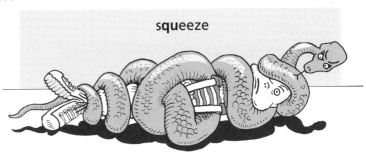

Test Your Skills

SPELLING
Long vowels, 'qu', common contractions and vowel/consonant blends

15 MIN

1 These words all end in a silent **e**. Add the missing vowel to each word.

m____ke   t____me   b____te

th____se   h____pe   t____be

____pe   sl____pe   th____me

r____be   c____be   ____se

c____ke   g____me   h____ke

c____me   r____pe   n____ce

r____ce   h____se   c____te

d____se   d____ce   n____te

pol____te   ____ce   h____de

r____te   h____te   k____te

2 Write a label for each drawing. Each answer has a silent **e**.

p_____   p_____

s_____   b_____

3 Add 'qu' to each word. Then write the whole word on the line.

s__ash _____   s__ish _____

s__elch _____   s__eeze _____

__iet _____   __ick _____

__ite _____   __ack _____

__ake _____   __arrel _____

__een _____   __estion _____

4 Write these words as contractions.

do not _____   did not _____

it is _____   we are _____

I am _____   you are _____

he is _____   she is _____

5 Choose the correct letters from the box to make words.

or	ar	ay	ow

f____   pl____   p____er

st____e   f____m   st____

sh____er   sh____t   al____m

bef____e   Mond____   h____

____l   h____d   g____den

Real Test

20 min

Please ask your parent or teacher to read to you the spelling words on page 214. Write the correct spelling of each word in the box.

1. Lee and I cooked a _____ for Mum's birthday.

2. We _____ to see you soon.

3. I only _____ one mistake in the test.

4. Let's _____ a fruit salad.

5. _____ your brain in the test.

6. Ben won a _____ for spelling.

7. I walked _____ from school.

8. Be kind to animals or they might _____ you.

9. It's _____ for bed.

10. Put the lid on the _____ of toothpaste.

11. Dad and I flew the _____ today.

12. Please shut the _____.

13. You have a lovely _____.

14. Our teacher _____ like us to talk during a test.

15. Sometimes I _____ with my sister.

16. I _____ like to eat squishy bananas.

17. Hold the _____ as you climb.

18. I will do gym this _____.

☞ **Answers and explanations on pages 184-185**

Real Test

SPELLING
*Long vowels, 'qu', common contractions
and vowel/consonant blends*

(continued)

Each sentence has one word that is incorrect. Write the correct spelling for each underlined word in the box.

19 I kicked my toe on a <u>ston</u>.

20 I <u>hayt</u> the taste of oysters.

21 Keep your hands by your <u>sid</u>.

22 <u>Sav</u> your money in the bank.

23 The bread was <u>stal</u>.

24 I <u>chos</u> Fred to be my partner.

25 I saw some dairy <u>cowhs</u> on the farm.

26 We had <u>rela</u> races for sport.

Each sentence has one word that is incorrect. Write the correct spelling for the word in the box.

27 Ned kwit the team when he hurt his foot.

28 I heard the duck kwack.

29 The story was about a king and kween.

30 You need to be kwick with the lunch orders.

31 There was an earthkwake in Mexico.

32 The teacher asked the children to keep kwiet
during the concert.

33 I dont like hot dogs.

34 Its' time for our library lesson.

35 Your'e a great goalkeeper.

☞ **Answers and explanations on pages 184-185**

GRAMMAR AND PUNCTUATION
Types of sentences, joining sentences and sentence punctuation

1 A **sentence** must make sense and it must have a verb. All sentences begin with a capital letter. They can end with a full stop, a question mark or an exclamation mark.

2 Sentences have different functions.

★ They can make **statements of fact**.

Example: My name is Cynthia.

★ They can make **statements of opinion**.

Example: I love dolphins.

★ They can ask **questions**. Questions often begin with question words: *who, what, where, when, how, why*.

Examples: What is your name? Why do you love dolphins?

★ They can make **exclamations**. Exclamations are spoken loudly or with emphasis, or in surprise.

Examples: Stop it! I love it!

★ They can give a **command** or make a **request**.

Examples: Say hello to Cynthia. Pass me the sauce, please.

★ *Note*: Sometimes full stops, question marks or exclamation marks are used in writing when the words don't make a sentence (e.g. Oh dear. Huh? Huh!). These words are interjections. Interjections are mostly single words or word groups. They do not have a verb.

3 Two sentences can be joined together using **connecting words**: *and, but, so, because*. Two sentences joined in this way make a compound sentence.

Examples: I love elephants <u>and</u> I love dolphins.
I love dolphins <u>but</u> elephants are my favourite animals.
I'm going to the zoo <u>so</u> I can see the elephants.
I'm going to the zoo today <u>because</u> there is a new baby elephant.

★ Some connecting words can go at the beginning of a sentence rather than in the middle.

Examples: <u>Because</u> it was raining, Sophie took an umbrella.
<u>Although</u> it was raining, Sophie decided not to take an umbrella.
<u>Until</u> it stopped raining, Sophie was staying indoors.
<u>Since</u> it's still raining, we'll stay inside.

4 Some connecting words join sentences in a time sequence.

Examples: We'll go to the shop <u>then</u> we'll go to Nonna's.
We'll visit Nonna <u>after</u> we do the shopping.

5 **Speech marks** are used to show when someone is speaking. You can use double or single speech marks. Speech marks go outside the words spoken and around other punctuation markers.

Examples: "Look!" exclaimed Craig.
'Where's the baby elephant?' asked Craig.

Test Your Skills

GRAMMAR AND PUNCTUATION
Types of sentences, joining sentences and sentence punctuation

15 MIN

Choose a punctuation mark from the box for each sentence.

!	.	?	.

1. "Be careful _____" shouted Mum.

2. Allan ate yoghurt and fruit _____

3. Where is the softball _____

4. Today is Monday _____

Write a statement to answer each question about yourself.

5. What is your name?

_____

6. How old are you?

_____

7. Where do you live?

_____

8. What is your favourite food?

_____

Write a question for each answer below.

9. _____

Answer: I live in Belrose.

10. _____

Answer: My favourite animal is a meerkat.

11. _____

Answer: I don't have any pets.

12. _____

Answer: I play soccer.

Write **fact** or **opinion** after each sentence.

13. *Charlotte's Web* is a great story.

_____

14. There are twelve months in a year.

_____

15. Bees make honey.

_____

16. I love honey on toast.

_____

17. Rewrite the sentence correctly using speech marks.
Can we go to the zoo? asked Harriet.

_____

18. Rewrite the sentence correctly using speech marks.
Stop that! yelled Liam.

_____

Real Test

GRAMMAR AND PUNCTUATION
Types of sentences, joining sentences and sentence punctuation

20 MIN

1 Which of the following is a sentence?
  A Grandma's garden.
  B Joe and his stepmother.
  C Rina lives with her stepfather.
  D a timber house.

2 Which words correctly complete this sentence?
  Lina was early for school ▭ .
  A but she helped the teacher
  B so she helped the teacher
  C then she helped the teacher
  D because she helped the teacher

3 Which sentence has the correct punctuation?
  A Grandpa lives with us?
  B Grandpa lives in Wagga Wagga?
  C Where does your grandfather live?
  D Grandpa was born in Athens?

4 Choose the correct word and punctuation mark to fill the gap.
  Did you invite your parents to the ▭
  A Concert!   B Concert.   C concert?   D concert

5 Choose the correct word and punctuation mark to fill the gap.
  "Look out, ▭ "
  A Nan   B Nan.   C Nan?   D Nan!

6 Which words correctly complete this sentence?
  Sachin is becoming a good cricket player ▭ .
  A so he practises every day
  B then he practises every day
  C but he practises every day
  D because he practises every day

7 Choose the correct punctuation mark to fill the gap.
  A car was coming. Mark shouted, "Careful ▭ "
  A .   B ,   C ?   D !

8 Which sentence has the correct punctuation?
  A Where is your brother.
  B Where is your brother!
  C Where is your brother?
  D Where is your brother

9 Which sentence has **incorrect** punctuation?
  A Where is Kenny.
  B Why is Nia here?
  C Where is your homework?
  D Are you ready?

☞ **Answers and explanations on page 186**

10 Which word should start with a capital letter?

I think aadrika is a good name for an elephant.

Ⓐ   Ⓑ   Ⓒ   Ⓓ

11 Which word should start with a capital letter?

The zoo in sydney has elephants and giraffes.

  Ⓐ   Ⓑ   Ⓒ Ⓓ

12 Shade one bubble to show where the missing full stop should go.

Tim had soccer practice yesterday Today he does gymnastics.

     Ⓐ   Ⓑ   Ⓒ   Ⓓ

13 Shade one bubble to show where the missing full stop should go.

It is raining today I hope it will be sunny tomorrow.

    Ⓐ   Ⓑ   Ⓒ   Ⓓ

14 Shade two bubbles to show where speech marks (" ") should go.

Ⓐ   Ⓑ   Ⓒ   Ⓓ

   Will you help me practise goal kicking? asked Jessica.

15 Shade two bubbles to show where speech marks (" ") should go.

Ⓐ Ⓑ   Ⓒ   Ⓓ

   Stop! Don't cross the road yet, shouted Keith.

16 Shade the bubble to show where the exclamation mark (!) should go.

"Yuk   " shrieked Julia . "That   tasted terrible."

     Ⓐ   ⒷⒸ   Ⓓ

☞ **Answers and explanations on page 186**

Real Test

GRAMMAR AND PUNCTUATION
Types of sentences, joining sentences and sentence punctuation

(continued)

17 Which words correctly complete this sentence?

He was late home _____ .

A but the bus was late   B because the bus was late
C although the bus was late   D and the bus was late

18 Which word correctly completes this sentence?

_____ the classroom was so hot, the teacher read to the class under a tree.

A Until   B Because   C Although   D And

19 Which word correctly completes this sentence?

_____ it was raining, Sara decided to walk to the park.

A Until   B Because   C Although   D Since

20 Which word correctly completes this sentence?

_____ it stopped raining, the dogs had to stay indoors.

A Until   B Because   C Although   D Since

Add a word from the box to complete each sentence.

because	and	until	so
A	B	C	D

21 Kate ran to school _____ she'd have time to play.

22 Carl ran to school _____ he wanted to race Frankie.

23 Matilda ran _____ she ran out of breath.

24 Jin ran to the corner _____ then he walked the rest of the way.

25 Which sentence below is closest in meaning to these sentences?

Yusuf's cat is very tiny. It is called Alpa which is a Hindu word meaning 'little'.

A Yusuf has a tiny cat called Alpa.
B Alpa is a Hindu word for Yusuf's cat.
C Yusuf's tiny cat is called Alpa which means 'little' in Hindu.
D Yusuf's cat is tiny and called Alpa.

☞ Answers and explanations on page 186

Key Points

1 **A narrative** tells a story. The main purpose of a narrative is to entertain. Narratives are about characters. Characters can have adventures or face real-life problems. Narratives can be set in real or imaginary places. They can be set in the past, present or future. All the events in a narrative make up the plot.

2 Narratives are told by a narrator. The narrator can be the author or a character in the story. When the narrator is a character in the story, pronouns such as *I*, *we*, *us* and *me* are used. This is a first-person narrative. It will give the point of view of the character who is telling the story.

A story told by the author is a third-person narrative. Pronouns such as *he*, *she* and *they* are used.

3 Narratives use noun groups to describe the characters and the setting.

4 Narratives usually have:

★ an **orientation** which sets the scene (It might introduce the main character and tell readers when and where the story is set.)

★ a **complication** (The complication is the problem that the main character has to solve. Without a complication a story would be boring.)

★ a series of events, called the **plot** (These build to a climax.)

★ a **resolution**. This is when life returns to normal for the character and any problems have been solved or overcome.

The spoilt prince on page 93 is a narrative that makes fun of fairytales. It has fairytale characters and a fairytale setting. It uses the language of fairytales: *Once upon a time in a kingdom far, far away*; *happily ever after*. If you know some fairytales you should understand how this narrative makes fun of fairytales.

A conversation with Grandma on page 94 is a conversation. Narratives often include conversations between characters. Conversations tell readers what characters are thinking or feeling. They tell how characters interact with each other. Conversations between characters in narratives make use of statements, questions and exclamations. Speech marks are used to mark what each character says.

Stuck on page 95 is a narrative. It introduces the main character, Jenny, and her cat, Pongo. There is a complication or problem which Jenny tries to solve. The story ends when Jenny's problem is resolved.

Test Your Skills

15 MIN

Read *The spoilt prince*. Circle the correct answers to the questions below.

1 **The spoilt prince**

2 Once upon a time in a kingdom far, far away there lived a
3 king and queen and their son, Johan. The king and queen
4 were kind and good but Johan was not kind or good. He
5 was lazy and rude. He demanded that the cook make him
6 special cakes. He was mean to everyone, even his parents.

7 On Johan's 21st birthday the king and queen announced that
8 it was time for Johan to marry. They sent letters to princesses
9 in kingdoms all around, inviting them to meet the prince.

10 Princesses came from far and wide but Prince Johan refused to marry anyone. He was
11 rude to all the princesses. He said that he wanted to live with his parents forever.

12 The princesses didn't want to marry a mean and rude prince, anyway. So, they went on
13 a holiday together to New Zealand. They had fun snow skiing and whale watching.

14 The prince never married. He lived happily ever after in his parents' castle. And, as for his
15 parents, they went on holidays to New Zealand as often as they could, without Johan.

1 Johan lived
   A in New Zealand. B in a kingdom.
   C in a village.   D with princesses.

2 Which words best describe Johan?
   A loud and angry
   B a very nice person
   C kind and good
   D mean and rude

3 Why do you think Johan's parents decided *it was time for Johan to marry*?

_____

_____

4 What is the main purpose of the text?
   A to explain how princes find wives
   B to tell about holidays in New Zealand
   C to describe life in the past
   D to tell a story to entertain

5 Why didn't the princesses want to marry Johan?
   A He ate too many special cakes.
   B He wasn't a nice person.
   C He didn't want to go to New Zealand.
   D They didn't like Johan's parents.

6 *Demanded* in the story means
   A begged for.   B insisted on.
   C hoped.   D needed.

7 Which words in the story tell you how Johan felt in the end?
   A The prince never married.
   B He lived happily ever after.
   C He wanted to live with his parents forever.
   D They had fun snow skiing and whale watching.

Answers: 1 B 2 D 3 Answers will vary.
4 D 5 B 6 B 7 B

☞ **Explanations on pages 186–187**

Real Test

Read *A conversation with Grandma*. Circle the correct answers to the questions below.

1 **A conversation with Grandma**

2 Cynthia and her grandmother were talking one afternoon.

3 "Where were you born, Zumu?" Cynthia asked.

4 "I was born in a farming village in China," replied her grandmother.

5 "What was it like there?" Cynthia asked.

6 "Beautiful," said Zumu. "It's an important wheat-
7 growing area now."

8 "Will you take me to see where you were born?"

9 "No, Cynthia. It is too far away," said Zumu.

10 "How far away is it?" Cynthia wanted to know.

11 "Too far," replied Zumu.

12 "I want to go!" Cynthia demanded.

13 "You can go when you are grown up. You can take yourself," said Zumu.

14 "That's a long time!" Cynthia declared in a sulky voice. She slumped her shoulders. She
15 pretended she might cry. She wanted Zumu to give in and agree to take her to China.

16 "You must be patient," declared Zumu.

17 "Oh! You always tell me to be patient," Cynthia declared. "I will go to China one day."

1 Zumu was born in
   A Australia.
   B a hospital.
   C China.
   D the countryside.

2 Zumu is Cynthia's
   A grandfather.
   B mother.
   C father.
   D grandmother.

3 The best word to describe Cynthia is
   A beautiful.
   B old.
   C silly.
   D determined.

4 Cynthia wants to go to China
   A to have a holiday.
   B to see where Zumu was born.
   C to see wheat farms.
   D to spend time with Zumu.

5 Cynthia slumps her shoulders because
   A she wants Zumu to feel sorry for her.
   B her shoulders were sore.
   C China is far away.
   D she is tired.

6 Which word best describes Zumu in the text?
   A sulky
   B patient
   C bossy
   D quick-tempered

7 At the end of the conversation Cynthia
   A thinks Zumu will take her to China.
   B is unhappy that she will not go to China.
   C thinks Zumu is mean.
   D declares she will go to China one day.

☞ **Answers and explanations on page 187**

Real Test

Read the text *Stuck*. Circle the correct answers to the questions below.

1 **Stuck**

2 "Pongo," called Jenny. "Pongo, come on down. Come on, Puss Puss."

3 Pongo had climbed a tree and Jenny wanted him to
4 come down. Pongo had been in the tree for ages.
5 Jenny was worried that Pongo didn't know how to
6 get back down. Jenny went inside the house to get
7 some chicken, Pongo's favourite food. She waved the
8 chicken at Pongo, then she placed the chicken on
9 the ground.

10 "Come and get some yummy chicken," she called.
11 Pongo just looked at her.

12 Now Jenny was really getting worried. She went
13 inside and told her mother that the cat was stuck
14 in a tree. Her mother said she'd have a look. But
15 when Jenny and her mother went outside, there was
16 Pongo, on the ground, eating the chicken.

17 "Oh, Pongo," said Jenny. "You are such a tricker!"

---

1 What is Pongo?

  A a bird   B a monkey
  C a cat   D a snake

2 What is Jenny's problem in the text?

  A Pongo has climbed a tree.
  B Jenny thinks Pongo can't get down
     from the tree.
  C Jenny has a tall tree in her backyard.
  D Jenny's father isn't at home.

3 Pongo's favourite food is

  A anything.   B Puss Puss.
  C chicken.   D leaves.

4 Who does Jenny ask for help?

  A her father   B no-one
  C her mother   D Pongo

5 How does Jenny feel at the end of the text?

  A bored   B upset
  C worried   D happy

6 Another title for the text could be

  A Tricky Pongo.
  B Chicken for dinner.
  C Mum to the rescue.
  D The tall tree.

7 Choose a word that could replace *worried* in the text.

  A angry   B concerned
  C shocked   D delighted

☞ **Answers and explanations on pages 187-188**

TIPS FOR WRITING NARRATIVES

Text structure and organisation

A **narrative** tells a story.

A narrative can be realistic, a fantasy, an adventure or a mystery.

It can be funny or sad.

It can be set in the past, the present or the future.

It can have imaginary characters, real-life characters or animal characters.

In some narratives the animal characters act like humans and have feelings like humans.

In some narratives animals talk and wear human clothes.

Before you start to write a narrative, think about:
● the **purpose** and **audience** for your text
● the **orientation** (This introduces the main character or characters. It tells readers where and when the story is set, e.g. in the jungle, in the future, on another planet, in the past.)
● the **plot** (The plot is the series of events in a story. The plot begins with a complication. This is a problem that upsets the normal lives of the characters. How characters deal with the complication or problem drives the story. The plot builds up to the climax.)
● the **resolution.** When characters have solved their problem the story ends with the resolution. The resolution needs to satisfy an audience. A narrative can have a sad ending or a happy ending but it needs to end so that readers know how the problem has been resolved.

Expressing and developing ideas

When you write a narrative remember to:

● use noun groups (Noun groups give descriptions. Descriptions help readers build a mental picture of characters and settings.)

● use verbs for characters' actions and to tell readers what characters are feeling and thinking (Let readers know whether a character is happy, sad, frightened or worried. This helps readers understand a character's behaviour and makes a story more enjoyable for readers.)

● use adverbs to tell when and where the events in the plot take place

● think about using alliteration and onomatopoeia (Alliteration is when a number of words start with the same sound, e.g. six sizzling sausages. Onomatopoeia is when words sound like the noise they are describing, e.g. whoosh, crack.)

● proofread your narrative and check that it makes sense

● check spelling and punctuation.

When you have finished your writing, give it to an adult to read and check.

(a sample answer to the question on page 99)

Akua and the leopard

Akua was frightened of leopards. He was now six years old and he was sleeping on his own, for the first time. His mother had told him to be a brave chimpanzee. She had told him to build his night nest high in the tree tops. He had remembered her advice. He had built his nest as high in the tree as he could.

It was very dark. Only a glimmer of moonlight filtered through the thick leaves. Akua listened to the noises of the night and tried to hear the leopard. His mother had warned him, "Leopards like to eat young chimps. They are good climbers so sleep high up in the tree and you'll be safe."

Akua was frightened of leopards. All alone in his night nest he listened to the noises of the forest and imagined the leopard silently sneaking closer.

A branch went *crack* but it was only another chimp, sharing his tree. A branch went *creak* but it was only a night bird shuffling its wings. *Rustle, rustle* went the leaves but it was only the wind. Akua heard a *whoosh* but it was only an owl.

All through the night Akua waited for the leopard to pounce. He didn't sleep a wink and he was very pleased to see the sun begin to rise the next morning. He looked around and saw other chimps climbing through the trees. Everything looked very friendly in the sunlight. He decided he would not be frightened of the dark ever again.

This text is beyond what would be expected of a typical Year 2 student. It is provided here as a model. The assessment comments are based on the marking criteria used to assess the NAPLAN Writing Test.

Vocabulary
- Noun groups provide detail.
- Onomatopoeia gives atmosphere to the narrative, e.g. *crack, creak*.
- Thinking and feeling verbs help readers empathise with Akua: *was frightened*.
- Terminology is relevant to subject matter: *night nests*.
- Alliteration helps build atmosphere.

Sentence structure
- Simple sentences build atmosphere: *Akua was frightened of leopards. It was very dark.*
- Compound sentences repeat the use of the conjunction *but*: *Akua heard a whoosh but it was only an owl.*
- Reported speech is used.
- Sentence lengths are varied for pace and emphasis.

Ideas
- Ideas demonstrate knowledge about chimpanzees: how they build night nests and sleep apart from their mother from the age of five or six. This knowledge makes the narrative credible.
- Akua is given human qualities (anthropomorphism).
- The narrative appeals to the senses of sight and hearing.

Punctuation
- Punctuation includes direct speech.

Spelling
- Words with silent letters are correctly spelt, e.g. *rustle, climbing*.
- Contractions are correctly spelt.

Audience
- This is a story for children. Themes include fear of being alone, fear of the dark, sleeping by yourself, growing up, overcoming fears.

Text structure
- The orientation introduces the main character and the setting. The complication is that it is Akua's first night sleeping alone and he is afraid of leopards. There is rising action during the night, building towards a climax. The resolution arrives with the morning.

Paragraphing
- Paragraphs are based on main ideas and elaboration.
- Paragraph 1 introduces the character and setting.
- Paragraphs 2, 3 and 4 describe what Akua can hear and what he imagines.
- The concluding paragraph provides the resolution. Akua realises that he has imagined danger. He has learned that he can be safe at night on his own.

Cohesion
- Suspense is built through repetition.
- Noun–pronoun referencing is accurate: *leopards—they*.
- Events are sequenced in time through the night to morning.

Character and setting
- A third-person narrator tells the story from the point of view of Akua. Readers are told what Akua is thinking, feeling, seeing, wondering, imagining. There is character growth: Akua is a dynamic character. He learns about himself. The setting is described to give atmosphere to the story.

Real Test

40 min

Before you start, read the **Tips for writing narratives** on page 96.

Today you are going to write a narrative. Your purpose is to entertain readers of your own age. You need to **finish this story**:

Something strange

Kim and Terry stopped walking. They looked at the shimmering silver ball beside the footpath. It was the size and shape of a soccer ball but looked to be made of metal. It was making a quiet rumbling noise like a motor. They had never seen anything like it. The children looked at each other. They wondered where the object had come from and what it was for.

Before you start to write, think about the shiny object.

- What could it be?
- Where might it come from? Is it from outer space?
- Is it magical?
- Does it have any special powers?
- What will Kim and Terry do with it?

Remember to:

- plan your writing—think about the sequence of events in your story and how the story will end
- use pronouns for Kim and Terry: *he, she, they*
- use sentence punctuation and take care with speech marks
- check spelling and punctuation
- write as neatly as you can so that readers can understand your writing
- ask a parent or teacher to read and check your finished work.

Use your own paper to write your narrative.

☞ **Marking guide on page 188**

Real Test

Before you start, read the **Tips for writing narratives** on page 96.

Today you are going to write a narrative. Your purpose is to write an **animal adventure** story.

You could write about a pet, a farm animal, a reptile, an insect, an ocean creature, or any other animal you wish. What adventure will the animal have?

Before you start to write, think about the animal.
- How would you describe it?
- Where and when will the story take place (the setting)?
- What happens to the animal (the plot)? What problem does it have?
- What conversations take place between characters in your story?

Remember to:
- plan your narrative—include orientation, complication, events in the plot and a resolution
- write in paragraphs
- use noun groups and adjectives to describe characters and setting
- write in sentences
- check spelling and punctuation
- write neatly so that readers can understand your writing
- ask a parent or teacher to read and check your finished work.

Use your own paper to write your narrative.

☞**Marking guide on page 189**

Real Test

Before you start, read the **Tips for writing narratives** on page 96.

Today you are going to write a **fairytale** or **folk tale**.

Think about tales that you know, such as *Cinderella, Red Riding Hood, The Billy Goats Gruff* or *The Three Little Pigs and the Big Bad Wolf.*

Choose a tale—any tale you like. Rewrite the tale, changing it in some way.

You could:

● imagine you are the wolf and write the tale of Red Riding Hood from the point of view of the wolf

● imagine you are the troll in the tale of the Billy Goats Gruff—write the troll's tale

● change the ending of a tale in some way.

Before you start to write, think about which tale you will use.
● What characters and events are in the tale?
● How do your characters feel about the events?
● How will you retell the tale?
Remember to:
● plan the tale
● use saying verbs for characters' speech
● write in sentences
● check spelling and punctuation
● write neatly so that readers can understand your writing
● ask a parent or teacher to read and check your finished work.

Use your own paper to write your narrative.

☞ **Marking guide on pages 189–190**

Only one week to go!

Week 4

This is what we cover this week:

Day 1   **Measurement and Geometry:** ◎ Location and transformation

Day 2   **Statistics and Probability:** ◎ Chance and Data

Day 3   **Spelling**: ◎ Singular and plural nouns, prefixes and suffixes

             Grammar and Punctuation: ◎ Personal pronouns, HOW adverbs and adjectives that compare

Day 4   **Reading:** ◎ Understanding persuasive texts

Day 5   **Writing:** ◎ Persuasive texts

Test Your Skills 1

MEASUREMENT AND GEOMETRY
Location and transformation

20 MIN

Look at this grid.

4	bank	butcher	bakery	post office
3	fruit shop	chemist	doctor	dentist
2	school	park	library	church
1	pool	skate park	gym	garage
	A	B	C	D

What is found at

1 B3?

2 C4?

3 D1?

4 A2?

Where is the

5 post office?

6 fruit shop?

7 library?

8 skate park?

Here is a picture of some friends.

Jo   Kim   Lee   Bill

Helen   Dan   Jane   Bob

Jo is standing on the left in the back row.

Who is standing

9 in front of Jo?

10 behind Dan?

11 between Kim and Bill?

12 second from the right in the back row?

13 third from the left in the front row?

Here is a map of Red Rock.

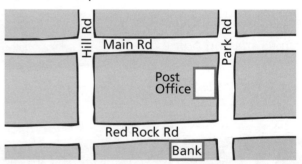

Hill Rd   Main Rd   Park Rd

Post Office

Red Rock Rd

Bank

14 On what road is the bank?

15 Zac leaves the bank and turns left. What is the next road he will come to?

16 On what road is the post office?

17 Sue leaves the post office and turns right. What is the next road she will come to?

MEASUREMENT AND GEOMETRY
Location and transformation

	A	B	C	D	E	F	G
5							
4							
3							
2				✈			
1							

1 What is the position of ✈ ?

What will the new position be if ✈ moves from its starting point

2 one square to the right?

3 two squares up?

4 three squares left?

5 one square down?

Fill in the number of squares and direction if ✈ moves from its starting point to

6 F2

_____ squares to the

_____

7 D5

_____ squares

_____

Choose the diagram that shows the shape in the first picture flipped over the dotted line.

8
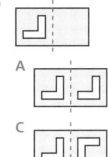

A   B

C   D

9

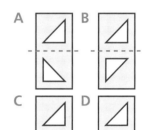

A   B

C   D

This arrow is being turned.

A   B   C   D

Write the letter that matches what the arrow will look like if it is turned

10 a full turn.

11 half a turn.

12 a quarter turn clockwise.

13 a quarter turn anticlockwise.

Key Points

MEASUREMENT AND GEOMETRY
Location and transformation

1 **A position on a grid is often shown using a letter and a number.**

The letter is found along the bottom (or top) of the grid.

The number is found along the side of the grid.

When giving a position the letter is put first, then the number.

Example:

4	bank	butcher	bakery	post office
3	fruit shop	chemist	doctor	dentist
2	school	park	library	church
1	pool	skate park	gym	garage
	A	**B**	**C**	**D**

- On this grid the chemist is found at B3.
- The bakery is found at C4.
- The garage is at D1 and the school is at A2.

4	bank	butcher	bakery	post office
3	fruit shop	chemist	doctor	dentist
2	school	park	library	church
1	pool	skate park	gym	garage
	A	**B**	**C**	**D**

- To find the location of the post office, first go down to read the letter D. Then go across to find the number 4. So the post office is at D4.
- The fruit shop is at A3.
- The library is at C2 and the skate park is at B1.

2 **When you look at pictures, the left side is our left and the right side is our right.**

Example:

Jo   Kim   Lee   Bill

Helen   Dan   Jane   Bob

- So in this picture, Jo is standing on the left in the back row.
- Helen is in front of Jo and Kim is behind Dan.
- The person standing between Kim and Bill is Lee.
- Bill is standing on the right in the back row so Lee is the second from the right in the back row.
- Helen is on the left of the front row, so Jane is third from the left in the front row.

3 **On a map, try to imagine following the directions.** Think about which way you will be facing, so that you know which way will be right and left.

Example: From the map of Red Rock on the next page you can see that the bank is in Red Rock Rd.

As Zac leaves the bank he will be in Red Rock Rd and facing Main Rd. So if he turns left the next road he will come to is Hill Rd.

MEASUREMENT AND GEOMETRY
Location and transformation

(continued)

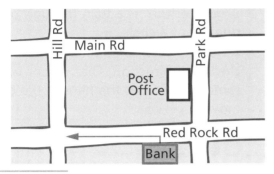

Example:

The post office is in Park Rd.

As Sue leaves the post office she will be in Park Rd and with her back to Hill Rd. So if she turns right the next road she will come to is Red Rock Rd.

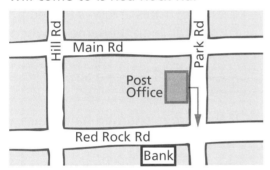

4 **Shapes can be moved or transformed by slides, flips or turns.**

5 **In a slide, a shape might move to the left or right or it might move up or down.** The shape will still look exactly as it did before the slide.

Example:

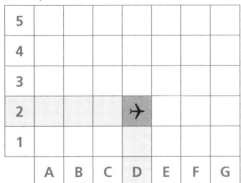

On this grid, the position of ✈ is D2.

■ If it moves one square to the right it will move to E2.

■ If it moves two squares up it will move to D4.

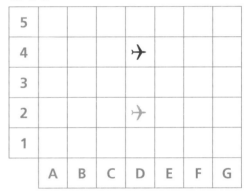

■ If it moves 3 squares to the left it will move to A2 and if it moves one square down it will move to D1.

■ If it moves to F2 it will move two squares to the right.

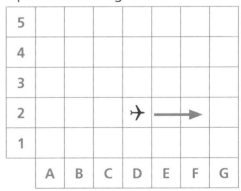

■ If it moves to D5 it will move three squares up.

MEASUREMENT AND GEOMETRY
Location and transformation

(continued)

6 **In a flip, a shape is reflected across a line.** If a shape is painted onto a piece of paper and then, while the paint is still wet, the paper is folded, a reflection of the original shape will appear as a flip on the paper.

Example:

So if this shape is flipped over the dotted line, the result will be this:

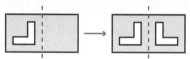

(You can imagine the paper being folded along the dotted line and the two parts matching exactly.)

Example:

If this shape is flipped over the dotted line, the result will be this.

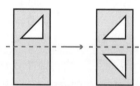

7 **In a turn, a shape is rotated.** If it turns through a full turn, it goes around in a circle and comes back to where it started.

★ **A half turn is a turn through half a circle.**

★ **A quarter turn is a turn through one quarter of a circle.**

★ A quarter turn can be made in a **clockwise** direction. That means in the same direction as the hands on a clock move.

★ A quarter turn can also be made in an **anticlockwise** (counter-clockwise) direction. That means in the opposite direction to the hands of a clock.

Example: If this arrow is turned a full turn it will look the same as when it started.

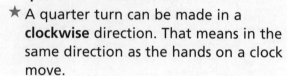

■ If the arrow is turned half a turn, it will look like this:

■ If the arrow is turned a quarter turn in a clockwise direction, it will look like this:

■ If the arrow is turned a quarter turn in an anticlockwise direction, it will look like this:

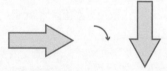

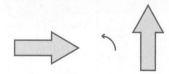

Excel Revise in a Month Year 2 NAPLAN*-style Tests

Real Test

MEASUREMENT AND GEOMETRY
Location and transformation

20 MIN

1 This is a plan of Jan's farm.

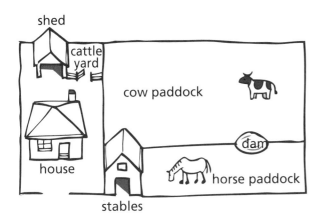

What is between the cow paddock and the shed?

A house   B dam

C cattle yard   D stables

2 This shape looks the same when it is flipped over the dotted line.

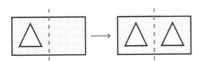

Which of these shapes will look the same when flipped over the dotted line? Choose all possible answers.

A 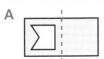   B

C 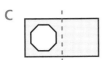   D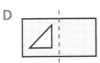

E 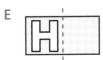   F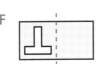

3

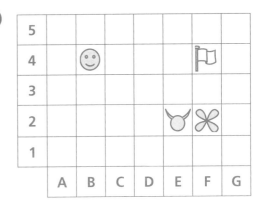

Which shape is at F2?

A   B   C   D

4 Elly turns this card half a turn.

What does it look like now?

A   B   C   D

5 Cam is playing a game.

He slides his counter 3 squares right. Which shows Cam's counter after the slide?

A 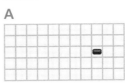   B

C    D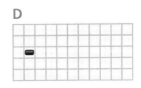

☞ **Answers and explanations on pages 190-191**

Real Test

MEASUREMENT AND GEOMETRY
Location and transformation

(continued)

6 Lucy folded this paper on the dotted line.

She cut out a shape.

Which is Lucy's paper when opened out?

A   B

C   D

7 Some tools are on a board.

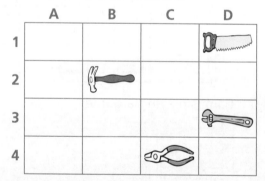

The hammer is at B2.
Where is the saw?

8 This arrow ⌐ looks like this ⌐

after a quarter turn in a clockwise direction.

What will this arrow ↗ look like after a quarter turn in a clockwise direction?

A   B   C   D

9 Billy made this shape.

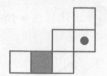

Which of these is Billy's shape?

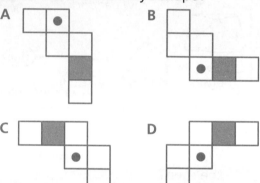

A   B

C   D

10 Nat is second from the left in this picture.

Which is Nat?

A   B

C   D

☞ **Answers and explanations on pages 190–191**

Test Your Skills 1

STATISTICS AND PROBABILITY
Chance and data

20 MIN

This table shows the number of races students won at a swimming carnival.

Name	Number of races
Max	3
Ben	7
Bella	5
Tara	4
Jack	2

1 How many races did Bella win?

2 Which student won exactly 4 races?

3 Who won the most races?

4 How many races did Max and Jack win altogether?

5 How many **more** races did Ben win than Tara?

Some students voted for their favourite fruit.

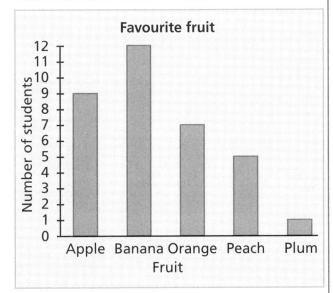

Favourite fruit

6 How many voted for apple?

7 Which fruit did exactly 7 students vote for?

8 Which fruit was the most popular?

9 How many students voted for peach and plum altogether?

10 How many **more** students voted for banana than for peach?

Some students chose their favourite animal at the zoo.

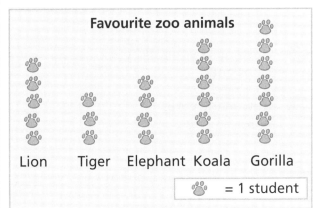

Favourite zoo animals

Lion   Tiger   Elephant   Koala   Gorilla

🐾 = 1 student

11 How many students chose elephant?

12 Which animal did exactly 5 students choose?

13 Which animal was chosen by the most students?

14 How many students chose lion and tiger altogether?

15 How many **more** students chose gorilla than koala?

Answers: **1** 5 **2** Tara **3** Ben **4** 5 **5** 3
6 9 **7** orange **8** banana **9** 6 **10** 7
11 4 **12** lion **13** gorilla **14** 8 **15** 1

Test Your Skills 2

STATISTICS AND PROBABILITY
Chance and data

20 MIN

Students voted for their favourite football team.

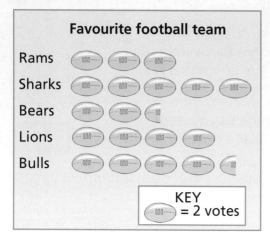

Favourite football team

Rams

Sharks

Bears

Lions

Bulls

KEY
= 2 votes

1 How many votes did the Lions get?

2 How many votes does = ?

3 How many votes did the Bulls get?

4 Which team got exactly 5 votes?

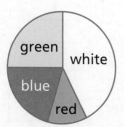

green
white
blue
red

This spinner is spun. Which colour is

5 most likely?

6 least likely?

This is a dice. It has the numbers from 1 to 6 on its faces, one number on each face. Jess rolls this dice in a game. Choose one of these words—likely, unlikely, impossible, certain—to describe the chance that Jess gets

7 1

8 less than 1

9 more than 1

10 7

11 less than 7

What numbers do these tally marks show?

12 |||

13 ℍ℩

14 ℍ℩ ||||

15 ℍ℩ ℍ℩ ℍ℩ ℍ℩

Key Points

1 **A table is a way of showing information.**

A table is made up of **rows** (going across) and **columns** (going up and down).

The headings at the top of the columns and at the side of the rows tell you what is in the table.

Example:

■ In this table the first column gives the names of the students and the second column gives the number of races each of those students has won.

Name	Number of races
Max	3
Ben	7
Bella	5
Tara	4
Jack	2

■ To find the number of races that Bella has won you need to look for the name Bella in the first column and then move across to the right to read the number of races that Bella has won.

Name	Number of races
Max	3
Ben	7
Bella	5
Tara	4
Jack	2

So Bella has won 5 races.

■
Name	Number of races
Max	3
Ben	7
Bella	5
Tara	4
Jack	2

To find the name of the student who has won exactly 4 races you need to look for the number 4 in the second column and then move across to the left to find the name of the student. So the person who won 4 races is Tara.

■ The largest number of races won is 7, so Ben won the most races.

■ Max won 3 races and Jack won 2 races, so altogether Max and Jack won 5 races because 3 + 2 = 5.

■ Ben won 7 races and Tara won 4 races. Now 7 − 4 = 3.

So Ben won 3 more races than Tara.

2 **A graph is another way of showing information.** Every graph should have a heading. The heading should tell us what the graph is about.

3 **A column graph is a special type of graph.**

The lines at the bottom and side of the graph are called **axes**. (Axes is the plural of axis. You have 1 axis but 2 or more axes.) The axes give information about the graph.

Example:

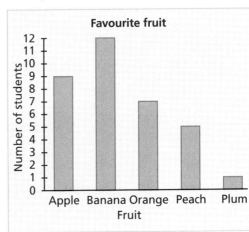

- In this graph, the heading tells you that the graph is about favourite fruit. The names of five different fruit are shown at the bottom of the columns. The number of students who chose each of those fruit is shown at the side.

- To find the number of students who voted for apple, find the top of the column for apple and go across to the left axis to read the number of students.

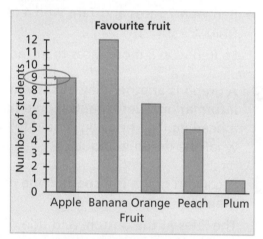

So 9 students chose apple.

- To find the fruit that 7 students chose, find 7 on the axis at the side and go across to find the top of a column.

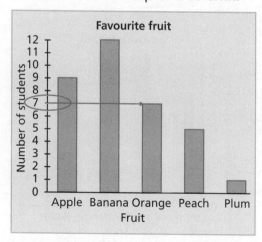

So the fruit that exactly 7 students chose was orange.

- The most popular fruit was banana because it has the tallest column.

- 5 students voted for peach and 1 student voted for plum.
  Now 5 + 1 = 6, so altogether 6 students voted for peach and plum.

- 12 students voted for banana and 5 voted for peach. Now 12 − 5 = 7 so 7 more students voted for banana than for peach.

4 **A picture graph uses symbols or pictures to show how many times something happens.**

There should be a **key** that tells you what each picture represents.

Example:

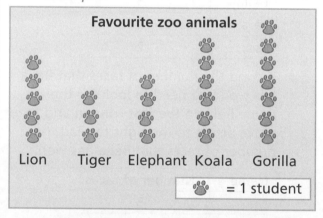

- In this graph each footprint symbol means one student. Count the symbols to answer the questions.

- There are four symbols for elephant so 4 students voted for elephant.

- Lion has five symbols so the animal that exactly 5 students voted for was lion.

- Gorilla has the most symbols so gorilla was chosen by the most students.

- 5 chose lion and 3 chose tiger.
  Now 5 + 3 = 8, so altogether 8 chose lion and tiger.

- 7 chose gorilla and 6 chose koala so one more student chose gorilla than koala.

Key Points

STATISTICS AND PROBABILITY
Chance and data

(continued)

Example:

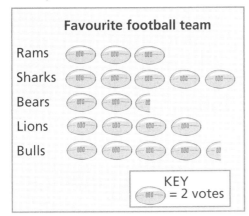

Favourite football team

Rams

Sharks

Bears

Lions

Bulls

KEY
= 2 votes

- In this graph, the key tells us that each football symbol means 2 votes.
- So, counting by twos, the Lions got 8 votes.
- As each football means 2 votes, half a football will mean 1 vote.
- To find the number of votes for the Bulls count the whole footballs by twos and add one more at the end. So the Bulls got 9 votes.
- 5 votes will be represented by 2 whole football symbols and half a symbol. So the team that got 5 votes was the Bears.

5 **The chance of something happening can be described using key words.**

If it cannot happen, it is **impossible**.
If it must happen, it is **certain**.
If there is a bigger chance of it happening than not happening it is **likely**.
If there is a bigger chance of it not happening than happening it is **unlikely**.

6 **A spinner is usually in the shape of a circle.** It is often divided into parts that are like the slices of a pizza. These parts are called **sectors**.

When a spinner is spun, it is most likely to stop on the largest sector. It is least likely to stop on the smallest sector.

Example:

- This spinner is most likely to stop on white.
- The colour on which it is least likely to stop is red because the smallest sector is red.

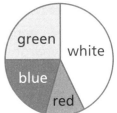

green

white

blue

red

7 **A normal dice has 6 faces.**

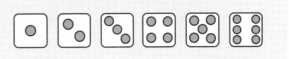

- When a dice is rolled each face has the same chance of ending up on top.
- So if a dice is rolled, you can describe the chance that the top number is 1 as unlikely.
- The chance that the number is less than 1 is impossible because there are no numbers on the dice that are less than 1.
- The chance that it is greater than 1 is likely.
- It is impossible for the top number to be 7.
- But, because all the numbers on the dice are less than 7, the chance that the top number is less than 7 is certain.

8 **You can use tally marks to help you count.** Each mark means 1. So ||| means 3.

Every fifth mark goes across to make a group of 5. So ||||| is 5 and ||||| |||| is 9.

Counting by fives you can see that ||||| ||||| ||||| ||||| is 20.

Real Test

STATISTICS AND PROBABILITY
Chance and data

20 MIN

1 Some students voted for their favourite movies.
How many more students voted for *Kangaroos* than voted for *Old Dogs*?

Favourite movie	
Movie	**Number of votes**
Good Times	7
Old Dogs	10
Red and Blue	8
Kangaroos	13

2 This dish holds some jelly beans.
Which describes the chance of taking a green jelly bean from this dish?

A impossible   B unlikely

C likely   D certain

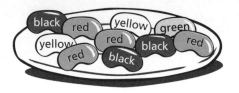

3 This graph shows the number of hours Mr Lee spent at work this week.

On what day did Mr Lee spend exactly 5 hours at work?

A Monday   B Tuesday

C Wednesday   D Friday

Hours Mr Lee spent at work

Monday 🕐🕐🕐

Tuesday 🕐🕐🕐🕐🕐

Wednesday 🕐🕐🕐(

Thursday 🕐🕐🕐🕐🕐🕐🕐

Friday 🕐🕐🕐🕐🕐🕐

KEY
🕐 = 1 hour

4 This graph shows the number of cars of different colours in a car park.

Which is correct? Select all possible answers.

A There were more black cars than silver cars.

B There were more red cars than black cars.

C There were more blue cars than white cars.

D There were more silver cars than blue cars.

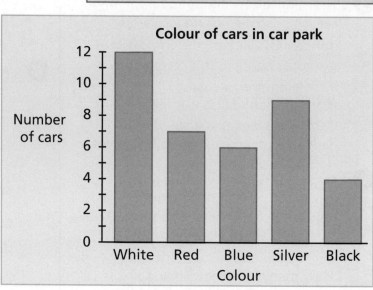

Colour of cars in car park

☞ **Answers and explanations on pages 191–192**

Real Test

STATISTICS AND PROBABILITY
Chance and data

(continued)

5 Some students voted for class captain.
How many students voted for Mia?

A 0   B 4
C 5   D 6

Name	Tally
Ahmed	卌 ll
Billy	llll
Mia	卌
Jenny	lll
Xavier	卌 l

6 On which number is this spinner most likely to stop?

A 1   B 2
C 3   D 4

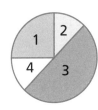

7 This table shows the number of boys and girls in three classes.

How many children are in 2P? ☐

Class	Boys	Girls
2K	13	14
2P	15	11
2Y	12	12

8 This graph shows the number of cherries some students ate.

How many cherries did Jill eat? ☐

Number of cherries eaten

🍒 = 2 cherries

Mike   Jill   Alice   Roy

9 These dice are rolled and the numbers added together.
Which is impossible?

A 1   B 5
C 9   D 11

10 Some students counted birds.

Name	Sid	Dana	Ruby	Nat	Eli	Sam
Birds	8	5	2	9	4	6

How many birds did Sid and Eli count altogether? ☐

☞ Answers and explanations on pages 191-192

Key Points

 When learning to spell a new word:
- listen for the individual sounds in the word
- look at the letter combinations that make the sounds
- use the strategy **LOOK, SAY, COVER, WRITE, SAY, CHECK** to practise spelling any words you find challenging.

Singular and plural nouns

1 Nouns can be **singular or plural**. One of something is singular (e.g. a cat). More than one of something is plural (e.g. the cats).

2 Most nouns are made plural by adding *s* or 'es'.

Examples: dog ➜ dogs, bench ➜ benches

3 If a noun ends in *y*, change the *y* to *i* and add 'es' to form the plural.

Examples: body ➜ bodies, baby ➜ babies

4 If a noun ends in a consonant and *o*, add 'es' to form the plural.

Example: tomato ➜ tomatoes

5 Some nouns that end in *f* drop *f* and add 'ves' to form the plural.

Example: loaf ➜ loaves

6 Some nouns change their spelling in other ways to form the plural.

Examples: child ➜ children, tooth ➜ teeth, mouse ➜ mice, man ➜ men

7 A few nouns don't change at all and have the same spelling for singular and plural.

Examples: sheep, deer, fish, bread, rice, celery

8 Letters such as *s* and 'es' which are added to the end of a word are called **suffixes**.

 dog   dogs

Prefixes and suffixes

9 **Prefixes** are letters added to the front of a word.

10 **Suffixes** are letters added to the end of a word.

11 Prefixes and suffixes change the meaning of words.

12 The prefix 'un' changes the meaning of a word to its opposite.

Examples: happy ➜ unhappy, comfortable ➜ uncomfortable
Note: Words that have opposite meanings are called **antonyms**.

13 Suffixes can be added to verbs to change tense.

Examples: play ➜ playing ➜ played
★ Remember that tense tells if something happened in the past, is happening now, happens all the time, or will happen in the future.

14 Common suffixes include:
★ 'ful' meaning 'full of'

Examples: respectful, helpful, hopeful
★ 'er', 'or' or 'ist' which are used to name people

Examples: teacher, gardener, cleaner, runner, doctor, professor, cyclist, dentist, florist
★ 'less' which means 'without'

Examples: hopeless, useless, thoughtless

SPELLING
Singular and plural nouns, prefixes and suffixes

`15 MIN`

Answer the questions below and then use a dictionary to check your spelling.

1 Write the plurals of these nouns.

bird	_____	whale	_____	teacher	_____
peach	_____	bench	_____	lunch	_____
body	_____	baby	_____	chilli	_____
child	_____	mouse	_____	foot	_____
man	_____	woman	_____	tooth	_____
sheep	_____	fish	_____	rice	_____
mango	_____	potato	_____	tomato	_____

2 Write the singular for these nouns.

races	_____	days	_____	puppies	_____
doctors	_____	dingoes	_____	shoes	_____
toothbrushes	_____	people	_____	foxes	_____
geese	_____	fairies	_____	ponies	_____

3 Use the prefix 'un' to write opposites for these words.

cover	_____	usual	_____	decided	_____
available	_____	tidy	_____	dress	_____
clean	_____	believable	_____	likely	_____
eaten	_____	finished	_____	done	_____

4 Add the suffixes to the following words. Write the new words on the lines.

–ful	help _____	hope _____	care _____
–less	help _____	hope _____	care _____
–ing	help _____	hope _____	care _____

Real Test

SPELLING
*Singular and plural nouns,
prefixes and suffixes*

20 MIN

Please ask your parent or teacher to read to you the spelling words on page 214. Write the correct spelling of each word in the box.

1. Li chopped the _____ for dinner.

2. Maya put lots of _____ in the salad.

3. I love _____.

4. Ten _____ attended the meeting.

5. Both of my _____ hurt after the race.

6. All the _____ cried at the same time.

7. The fruit shop sells nice _____.

8. Five _____ ran to the fence.

9. Boys and girls sat on separate _____.

10. The dentist looked at my _____ today.

11. The _____ ran around the bush at dusk.

12. The _____ waddled next to the creek.

13. The _____ ate all the cheese.

14. I went in a number of _____ at the sports carnival.

15. The duckling was _____ against the current.

16. We bought two _____ of bread for the picnic.

17. Dad said to be _____ of people's opinions.

18. The pod of _____ swam along the coast.

☞ **Answers and explanations on pages 192-193**

Each sentence has one word that is incorrect. Write the correct spelling of the underlined word in the box.

19 That chair is <u>unncomfortable</u>.

20 My shoes always come <u>unndone</u>.

21 Katy's work was <u>unfinisht</u>.

22 The teacher said to <u>unnfold</u> the paper.

23 Be <u>carefull</u> crossing the road.

24 Kara is <u>helpping</u> Mindi with her story.

25 The child was <u>careliss</u> with her bike.

26 My sister is <u>hopeliss</u> at cleaning her room.

Each line has one word that is incorrect. Write the correct spelling of the word in the box.

27 The gardnor mowed the grass.

28 The runnor hurt her foot.

29 The cyclest fell off his bike.

30 Mum bought flowers from the florest.

31 My dentest rides her bike to work.

32 Our local bakor makes delicious bread rolls.

33 The docter looked at my tonsils.

34 The plumba fixed our leaking roof.

35 Mr Chen is my teacha.

☞ **Answers and explanations on pages 192-193**

Key Points

GRAMMAR AND PUNCTUATION
Personal pronouns, HOW adverbs and adjectives that compare

1 **Personal pronouns** are words that replace nouns, or which refer to nouns in a text.

Examples: I, us, we, me, you, he, she, it, they, him, her, them

★ Use pronouns to refer to yourself.

Examples: <u>I</u> borrowed a book. <u>We</u> walked to the park.
Give <u>me</u> the book. Come to the park with <u>us</u>.

★ Use pronouns to address others.

Examples: <u>You</u> can walk to the park from here. (addresses one person)
<u>You</u> will all need to take turns. (addresses more than one person)

★ Use pronouns to refer to other people or things.

Examples: Sanjay—he, him; Ella—she, her; the table—it; the books—they, them; the children—they, them

2 **HOW Adverbs** add meaning to **verbs**.

Examples: run <u>swiftly</u>, chew <u>slowly</u>, work <u>quietly</u>

★ Adverbs that tell HOW often end in 'ly'.

Examples: slowly, quickly, swiftly, happily, quietly

★ Only adverbs can add meaning to verbs.

Examples: My brother ran <u>well</u> in the race.

★ Be careful not to use adjectives to describe verbs. Adjectives can only be used to describe nouns.
This is <u>incorrect</u>: "My brother ran <u>good</u> in the race".

3 **Adjectives** are used to compare nouns.

Examples: good, better, best
This pie is good. That pie is better. The chicken pie is the best.

★ To compare two things add 'er' to the adjective.

Example: Hannah is <u>taller</u> than Tom.

★ To compare more than two things add 'est' to the adjective.

Examples: Lucy is the <u>tallest</u> in the class.
happy, happier, happiest; hungry, hungrier, hungriest; sad, sadder, saddest; furry, furrier, furriest

★ Three-syllable adjectives need <u>more</u> for comparing two things and <u>most</u> for comparing more than two things.

Examples: The kite <u>is colourful</u>. This kite is <u>more colourful</u> than that kite. This is the <u>most colourful</u> kite of them all.
The sunset is <u>beautiful</u>. Yesterday's sunset was <u>more beautiful</u>. Last Friday's sunset was the <u>most beautiful</u>.

★ Some adjectives can't compare.

Examples: dead, full, empty, closed, open

Test Your Skills

GRAMMAR AND PUNCTUATION
Personal pronouns, HOW adverbs and adjectives that compare

15 MIN

Choose an adverb from the box that means the opposite for each word below.

Example: thickly—thinly

| loudly | happily | quickly | kindly |

1 slowly _____

2 quietly _____

3 sadly _____

4 angrily _____

5 Choose a pronoun to complete the sentence.
Tim and Elli are in the library. ▓▓▓▓ are reading.
A They   B Them C Us   D We

The HOW adverbs are written incorrectly. Write them correctly on the lines.

Example: The cat purred happy. happily

6 The lizard flicked its tongue out quick.

_____

7 Possums climb good.

_____

8 The turtle crawled slow.

_____

9 The parrot cracked the seed easy.

_____

10 The turtle snapped hungry at the fish.

_____

11 The page was bad torn.

_____

12 The lorikeet squawked loud.

_____

13 Choose a word or words to complete the sentence.
Which painting is ▓▓▓▓ ?
A colour fullest
B the most colourful
C colour fuller
D colouring

14 Choose an adjective to complete the sentence.
"My bag is ▓▓▓▓ than yours," said Frank.
A heavy   B heaviest
C heavily   D heavier

Write a personal pronoun from the box on each line to complete the sentences.

| she | them | it | We |

15 Shane is my best friend. _____ play soccer together.

16 Pass the ball to Leanne so _____ can kick the goal.

17 The children had worked well so the teacher gave _____ a surprise.

18 The dog was barking so I told _____ to be quiet.

Answers: 1 quickly 2 loudly 3 happily
4 kindly 5 A 6 quickly 7 well 8 slowly
9 easily 10 hungrily 11 badly 12 loudly
13 B 14 D 15 We 16 she 17 them 18 it

Real Test

GRAMMAR AND PUNCTUATION
Personal pronouns, HOW adverbs and adjectives that compare

20 min

1 Which word best completes the sentence?
The goanna walked ▧▧▧▧ .

   A lost   **B** loud   **C** soft   **D** softly

2 Which word best completes the sentence?
The beetle munched ▧▧▧▧ .

   A noisily   **B** thickly   **C** thinly   **D** crunching

3 Which word best completes the sentence?
Smile ▧▧▧▧ for the class photo.

   A wrongly   **B** nicely   **C** hopefully   **D** loudly

4 Which word best completes the sentence?
Hit the nail ▧▧▧▧ with the hammer.

   A fast   **B** carefully   **C** hungrily   **D** quick

5 That is Jack's book. Give it to him.
In this sentence the word *it* is used instead of

   A Jack.   **B** him.   **C** the book.   **D** a handshake.

6 These shoes are full of mud. Clean them.
In this sentence the word *them* is used instead of

   A mud.   **B** Jack.   **C** these shoes.   **D** cleaning.

7 Which word or words tell how you would pat a kitten?

   A outside   **B** then   **C** in the dark   **D** gently

Choose a word to complete each sentence.

him	They	I	me

8 I asked Kia to come to the park with _____.

9 Liam sits next to me so I help _____ with maths.

10 Koalas are marsupials. _____ eat eucalyptus leaves.

11 My name is Zac. _____ live in Padstow.

12 Which word correctly completes the sentence?
Some people like cats ▧▧▧▧ than dogs.

   A best   **B** better   **C** more better   **D** good

☞ **Answers and explanations on page 193**

Real Test

GRAMMAR AND PUNCTUATION
Personal pronouns, HOW adverbs and adjectives that compare

(continued)

Choose a word for each sentence.

biggest	big	bigger

13 That elephant is _____.

14 The red balloon is _____ than the green balloon.

15 The blue balloon is the

_____ of them all.

16 Which word or words correctly complete the sentence?

This yoghurt tastes _____ than that yoghurt.

A best   B better
C more best   D more good

17 Which word correctly completes the sentence?

My sister ran _____ in the race.

A great   B well
C good   D wonderful

18 Which word correctly completes the sentence?

A carpet snake lived _____ in our roof.

A quiet   B silent
C quietly   D quitly

19 Which sentence is correct?

A Stack the books carefully on the shelf.
B Stack the books carefully at the shelf.
C Stack the books careful over the shelf.
D Stack the books towards the shelf careful.

20 Which word or words correctly complete the sentence?

"I am the _____ runner in the class," said Paulo.

A fastest   B faster
C most fast   D more fast

21 Which word correctly completes the sentence?

The kookaburra sang _____.

A loud   B loudly
C silently   D happy

22 Which word correctly completes the sentence?

Are you going to the park? Can I come with _____?

A them   B him   C she   D you

23 Which word correctly completes the sentence?

This pencil belongs to Lara. Give it to _____.

A you   B her   C us   D I

24 Which sentence is correct?

A The magpies flew swift.
B The magpies flew good.
C The magpies flew swiftly.
D The magpies flew softly.

25 Which word correctly completes the sentence?

Mum said the battery was _____.

A deader   B dead
C deadest   D deadly

☞ Answers and explanations on page 193

Key Points

1 The purpose of a **persuasive text** is to persuade an audience to a point of view.

2 **Advertisements** are persuasive texts. They try to persuade you to buy something.

3 **Arguments** are persuasive texts. They try to influence your opinion about something.

4 Persuasive texts can be entertaining as well as informative.

5 Persuasive texts can have the following structure:

a an **opening statement** to let readers know what the text is about and to introduce the point of view—the opening statement can be a heading, a sentence or a whole paragraph

b a **sequence of arguments** and reasons (The strongest argument is usually made first. One paragraph is used for each argument. Some persuasive texts include ideas for and against a topic. You can point out arguments for and against the topic and then make a recommendation.)

c a **conclusion**. This is the summing-up statement.

6 Persuasive texts might use:

★ persuasive words

Examples: must, should, must not, do not

★ thinking and feeling verbs

Examples: I think, I believe

★ commands

Examples: Buy this product! Recycle your bottles.

★ adjectives

Examples: healthy, clever, fresh, cheap.

7 When reading a persuasive text look for the point of view. Decide for yourself whether you agree or disagree with the point of view given.

Be kind to possums on page 125 is an argument. It is written in paragraphs. The heading tells the writer's opinion. The first paragraph outlines the problem. The text then gives reasons or arguments that support the writer's opinion. The final paragraph makes a recommendation: *build a possum-house.*

Circuses are NOT good for animals on page 126 is an argument. The heading tells the writer's opinion. The rest of the text gives reasons for the opinion. The final paragraph is a summing up of the writer's opinion.

Be a winner on page 127 is an advertisement. The advertisement:

● uses commands: *Be a winner.*

● ends with a call to action: *Think of the planet…eat the skin or recycle it: No waste.*

● appeals to readers' feelings about their appearance, identity, belonging and friendship

● uses adjectives: *crisp, crunchy, juicy, shiny, green, red; healthy, better*

● appeals to readers' values: *Think of the planet*

● addresses readers as 'you': *helping you win*

● uses repetition: *win, winning*

● uses upper-case letters to seem more persuasive: *NOW!*

READING
Persuasive texts: argument

15 MIN

Read the text *Be kind to possums*. Circle the correct answers to the questions below.

1 **Be kind to possums**

2 Brush-tailed possums are common in Australia. They live in the bush and in people's
3 backyards. They prefer to live in hollow trees but they also make their homes in
4 people's roofs. Many people don't like having a possum in the roof.

5 Sometimes people trap the possum in the roof and set it free somewhere else. But
6 this is a problem for the possum. Possums are territorial, which means they have an
7 area that they call their own. They do not let new possums come into their area.
8 They chase away any new possums. Possums usually die when people move them out
9 of their own territory. They starve. I think that is very sad.

10 If you have an unwelcome possum in your roof, the best
11 thing to do is to build a possum-house in a tree in your
12 own backyard. You can attract the possum to the possum-
13 house using bananas. Possums love bananas. Once the
14 possum is out of your roof and in its new house you can
15 cover over any holes in your roof. Then it won't be able to
16 get back inside your roof.

1 The word *common* in the text means
A there are many of them.
B there are only a few of them.
C they only live in Australia.
D they are rare.

2 The best place for a possum to live is in
A a roof.   B a hollow tree.
C a possum-house.   D a zoo.

3 What does *Possums are territorial* mean?
A Possums don't like sharing their area with new possums.
B Possums have homes everywhere.
C Possums always live alone.
D Possums can't find a new place to live and so they die.

4 Where should you build a possum-house?
A in a neighbour's roof
B in a backyard tree
C in the forest
D in your roof

5 How does the writer feel when possums are moved out of their own territory?
A sad   B pleased
C angry   D hungry

6 The text says you should cover over holes in your roof
A so rain can't get in.
B so the possum can't get out.
C so the possum dies of starvation.
D so the possum can't get back inside.

7 What is the writer's purpose in the text?
A to describe possums
B to tell how to catch a possum
C to give opinions about possums
D to tell you how to make a possum-house

Answers: 1A 2B 3A 4B 5A 6D 7C

☞ **Explanations on pages 193-194**

Real Test

READING
Persuasive texts: argument

15 MIN

Read the text *Circuses are NOT good for animals*. Circle the correct answers to the questions below.

---

1 **Circuses are NOT good for animals**

2 I don't like circuses that use animals.

3 I feel sorry for the animals in circuses. Lions, tigers and
4 elephants don't belong in circuses. They need room to roam
5 around. They should not be kept in cages. They should not
6 be made to do tricks. They belong in the wild.

7 Some people think that it's all right to use animals such as horses in circuses. I
8 disagree. Circuses drive around from one place to the next. The horses wouldn't like
9 being driven around in a truck for hours and hours. That's not fair.

10 I don't think circuses should use any animals at all. Circuses should just have
11 human performers. In Circus Oz, the Flying Fruit Fly Circus and Cirque du Soleil the
12 humans do the tricks and perform. I love these kinds of circuses. I love the trapeze,
13 trampolining, juggling and stilt walking. My favourite act is the flying trapeze. It is so
14 much fun to watch.

15 Human circuses are entertaining. Animal circuses are cruel. Some countries don't let
16 circuses use lions, tigers or elephants. I am happy about that.

17 *Sanjay, age 10*

---

1 What does the writer think about circuses that use animals?

　A It's a good thing.
　B It's wrong.
　C It's fun.
　D It's entertainment.

2 The writer says elephants belong in

　A zoos.　　　　B the wild.
　C cages.　　　 D circuses.

3 How does the writer feel about circuses with human performers?

　A He doesn't like them.
　B He loves them.
　C He thinks it's wrong.
　D It's not fair.

4 The Flying Fruit Fly Circus has performing

　A lions.　　　　B dogs and horses.
　C humans.　　 D flies.

5 The writer's favourite circus act is

　A the flying trapeze.　B elephants.
　C juggling.　　　　　 D the clown.

6 The word *cruel* means

　A entertaining.　　　B unkind.
　C pleasant.　　　　　D foolish.

7 What is the purpose of the text?

　A to give an opinion about circuses
　B to convince people to see the circus
　C to describe the best circus acts
　D to explain what circuses do

☞ **Answers and explanations on page 194**

Real Test

15 MIN

Read the magazine advertisement *Be a winner*. Circle the correct answers to the questions below.

1 What does the text tell people to do every day?

  A Be a winner.
  B Eat an apple.
  C Win games.
  D Think of the planet.

2 Who is the *you* in the advertisement?

  A parents   **B** children
  C apples   **D** pirates

3 The text says that eating apples will help you win

  A apple power.
  B a smile.
  C a brain.
  D at sports and computer games.

4 *crisp, crunchy, juicy* The text says this

  A to make you want to eat an apple.
  B to tell you what apples look like.
  C to show that apples are healthy.
  D to show what apples are made of.

5 The text says a winning personality will get you

  A a winning attitude.   **B** extra apples.   **C** more friends.   **D** a better smile.

6 An apple has sustainable packaging because

  A its skin can be eaten.   **B** its skin is shiny.
  C its skin can be eaten or recycled.   **D** it makes readers think of the planet.

7 Which sentence is true about the advertisement?

  A It's trying to make parents buy apples.
  B It's trying to make children want to eat more apples.
  C It proves that apples are good for you.
  D It shows that apples make you a happier person.

☞ **Answers and explanations on pages 194–195**

TIPS FOR WRITING PERSUASIVE TEXTS

Text structure and organisation

A **persuasive text** presents a point of view about an issue. The purpose of a persuasive text is to convince others to agree with that point of view.

Persuasive texts include arguments, debates, discussions, advertisements, book reviews and film reviews.

Persuasive texts:

- need to sound convincing
- can be entertaining or funny as well as informative.

Before you start to write a persuasive text, think about:

- the **purpose** and **audience** for your text— is it an argument or an advertisement?
- the **opening statement**—use this to introduce the topic: make a statement to tell readers your opinion
- the **reasons** for your point of view (In an argument you can give both sides of the argument rather than just one side but you'll need to make your recommendation or summing-up position at the end of the text. In an advertisement, you need to point out all the good things about the product you are trying to sell. List these in order, from the most important to the least important. Exaggerate your claims, e.g. Miracle cleaner. Great value.)
- the **conclusion**. This is the summing-up statement. It draws all the arguments together. It might tell people to act or it might make a recommendation, e.g. *BUY NOW. Let's say NO to bullying*.

Expressing and developing ideas

When you write a persuasive text, remember to:

- use words such as *must* and *should*
- use commands to tell the reader what to do (e.g. buy this, act now)
- use emotive language (e.g. This is unfair. Children are suffering.)
- use thinking verbs (e.g. want, believe, hope, think)
- proofread your text and make sure it makes sense
- check spelling and punctuation.

When you have finished your writing, give it to an adult to read and check.

(a sample answer to the question on page 157)

Bullying

I don't like bullies. Bullies are people who keep saying things or doing things that hurt you. Bullies make you feel scared. They hurt you or embarrass you. Sometimes they take things from you. Sometimes they break your things.

I don't know why people become bullies. Maybe they think that bullying makes them look tough. Maybe bullying makes them feel powerful. Maybe they think bullying will make them popular. I think some bullies might be jealous of the people they bully. Or, maybe they just feel bad about themselves and want other people to feel bad too. Whatever the reasons, bullying is wrong.

Everyone needs to work together to let bullies know that we won't allow bullying in our school. We won't ignore bullying. If we ignore bullying, then the bullies get away with it. If we let bullies continue hurting others, then we are just as bad as them. We all need to let bullies know that they have to stop. We need to tell them we don't like it. We must stick up for people who are being bullied.

Let's say 'No' to bullying. Our school is a NO BULLYING Zone!

Jackson, 11

This text is beyond what would be expected of a typical Year 2 student. It is provided here as a model. The assessment comments are based on the marking criteria used to assess the NAPLAN Writing Test.

Vocabulary
- Terminology is relevant to the topic, e.g. *hurt, scared, embarrass, powerful, popular.*

Sentence structure
- Sentences are grammatically correct and make sense.

Ideas
- Ideas are logical and well thought out.

Punctuation
- The writer uses accurate punctuation: full stops, capital letters at the beginning of sentences, commas, an exclamation mark and contractions.

Spelling
- Challenging words are spelt correctly.
- Suffixes are accurate: *bullies, bullying.*
- Apostrophes are correct in contractions: *Let's, don't.*

Audience
- The audience for the text is schoolchildren. The opening sentence tells readers the writer's opinion about the topic.

Text structure
- The heading lets readers know what the text will be about.
- The first paragraph introduces the topic. It gives a definition of bullying. It states the writer's opinion.
- The second paragraph outlines reasons why people might bully.
- The third paragraph persuades readers to take action against bullies.
- The final paragraph is a strong final statement. It is a call to action: *Let's say 'No' to bullying.*

Paragraphing
- Paragraphs are sequenced and logical. Each is built around a main idea with supporting detail. The last paragraph has two simple sentences for emphasis.

Cohesion
- Correct use of pronoun reference: *bullies—they.*

Persuasive devices
- Upper-case letters emphasise the final point: NO BULLYING.
- High modality is used.

© Pascal Press ISBN 978 1 74125 419 8

Real Test

40 MIN

Before you start, read the **Tips for writing persuasive texts** on page 128.

Today you are going to write an **argument**. Your purpose is to give your opinion about the topic and persuade readers to agree with you.

The topic is **Television is bad for children.**

What do you think about television? Do you think television is bad for children? Are some programs bad for children to watch? Is it bad for children to see so many advertisements? Do you think children spend too much time watching television? Think about what television means to you, your friends and your family.

Before you start to write, think about the topic.
- Do you agree or disagree?
- What will you say in the introduction to let your readers know what you think?
- What will be the arguments and reasons for your opinion?
- How will the conclusion sum up all your ideas?

Remember to:
- plan your writing
- use a new paragraph for each idea
- think about words that will make your arguments sound convincing
- write in sentences
- check spelling and punctuation
- write neatly so that your readers can understand your writing
- ask a parent or teacher to read and check your finished work.

Use your own paper to write your argument.

☞ **Marking guide on page 195**

Real Test

Before you start, read the **Tips for writing persuasive texts** on page 128.

Today you are going to write an **argument**. Your purpose is to give your opinion about the topic and persuade readers to agree with you.

The topic is **People eat too much junk food.**

Most people like to eat burgers, fries, cakes, lollies and soft drinks. People often call this kind of food 'junk food' because it is not good for us to eat too much of it. Many people think we should not eat any of these foods. What do you think?

Before you start to write, think about the topic.
- Do you agree or disagree?
- What will you say in the introduction to let your readers know what you think?
- What will be the arguments and reasons for your opinion?
- How will the conclusion sum up all your ideas?

Remember to:
- plan your writing
- use a new paragraph for each idea
- think about words that will make your arguments sound convincing
- write in sentences
- check spelling and punctuation
- write neatly so that your readers can understand your writing
- ask a parent or teacher to read and check your finished work.

Use your own paper to write your argument.

☞ **Marking guide on pages 195-196**

WRITING
Persuasive text 3

40 MIN

Before you start, read the **Tips for writing persuasive texts** on page 128.

Today you are going to write an **advertisement** to display in your school. Your purpose is to persuade others to buy a product or a service. You can advertise to sell something that you own or something you have invented or made. Or you could advertise a service: something you can do to earn money. This could be car washing, dog washing, gardening, helping another child with their homework or any other service you can think of. Be as imaginative as you like. You can add illustrations or use layout to make your advertisement more persuasive.

Before you start to write, think about the advertisement.
- What will it be advertising?
- How can you make your advertisement sound convincing? You want readers to buy your product or service.
- How can you exaggerate how good your product or service is?
- Think about ways you might illustrate your advertisement.

Remember to:
- use strong language
- use descriptive adjectives
- use commands
- use a font or writing style that makes your advertisement stand out
- check spelling and punctuation
- write neatly so that readers can understand your writing
- ask a parent or teacher to read and check your finished work.

Use your own paper to write your advertisement.

☞ **Marking Guide on pages 196-197**

Sample NAPLAN Online-style tests

DIFFERENT TEST LEVELS

- There are eight tests for students to complete in this section. These sample tests have been classified as either Intermediate or Advanced according to the level of the majority of questions. This will broadly reflect the NAPLAN Online tailored testing experience where students are guided into answering questions that match their ability.
- The following tests are included in this section:
  - one Intermediate-level Test for each of Reading, Conventions of Language and Numeracy
  - one Advanced-level Test for each of Reading, Conventions of Language and Numeracy
  - two Writing Tests.

CHECKS

- The NAPLAN Online Reading, Conventions of Language and Numeracy tests will be divided into different sections.
- Students will have one last opportunity to check their answers in each section when they have reached the end of that section.
- Once they have moved onto a new section, they will not be able to go back and check their work again.
- We have included reminders for students to check their work at specific points in the Sample Tests so they become familiar with this process before they take the NAPLAN Online tests.

EXCEL TEST ZONE

- After students have consolidated their topic knowledge by completing this book, we recommend they practise NAPLAN Online–style questions on our website at www.exceltestzone.com.au.
- Students will be able to gain valuable practice in digital skills such as dragging text across a screen, using an onscreen ruler, protractor and calculator to answer questions, or listening to audio recording of a spelling word which they then type into a box.
- Students will also become confident in using a computer or tablet to complete NAPLAN Online–style tests so they will be fully prepared for the actual NAPLAN Online tests.

Today you are going to write a **narrative**. The title for your narrative is **Help me!** Imagine you are a character in this story and that you are outdoors somewhere and can hear a tiny voice. It calls to you. You look around and see a bird. The bird is speaking to you. It says "Help me!" What problem does the bird have? What does it want you to do? Are you able to help it? Try to make your story exciting.

Before you start to write, think about:
- the setting (Where are you? Use your senses to describe the setting.)
- the characters (What does the bird look like? What does it say? How does it sound?)
- the plot—what happens in your story?
- the resolution. How does your story end?

Remember to:
- plan your writing
- use noun groups with adjectives to describe the characters and the setting
- use pronouns consistently (e.g. I, me, it)
- write in paragraphs and sentences
- check your punctuation and spelling
- write neatly so that your readers can understand your handwriting
- ask a parent or teacher to read and check your finished work.

Use your own paper to write your narrative.

☞ Marking guide on page 197

Online-Style Sample Test

Read the poem *Nana's cat* and answer questions 1 to 5.

1 The cat's name is
A Cat.
B Des.
C Nana.
D Tubbs.

2 A *pushchair* is an old-fashioned word for a
A chair.
B pram.
C bed.
D pushbike.

3 How does the cat feel about food?
A He won't eat.
B He's fussy.
C He hates food.
D He loves food.

4 Where does the cat sleep?
A beside Nana's bed
B on Nana's lap
C in the bed
D in the heat

5 Choose the best diagram to show how Nana sits with Des.

1 **Nana's cat**
2 by Tanya Dalgleish

3 My nana has a big old cat.
4 She carts him everywhere.
5 He's black and white and much too fat.
6 He has his own pushchair.

7 My nana's cat just lives to eat
8 Or so my nana says.
9 He is a sneak. He hates the heat.
10 My nana calls him Des.

11 When Nana stops to take a nap,
12 Des lies upon her knees.
13 His tummy fits upon her lap.
14 The rest hangs in the breeze.

15 My nana keeps him in at night.
16 He sleeps beside her bed.
17 If Nana wakes up in a fright
18 she pats him on the head.

A   B   C   D

☞ **Answers and explanations on page 198**

Read *Ride a bike* and answer questions 6 to 12.

1 **Ride a bike**

2 More people should ride bikes instead of driving cars. Bike
3 riding is fun. It is good exercise. It is also helpful for the
4 environment.

5 Cycling helps to keep people fit and healthy. It's great
6 to cycle for fun with friends or family. There are lots of
7 footpaths for children to ride on safely.

8 People should use bicycles instead of cars whenever they
9 can. Cycling saves fuel costs and helps the environment.
10 Bicycles don't make any pollution. If more people used
11 bikes instead of cars there wouldn't be so much pollution.

12 Children can ride bikes to school or around the neighbourhood. Older people can use
13 bikes too. My Papi rides a tricycle. It has three wheels. He says he can't balance on a
14 two-wheeled bicycle any more. He rides his tricycle to the shops. He has a basket on
15 the back of his bike to carry his groceries. Sometimes he cycles with his little dog in the
16 basket. Papi loves cycling. It's not an electric cycle so he has to use pedal power to get
17 anywhere. He says that keeps him fit.

18 People should use bikes instead of cars whenever they can for their own health
19 and the health of the planet.

20 *Leilani, age 10*

6 Another word for *bike riding,* used in the text, is
A cycling.　　B tricycle.
C bicycle.　　D exercise.

7 The writer wants more people to
A ride tricycles.　B have fun.
C ride bikes.　　D get more exercise.

8 What might Papi carry in his basket?
A Grandma　　B his cat and dog
C his bag　　D groceries and a dog

9 How many wheels does a tricycle have?
A 3　　B 2　　C none　　D 4

10 Papi doesn't ride a bicycle because
A it has two wheels.
B he can't balance on it.
C it goes too fast.
D he needs a bike with an electric motor.

11 Where does Papi go on his tricycle?
A to the petrol station
B to the shops
C to school
D around the neighbourhood

12 What does *pedal power* mean?

_____

_____

It would be a good idea to check your answers to questions 1 to 12 before moving on to the other questions.

☞ **Answers and explanations on page 198**

Read *Eating for health* and answer questions 13 to 17.

1 **EATING FOR HEALTH**
2 *For good health, energy and growth, as well as strong teeth and bones, eat these foods.*

3 *fruit and vegetables*
4 *These foods provide fibre,*
5 *as well as vitamins*
6 *and minerals.*

lean meat, eggs, fish,
legumes, nuts
These foods provide protein
for muscles and growth.

wholegrain cereals
such as oats
These foods provide energy,
as well as fibre for digestion.

7 **fats and oils,*
8 *such as olive oil*
9 ** In small amounts only*

10 *dairy foods such as milk*
11 *and yoghurt*
12 *These foods provide calcium*
13 *for bones and teeth.*
14

natural foods rather than
processed foods
Processed foods sometimes
have too much salt and sugar,
and no fibre.

And remember to drink
lots of water.

13 Which foods are good for teeth and bones?
A milk
B apples
C dairy foods
D vitamins

14 Choose all that apply.
Whole grain cereals
A provide fibre for digestion.
B give energy.
C help your muscles.
D taste good.

15 Meat is a
A fish food.   B protein food.
C energy food.   D packaged food.

16 You get vitamins from
A strong teeth and bones.
B fruit and vegetables.
C water.
D sugar.

17 Oats are
A a horse food.   B a protein food.
C a vegetable.   D a cereal.

☞ Answers and explanations on page 198

Read *Join Earth Hour* and answer questions 18 to 23.

1 **Join Earth Hour**

2 I think that Earth Hour is a really good way to let people know
3 that little things they do can make a big difference to the planet.

4 Earth Hour started in Sydney, Australia, in March 2007. Now, cities
5 all around the world join in for Earth Hour. During Earth Hour
6 people are asked to switch off their lights to save the planet.
7 'Switching off' also includes turning off televisions and computers.

8 A lot of energy is saved around the world during Earth Hour but people should think
9 beyond one hour of energy saving. People should help the planet every hour of every
10 day. Walking to school or the shop, instead of going by car, saves energy. Buying
11 local products rather than imported products saves energy. Buying products with less
12 packaging saves energy. Reducing waste and recycling save energy. When you stop
13 and think about it, there are so many simple things people can do every day to help
14 the planet.

15 Being part of Earth Hour connects people around the world for a good cause. I am
16 going to be part of Earth Hour again next year. I hope you will be too.

17 *Owen, age 10*

18 Earth Hour started in
A homes.　　　B cities.
C Australia.　　D around the world.

19 *Join Earth Hour*
A gives an opinion.　B tells a story.
C is a factual report.
D is a set of instructions.

20 The purpose of the text is to
A encourage people to help the planet.
B connect people around the earth.
C make children walk to school.
D tell people to switch off televisions
and computers.

21 The writer is best described as a person
who
A saves electricity.
B cares about the environment.
C works well with others.
D has a good imagination.

22 Which of the following does <u>not</u> save
energy?
A buying local products
B walking to school
C walking to the shop
D watching television

23 What is another suitable title for this text?
A Help planet Earth
B The history of Earth Hour
C Owen turns off his lights
D Turn that computer off!

**It would be a good idea to check your
answers to questions 13 to 23 before
moving on to the other questions.**

☞**Answers and explanations on pages 198-199**

Read *How to choose the right pet* and answer questions 24 to 29.

1 **How to choose the right pet**

2 It's great to have a pet but it's important
3 to choose the right pet for your family.

4 When choosing a pet you need to think about:
5 ● how much time you have to spend with your pet
6 ● the size of the pet and how much space it needs
7 ● how active it is
8 ● its housing; where it will sleep and where it can
9   shelter from the sun, rain or cold
10 ● where it will go to the toilet
11 ● what it will do when you are not home
12 ● how much grooming it needs (washing, combing, clipping its fur)
13 ● cleaning up after it (picking up its droppings)
14 ● cleaning its housing (kennel, aviary, enclosure, bedding)
15 ● how it will affect your neighbours (barking dogs can annoy neighbours).

16 You also need to think about the cost of caring for your pet. Costs include: food,
17 housing, medical bills (vaccinations, medicines, worming), registration and equipment
18 (leash, collar, car harness, carry cage, grooming tools, play toys).

24 Select one or more answers. Pets need to have shelter from
   A the sun.   B the dark.
   C their toys.   D scary things.
   E the rain.   F the cold.

25 Grooming a pet <u>doesn't</u> mean
   A washing it.
   B picking up its droppings.
   C combing it.
   D clipping its fur.

26 Pet dogs can annoy neighbours when they
   A travel in the car.
   B need worming.
   C bark.
   D sleep.

27 You might need this to house pet birds.
   A leash   B kennel
   C aviary   D comb

28 Medical bills for a pet dog can include
   A play toys.   B registration.
   C grooming tools. D vaccinations.

29 The purpose of the text is to
   A help people choose the right pet.
   B tell an animal story.
   C describe different kinds of pets.
   D tell people not to buy pets.

☞ Answers and explanations on page 199

Online-
Style Sample
Test

READING TEST 1
Intermediate Level

(continued)

Read *Simple Fried Rice* and answer questions 30 to 35.

---

1 **Simple Fried Rice**

2 *This fried rice is easy to cook.*

3 **Ingredients**

4 $\frac{1}{3}$ cup peanut oil

5 1 onion, finely chopped

6 1 cup frozen peas

7 3 cups cooked rice

8 150 g cooked chicken, cut into strips

9 2 tablespoons soy sauce

10 1 tablespoon oyster sauce

Method 11

1 Heat the peanut oil in a 12
wok or large frypan. 13

2 Fry the onion for 14
2 minutes. 15

3 Add peas and cook 16
through. 17

4 Add all other ingredients. 18

5 Stir until everything is 19
hot. 20

Serve as a main meal or a 21
side dish. 22

---

30 This recipe can be cooked in

A the oven. B a frypan. C a cup. D a microwave oven.

31 What does *finely* mean?

A really B slowly C thinly D carefully

32 Which ingredient is used first?

A onion B capsicum C rice D peanut oil

33 What sort of chicken is needed?

A cooked B baked C frozen D raw

34 The fried rice is ready when

A it is served as a main dish or a side dish.
B it is hot.
C the chicken is cooked.
D you add the oyster sauce.

35 Select one or more answers. A good reason to use this recipe is because

A it says it's easy. B it takes 2 minutes.
C it's popular. D it looks tasty.
E it seems healthy.

☞ **Answers and explanations on page 199**

Read *Lost and found* and answer questions 36 to 39.

1 **Lost and found**

2 Vicki and Henry looked at each other. They were lost.
3 They had been to the park with their dog. It had chased
4 another dog into the bushes to play. They had chased
5 it and now they were definitely lost. And it was getting
6 dark. Their mother would be worried.

7 Vicki was the oldest so she tried to be brave and not
8 frighten Henry but she knew he was worried. He had
9 that look on his face, the look that said he was close to tears.

10 "Don't worry," she said. "Mum will come and find us." Henry's bottom lip trembled
11 but he didn't cry.

12 Just then they heard their dog's bark. The children called out excitedly, "Holly!" Holly
13 came crashing through the bushes towards them. The children hugged her. She licked
14 them joyfully.

15 Vicki stood up and said, "Home Holly." Holly wagged her tail and led them out of the
16 bushes, across the park, down the street, through the vacant block and into the front
17 yard of their own home, where their mother was waiting.

18 The children's mother said, "I knew Holly would bring you home."

36 Why did the children get lost?
  A Holly chased another dog.
  B They followed their dog into the bushes.
  C It was getting dark.
  D They had been to the park.

37 The mother wasn't worried because she knew that
  A the children knew the way home from the park.
  B Henry was easily frightened.
  C Vicki was the oldest.
  D Holly would bring the children home.

38 The children's mother was waiting
  A in the front yard.
  B at the park.
  C by the back steps.
  D on the street.

39 Holly licked the children *joyfully* because
  A she wanted to play with the other dogs.
  B the children were happy to see her.
  C their mother would be worried.
  D it was dinner time.

☞ Answers and explanations on page 200

1 Which word correctly completes this sentence?

Three dogs [_____] swimming in the lake.

A was	B were	C is	D has

2 Which word correctly completes this sentence?

I [_____] at the doctor's yesterday.

A gone	B is	C am	D was

3 Which word in this sentence is a noun?

We went to the museum.

A We	B went	C the	D museum

4 Which word in this sentence is used as an adjective?

Wendy slipped on the [_____] path.

A heavy	B pretty	C muddy	D little

5 Which word in this sentence tells how the children walked across the road?

The children walked quickly across the road.

A children	B walked	C quickly	D road

6 Which sentence is written correctly?

A today is the first day of april   B Today is the first day of april
C Today is the first day of April.   D Today is the first day of april.

7 Which sentence is written correctly?

A Jay has an new school bag.   B Jenna is an great runner.
C Robert is a fast reader.   D Kim is a excellent cook.

8 Which word correctly completes this sentence?

Dad [_____] tennis each Saturday.

A plays	B played	C playing	D player

9 Circle **three** proper nouns in this sentence.

Damon and Rina went to the library on Wednesday.

10 Which word correctly completes this sentence?

Luke [_____] his bike to school today.

A rode	B ride	C riding	D rid

☞ **Answers and explanations on pages 200–201**

11 Which word or words correctly complete this sentence?

I ▒▒▒▒▒▒ the grapes later.

A eating   B has eaten   C will eat   D been eaten

12 Which punctuation mark correctly completes this sentence?

Matilda shouted, "Look out ▒▒▒▒▒ "

A .   B ,   C ?   D !

13 Which words correctly complete this sentence?

It was Molly's birthday ▒▒▒▒▒ .

A then Ted decided to give her a flower

B because Ted decided to give her a flower

C so Ted decided to give her a flower

D otherwise Ted decided to give her a flower

14 Which word can replace the pronoun *her* in this sentence?

Give the pencil to her.

A me   B Ben   C Mum   D I

15 Write the words in the correct order to make a sentence.

/ on Wednesday / has / gym / . / Jesper /

16 Which word correctly completes this sentence?

The paint is stored ▒▒▒▒▒ .

A safely   B safe   C safest   D safer

17 Which sentence is punctuated correctly?

A We cant find the cricket balls.   B Where are the keys?

C Mum can't find her key's.   D Dad lost his keys yesterday?

18 Which sentence is written correctly?

A Ted bought apples oranges bananas and a pineapple.

B Ted bought apples, oranges, bananas and a pineapple.

C Ted bought apples, oranges, bananas, and a pineapple,

D Ted bought apples, oranges, bananas, and a pineapple

☞ Answers and explanations on pages 200–201

19 Choose the word group that <u>them</u> refers to in the text.

Those books have been marked. Hand <u>them</u> out.

A marked   B Those books   C Hand   D out

20 Which word correctly completes the sentence?

My brother swam ▬▬▬ in the carnival.

A great   B well   C good   D wonderful

21 Circle the correct article for each phrase.

A a / an butterfly   B a / an orange   C a / an egg   D a / an pineapple

22 Which word or words correctly complete the sentence?

This apple tastes ▬▬▬ than that one.

A best   B better   C gooder   D more good

23 Which word correctly completes the sentence?

Julie ran ▬▬▬ up the stairs.

A quiet   B quietly   C most quiet   D more quiet

24 Which sentence is punctuated correctly?

A "I love spelling tests, said Ryan."   B "I love spelling tests said Ryan"

C I love spelling tests, "said Ryan."   D "I love spelling tests," said Ryan.

25 Which word correctly completes this sentence?

It had stopped raining ▬▬▬ Sukie decided to walk to the park.

A because   B so   C or   D but

> **It would be a good idea to check your answers to questions
> 1 to 25 before moving on to the other questions.**

Please ask your parent or teacher to read to you the spelling words on page 215. Write the correct spelling of each word in the box.

26 Jack missed ▬▬▬ on Monday.   ☐

27 We ▬▬▬ the tomatoes to Peter.   ☐

28 Jordon collected the ▬▬▬ from the letterbox.   ☐

29 Early explorers rode ▬▬▬ in the desert.   ☐

30 Mina's ▬▬▬ is in May.   ☐

☞ **Answers and explanations on pages 200–201**

31 The door was ▨▨▨ .

32 The teacher ▨▨▨ the parents for visiting.

33 Gemma made ▨▨▨ mistakes in the spelling test.

34 The children collected water in a ▨▨▨ .

35 We ▨▨▨ go swimming later.

36 Sara had a ▨▨▨ of her grandparents.

37 The sky is a lovely ▨▨▨ today.

38 Mum and Greg ▨▨▨ into the kitchen.

39 Greg wanted to ▨▨▨ spaghetti for dinner.

40 Greg ▨▨▨ a lot of noise.

The spelling mistakes in these sentences are underlined. Write the correct spelling in the boxes.

41 <u>Wen</u> the spaghetti was ready Mum called me.

42 The spaghetti tasted <u>grate</u>.

43 I <u>thankt</u> Mum and Greg.

44 It's Heather's birthday <u>toomorow</u>.

45 Tim likes <u>rideing</u> his bicycle.

Each line has one word that is incorrect. Write the correct spelling of the word in the box.

46 Don't scrach your insect bites.

47 The cat ran quikly across the road.

48 We go to the library on Wensday.

49 The baby bird coodn't fly.

50 We looked evrywhere for the key.

☞**Answers and explanations on pages 200-201**

NUMERACY TEST 1
Intermediate level

1 What time is shown on this clock?

A quarter past five
C quarter past six

B quarter to six
D half past nine

2 What number comes next in this pattern?

15, 20, 25, 30, 35, ?

3

Using this ruler, how long is the pencil? _____ cm

4 This graph shows the number of cats owned by students.

 Number of cats

Key
= 1 cat

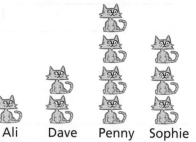

Ali   Dave   Penny   Sophie

Which student has 2 cats?

A Dave   B Sophie   C Penny   D Ali

5 Which of these is 762?

A 7 + 6 + 2   B 7 + 60 + 200   C 700 + 6 + 20   D 700 + 60 + 2

6 Here is a picture of some boys.

Max   Billy   Angus   Con

List the boys from tallest to shortest.

tallest   shortest

☞ **Answers and explanations on pages 201-204**

7 Sally is placing stamps on a board.

How could Sally work out the total number of stamps that could go on the board?

A 5×6

B $6 + 5$

C $2 \times 5 \times 5$

D $5 + 5 + 5$

8 Write nine hundred and twenty-eight as a number.

9 Jon flipped this card over the dotted line.

What did it look like after the flip?

A   B   C   D

10 Tess drew five shapes.

How many of these shapes are triangles?

A 1   B 2   C 3   D 4   E 5

11 $28 + 7$ has the same value as $30 +$ ☐

12 Meg put half of these plants in the garden.
How many plants did Meg put in the garden? ☐

It would be a good idea to check your answers to questions 1 to 12 before moving on to the other questions.

☞ Answers and explanations on pages 201-204

13 Which is a cone?

A

B

C

D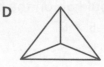

14 Which of these are used to measure mass? Select **all** the correct answers.

A

B

C

D

E

F

15 Which object is made from the most cubes?

A

B

C

D

16 Write the numbers 835, 853, 809 and 840 in order from lowest to highest.

lowest   highest

17 The calendar shows the month of March in 2018.

March						
Sunday	Monday	Tuesday	Wednesday	Thursday	Friday	Saturday
				1	2	3
4	5	6	7	8	9	10
11	12	13	14	15	16	17
18	19	20	21	22	23	24
25	26	27	28	29	30	31

What day of the week is 15 March?

A Thursday   B Sunday   C Saturday   D Monday

☞ **Answers and explanations on pages 201-204**

18 This arrow is being turned through a quarter turn each time.

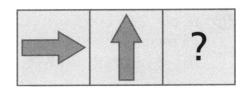

What will the arrow look like next?

A   B   C   D

19 Ed has some marbles in a dish.

He takes a marble from the dish. Which is impossible?

A red B blue

C yellow D green

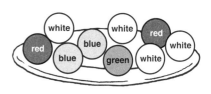

20 Which of these have exactly 5 faces? Select all correct answers.

A 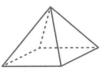 B   C  D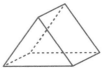

21 Mia has these coins.

How much money does she have?

A $3.10

B $3.90

C $4.10

D $4.90

22 Kim has this counter.

Kim moves the counter up 2 squares.

Then she moves the counter to the right 3 squares.

Which shows Kim's counter now?

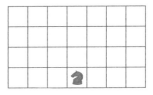

A  B C D

23 $2 \times 6 = 3 \times \boxed{}$

☞ **Answers and explanations on pages 201–204**

24 Jai put some cakes on 5 plates. Each plate has 3 cakes. Which shows the cakes that Jai needed?

A   B   C   D

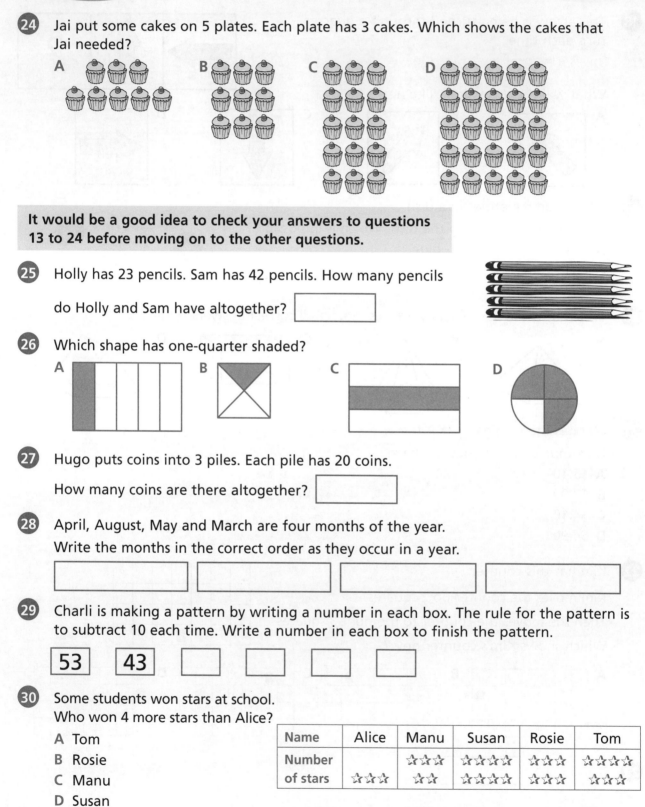

It would be a good idea to check your answers to questions
13 to 24 before moving on to the other questions.

25 Holly has 23 pencils. Sam has 42 pencils. How many pencils

do Holly and Sam have altogether? [ ]

26 Which shape has one-quarter shaded?

A   B   C   D

27 Hugo puts coins into 3 piles. Each pile has 20 coins.

How many coins are there altogether? [ ]

28 April, August, May and March are four months of the year.
Write the months in the correct order as they occur in a year.

[ ] [ ] [ ] [ ]

29 Charli is making a pattern by writing a number in each box. The rule for the pattern is to subtract 10 each time. Write a number in each box to finish the pattern.

| 53 | 43 | [ ] | [ ] | [ ] | [ ] |

30 Some students won stars at school.
Who won 4 more stars than Alice?

A Tom
B Rosie
C Manu
D Susan

Name	Alice	Manu	Susan	Rosie	Tom
Number of stars	☆☆☆	☆☆☆ ☆☆	☆☆☆☆☆ ☆☆☆☆☆	☆☆☆ ☆☆☆	☆☆☆☆ ☆☆☆

☞ **Answers and explanations on pages 201-204**

31 68 + 35 = [   ]

32 This is a map of my town. I leave the school and turn right. At the next corner I turn left.

Where might I be going?

A pet shop   B park

C bank   D pool

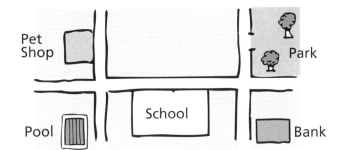

33 Zac counted some cars.

He showed the numbers in this table.

How many red cars did Zac count?

A 3   B 6

C 7   D 8

Colour of cars	
Colour	Tally
White	ЖЖ ЖЖ I
Red	ЖЖ III
Blue	IIII
Silver	ЖЖ II
Black	ЖЖ
Other	III

34 Complete the number sentence to show the total number of stars.

[   ] × 4 = [   ]

35 Which spinner is most likely to stop on 2?

A   B   C   D

36 These marbles are shared between 4 boys.
The boys all get the same number of marbles.

How many marbles do each of the boys get?

A 7   B 6

C 5   D 4

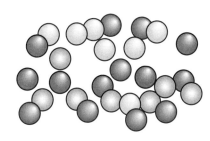

☞ **Answers and explanations on pages 201-204**

Today you are going to write a persuasive text. Write your opinion about the topic:

School should start at 7 am and finish at 1 pm.

Do you agree or disagree with the topic?

Is it a <u>good</u> idea to start school at 7 o'clock in the morning? Think about all the things you could do in the afternoon if school finished at 1 pm.

Do you think it is a <u>bad</u> idea to start school at 7 am? Will you be able to get out of bed to get to school on time?

What reasons can you think of to support your opinion?

Before you start to write a persuasive text, think about:
- your opinion—whether you agree or disagree with the topic
- the introduction—tell readers your opinion
- your arguments and reasons
- a conclusion which will sum up all your arguments and ideas.

Remember to:
- plan your writing
- write in paragraphs
- make sure you sound convincing
- write in sentences
- check spelling and punctuation
- write neatly so that readers can understand your handwriting
- ask a parent or teacher to read and check your finished work.

Use your own paper to write your persuasive text.

☞ Marking guide on page 204

Online-
Style Sample
Test

READING TEST 2
Advanced level

45 min

Read *Bullying* and answer questions 1 to 5.

1 **Bullying**

2 There are four main ways bullies hurt you.

3 1 Bullies can hurt you physically by hitting, pushing or
4 tripping you.

5 2 Bullies can hurt you with their words. This is called verbal
6 bullying. Bullies might threaten you. They might say nasty
7 things to you or they might say hurtful things about you to
8 others. It is bullying if someone keeps spreading lies about you.

9 3 Bullies can make you feel left out. This means not letting you join in with games or
10 other activities. If it happens often it is bullying. Being left out all the time makes
11 you feel terrible.

12 4 Bullying can also happen through technology. This means using the internet or a
13 mobile phone to say mean things about you, or using a camera to take photos of
14 you when you don't know it. This is called cyberbullying.

15 Bullying can happen to anyone. It can happen anywhere. It can happen to you when
16 you don't even know why. If you are being bullied you need to tell someone. You can
17 tell a teacher, a parent or relative or a friend. They will help you work out what to do.
18 If you see someone else being bullied you should tell an adult. Don't ignore bullying.

19 *Amanda, age 10*

1 Physical bullying means
  A someone keeps spreading lies about you.   **B** being picked on.
  C being left out.   **D** being hit, pushed or tripped.

2 An example of a bully hurting you with their words is when
  A people don't believe what you tell them.**B** someone keeps calling you names.
  C you feel bad.   **D** you have a mobile phone.

3 Cyberbullies
  A bully at school.   **B** use technology to bully people.
  C use robots to bully people.   **D** call you on their mobile phones.

4 What should you do if you are being bullied?
  A Tell someone.   **B** Complain to the bully.
  C Try to ignore the bully.   **D** Become a bully yourself.

5 Being left out is bullying if
  A it is an activity you really want to do.   **B** everyone is allowed to join in except you.
  C it makes you feel sad.   **D** it happens often.

☞ **Answers and explanations on pages 204–205**

Read *How to make a worm farm* and answer questions 6 to 11.

1 **How to make a worm farm**

2 **What you need**

3 2 foam boxes (one with a lid)

4 insect screen (to fit the bottom of one box)

5 newspapers

6 worms

7 **What you do**

8 1 *For the worm farm*: Make some holes in the
9 bottom of one of the boxes using a biro or
10 screwdriver. (You need holes so that the worm
11 wee drains out.) Line the bottom of the box with insect screen to stop worms from
12 falling through the holes. Add shredded newspaper, soaked in water, for worm
13 bedding. Add worms that you have bought from a nursery. Use Tigerworms or
14 Redworms, but not earthworms. Cover the farm with a foam lid with air holes.

15 2 Place the worm farm box on top of the second box. Place a brick in the bottom
16 box so that if worms do fall through, they won't drown. (They can climb onto the
17 brick until you rescue them.)

18 3 Keep your worm farm in the shade. Add fresh bedding regularly.

19 4 Feed your worms kitchen waste. BUT: No meat. No dairy. No oranges, lemons or
20 grapefruits. No raw onions, raw garlic or raw potato.

21 5 Mix worm wee with water for use in your garden.

6 Select one or more answers. Don't feed worms
A carrots. B oranges.
C watermelon. D lettuce.
E raw onions. F lemons.

7 Use worm wee
A on vegetables. B for cooking.
C in the garden. D in the kitchen.

8 You need a brick in the bottom box
A because worms like to climb.
B to stop the box blowing away.
C so worms don't drown if they fall in.
D because the top box is full of shredded newspaper.

9 A worm farm needs
A earthworms.
B special worms bought from a nursery.

C any worms found in the garden.
D a variety of different kinds of worms.

10 Worms sleep
A in warm beds.
B in damp newspaper.
C in damp dirt.
D in fresh hay or straw.

11 The worm farm should be kept
A in the dark. B in the sun.
C in the shade. D under the house.

It would be a good idea to check your answers to questions 1 to 11 before moving on to the other questions.

☞ **Answers and explanations on page 205**

Read *The Greater Bilby* and answer questions 12 to 17.

1 **The Greater Bilby**

2 The Greater Bilby is in danger of becoming extinct throughout Australia. Once upon
3 a time bilbies could be found over most of Australia. Now they can only be found in
4 small areas of the country. There are two main reasons why bilbies are endangered.
5 One is because cattle, sheep and feral rabbits eat the same foods as bilbies. The
6 second reason is that foxes and feral cats attack and eat bilbies.

7 The Greater Bilby is the size of a rabbit. It has huge ears. It has greyish fur and a long
8 pointy pink nose with whiskers. Its inner ears are pink and so are its feet. It has a long black
9 and white tail. The bilby has very good hearing. It has a good sense of smell. This helps
10 it find food. It doesn't see very well. Bilbies eat seeds, fruit,
11 bulbs, termites and other insects, as well as spiders.

12 Bilbies dig deep burrows to keep safe from predators and
13 to keep cool on hot desert days. Each bilby can have a
14 number of burrows. Female bilbies have backwards-facing
15 pouches. This is so dirt doesn't get in the pouch when they
16 are digging and harm the bilby babies. The female usually
17 has two babies at a time.

18 Using the bilby at Easter time, to replace the Easter bunny,
19 raises awareness of the bilby's problems in the wild.

12 Bilbies are killed by
  A rabbits.
  B sheep and cattle.
  C dogs.
  D foxes and cats.

13 Bilbies eat
  A plant food.
  B grass and leaves.
  C plants and animals.
  D only insects and spiders.

14 A female bilby's newborn babies live in
  A a nest.   B an egg.
  C a pouch.   D a burrow.

15 Rabbits cause problems for bilbies because
  A people buy more Easter bunnies than Easter bilbies.
  B they eat the plants bilbies like.
  C they are the same size as bilbies.
  D they attack and eat bilbies.

16 A bilby's feet are
  A white.   B greyish.
  C black and white. D pink.

17 Select one or more answers. Bilbies use their burrows
  A to trap cats.   B for safety.
  C to trap foxes.   D to keep cool
  E to dig holes.

☞ **Answers and explanations on page 205**

Read *Class discussion* and answer questions 18 to 23.

18 What was Lily's favourite artwork?
   A the sculpture of the clothes line
   B 'Swimming before school'
   C a painting by Lin Onus
   D Ian Abdulla

19 What did Selina like about the sculpture?
   A She could walk around it.
   B It was colourful.
   C She likes fruit bats.
   D It was a clothes line.

20 What reason did Ralph give for bats hanging on clothes lines?
   A There are no trees.
   B Lots of people don't like bats.
   C Bats are native animals.
   D The bats were made of fibreglass.

21 How do fruit bats help forests?
   A They live in groups or colonies.
   B They spread seeds and pollen.
   C They help forests.
   D They are important in Aboriginal culture.

22 The bat droppings on the sculpture were made of
   A lots of colours.
   B lines and cross-hatching.
   C wooden disks.   **D** fibreglass.

23 What did Lien mean when he said *the sculpture is about everyone and everything living in harmony*?
   A Fruit bats like to use clothes lines.
   B Aborigines are the traditional owners of the land.
   C The children in the class are friendly.
   D All people and animals need to share the environment.

It would be a good idea to check your answers to questions 12 to 23 before moving on to the other questions.

1 **Class discussion**

2 The students in Class
3 4W were talking
4 about artworks they
5 saw at the art gallery
6 on an excursion.

7 Lily: I loved the painting by Ian
8   Abdulla, 'Swimming before
9   school'.
10 Ms Rose: What did you like about that
11   painting, Lily?
12 Lily: I liked the idea of swimming
13   before school.
14 Ms Rose: What do other people think?
15 Harry: I liked the sculpture of the
16   clothes line with the fibreglass
17   bats hanging on it.
18 Ralph: That was my favourite too. The
19   artist was making a joke.
20 Selina: I liked it because I could walk
21   around it.
22 Ms Rose: The artist's name is Lin Onus.
23   What do you think his
24   artwork is about?
25 Ralph: Well, lots of people don't
26   like bats in their garden but
27   where can the bats go if there
28   are no trees? My mum says
29   fruit bats are really important
30   for forests. Bats spread plant
31   seeds and pollen.
32 Ms Rose: That's a good point.
33 Julia: I liked the wooden disks that
34   were the bats' droppings. I
35   liked the colours on them.
36 Ms Rose: Do you think the sculpture
37   is also about Aboriginal
38   culture?
39 Selina: Yes, because of the colours
40   and the way it's painted.
41 Lien: I think the sculpture is about
42   everyone and everything
43   living in harmony.

☞ **Answers and explanations on pages 205-206**

Read *African child* and answer questions 24 to 29.

1 **African child**

2 Mariama walked quickly. She needed to hurry. She had to
3 fetch the water and take it home before she could go to
4 school. It took her three hours every morning to fetch the
5 water. Her village's well was dry. The closest village had
6 contaminated water in its well. So now she had to walk
7 a long way to another village to get clean water for her
8 family. She was hungry but there had been little food for months, since the drought.

9 Mariama's mother usually fetched water with her but Mariama's little brothers
10 were both sick. They had been drinking dirty water and they had diarrhoea. The aid
11 worker had given them medicine but they were still very sick. The aid worker said
12 that diarrhoea kills too many little children. Mariama was worried about the boys.
13 They were so skinny and so sick.

14 Mariama was also frightened of wild animals in the scrub. The animals were hungry
15 and thirsty too. And they were coming closer to the villages in search of food. Last
16 month her friend was taken by a lion while she was fetching water.

24 Why was Mariama worried about her brothers?

A They were frightened of lions.
B They were sick.
C They needed water.
D They were missing school.

25 Why was Mariama in a hurry?

A She wanted to get to school.
B The village well was far away.
C She wanted to check on her brothers.
D Her mother needed her help.

26 Why was the village well dry?

A There was a drought.
B The wild animals were thirsty.
C Other villages had used it up.
D Her mother fetched water with her.

27 How did the boys get diarrhoea?

A They were too skinny.
B There was a drought.
C They had been given the wrong medicine.
D They had drunk dirty water.

28 Why was Mariama hungry?

A She had missed breakfast.
B There wasn't enough food.
C Her mother had given the food to the boys.
D The well was dry.

29 What had happened to Mariama's friend?

A She was hungry.
B She missed school.
C She had diarrhoea.
D A lion had killed her.

☞ Answers and explanations on page 206

Read *Children spend too much time on computers* and answer questions 30 to 35.

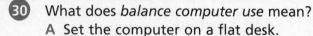

1 **Children spend**
2 **too much time**
3 **on computers**

4 Some people think
5 all children spend
6 too much time using
7 computers. I don't
8 agree with them.
9 I think computers are good for children.

10 I think it's good to use the computer
11 for homework or reading or doing
12 research or learning things about
13 nature. Those things are a great use of
14 your time on a computer. You can also
15 use a computer for fun and games.

16 I think it's important to balance
17 computer use with other activities
18 such as playing sport and having fun
19 outdoors.

20 If you do spend a lot of time on a
21 computer you have to be careful about
22 some things. You have to sit correctly so
23 you don't hurt your back. You have to
24 be careful not to strain your eyes. You
25 need to think about being safe online:
26 don't chat with people you don't know
27 or who your family doesn't know. Don't
28 post things like photos online. Don't
29 post personal information online.

30 If you use a computer sensibly then
31 there is no such thing as spending too
30 much time on it.

31 *Kylie, age 9*

30 What does *balance computer use* mean?
A Set the computer on a flat desk.
B Use the computer for fun and games.
C Give equal time to computers and other activities.
D Use the computer for homework.

31 The writer thinks that
A all children spend too much time on computers.
B computers should only be used for fun and games.
C she spends too much time on computers.
D computers are good for children.

32 You need to sit correctly at the computer
A so you don't hurt your back.
B so you don't block the view of other people.
C so you can video call.
D so you can take photos to post online.

33 *Being safe <u>online</u>* means
A avoiding eye strain.
B not telling strangers where you live.
C only posting nice photos of yourself.
D not letting strangers into your house.

34 The writer says that children need to spend time
A chatting online.
B having fun outdoors.
C watching television.
D being careful not to strain their eyes.

35 Which of the following <u>is not</u> an <u>online</u> safety risk?
A posting personal photos
B giving out personal information
C chatting with strangers
D straining your back

☞**Answers and explanations on page 206**

Read *Our edible school garden* and answer questions 36 to 40.

1   **Our edible school garden**

2   Our school
3   has an edible
4   garden that
5   we planted
6   three years ago. We have been learning how to grow our own food and how to
7   cook. We enjoy eating the foods we grow ourselves. We grow vegetables such as
8   carrots, tomatoes and lettuce. We use the food for cooking in class. We are learning
9   about environmental stewardship. This means taking care of the earth.

10   We want to make our edible garden bigger. We want to grow lots of different kinds
11   of foods. We have asked the government for some money to create an organic kitchen
12   garden. The money will help us buy organic fertilisers, worms, seeds and weed mats.

13   Organic gardeners compost all garden matter into the soil. This creates healthier
14   gardens. Organic gardeners don't use any chemicals. This means the food grown is
15   better for people and the environment. Organic gardens are safer for birds, too, as
16   well as the earthworms, bacteria, fungi and insects that a healthy garden needs.

36   What is *environmental stewardship*?

A taking care of the earth
B growing your own food
C learning about the earth
D being an organic gardener

37   What does the school need to buy for the organic kitchen garden?

A earthworms, bacteria, fungi and insects
B carrots, tomatoes and lettuce
C fertilisers, worms, seeds and weed mats
D a greater variety of food

38   How do students use the food they grow?

A They compost it.
B They eat it.
C They feed it to the birds.
D They sell it to parents and teachers.

39   Organic gardeners don't use

A compost.
B gardens.
C birds.
D chemicals.

☞ Answers and explanations on page 206

1 Which word in this sentence is used as an adjective?

Mum wore her yellow dress.

A Mum   B wore   C yellow   D dress

2 Which of these is a complete sentence?

A Ellie loves bananas.   B Ellie and me.

C Yesterday, in assembly.   D The dog with the sore foot.

3 Which word correctly completes this sentence?

George ate all the cherries ▆▆▆▆▆ he was hungry.

A until   B because   C then   D so

4 Which word in this sentence is a noun?

We bought delicious apples.

A We   B bought   C delicious   D apples

5 Which of these is correct?

A an monkey   B an donkey   C a elephant   D an insect

6 Which sentence is punctuated correctly?

A Tom invited Lisa Ben Jai and Sachar to his party.

B Tom invited Lisa, Ben, Jai and Sachar to his party.

C Tom invited Lisa, Ben, Jai, and Sachar, to his party.

D Tom, invited Lisa Ben Jai and Sachar, to his party.

7 Which word correctly completes the sentence?

Hannah ▆▆▆▆▆ in three races.

A swim   B swimming   C swam   D swum

8 Which word correctly completes the sentence?

Zoe is good at ▆▆▆▆▆ people.

A drew   B drawing   C drawn   D draws

9 Which word correctly completes the sentence?

▆▆▆▆▆ it's still raining, we'll stay inside.

A Because   B Until   C Although   D And

10 Which word correctly completes the sentence?

We'll visit Gran ▆▆▆▆▆ we wash the car.

A until   B after   C because   D so

☞ **Answers and explanations on pages 206–208**

11. Which words correctly complete this sentence?

    ▬▬▬▬▬ Sharon still made it to school on time.

    A But the bus was late   B Because the bus was late

    C Although the bus was late   D Then the bus was late

12. Which word can replace the underlined words in this sentence?

    Jenny and Leanne worked on the painting.

    A Them   B They   C He   D She

13. Which word or words correctly complete the sentence?

    Mario played ▬▬▬▬▬ in the game today.

    A good   B more best   C more better   D well

14. Which word tells how to hold the baby?

    Hold the baby carefully.

    A Hold   B the   C baby   D carefully

15. Which words can replace the pronoun *They* in this sentence?

    They walked into the classroom.

    A The teacher   B The children   C Jim and I   D Me and my mother

16. Which word correctly completes the sentence?

    Look at ▬▬▬▬▬ ducks on the pond over there.

    A them   B those   C this   D these

17. Which word or words correctly complete the sentence?

    David is ▬▬▬▬▬ than Mark.

    A shortest   B shorter   C more short   D most short

18. That puppy is fatter than this one.

    In this sentence the word *one* is used instead of

    A kitten.   B baby.   C puppy.   D dog.

19. Which sentence below is closest in meaning to these sentences.

    The magpie babies are very noisy. They squawk all day for food.

    A The magpies are very noisy.

    B The magpies are babies.

    C The noisy baby magpies squawk for food all day.

    D The hungry baby magpies eat all day.

☞ **Answers and explanations on pages 206-208**

Online-
Style Sample
Test

CONVENTIONS OF LANGUAGE TEST 2
Advanced level

(continued)

20 Which sentence is correct?

A You should of did it by now.
B You should have done it by now.
C You should of do it by now.
D You should of done it by now.

21 Which sentence is correct?

A The bucket is full.
B The bucket is more full.
C The bucket is most full.
D The bucket is fuller.

22 Which word correctly completes the sentence?

Jack asked Katy to go to the park with ________ .

A her B they C him D he

23 Which contraction correctly completes the sentence?

We need to hurry or ________ miss the train.

A we've B we'll C we'd D we're

24 Which sentence is punctuated correctly?

A "Where's my hat?" asked Fillipo.
B Where's my hat?"asked Fillipo."
C "Where's my hat? asked Fillipo."
D "Where's my hat"? asked Fillipo.

25 Which sentence is punctuated correctly?

A "Stop?" shouted the police officer.
B "Stop! shouted the police officer."
C "Stop" shouted the police officer
D "Stop!" shouted the police officer.

It would be a good idea to check your answers to questions 1 to 25 before moving on to the other questions.

Please ask your parent or teacher to read to you the spelling words on page 215. Write the correct spelling of each word in the box.

26 Leo asked when the movie ________ going to start.

27 The banana got ________ in my bag.

28 Dad ________ the football team when he hurt his knee.

29 Call 000 in an ________ .

30 It's ________ to climb on the roof.

31 Helen ran around the oval ________ .

Answers and explanations on pages 206–208

32 We saw ▭▭▭ horses in the parade.

33 The class had a ▭▭▭ of tee-ball or cricket.

34 Jake is learning to ▭▭▭ hip-hop.

35 The ▭▭▭ showed the wrong time.

36 The ▭▭▭ had a meeting before school.

37 The Shetland ▭▭▭ were small and cute.

38 The smallest kitten looked so ▭▭▭ .

39 The kitten was ▭▭▭ in colour.

40 The kitten had ▭▭▭ feet.

The spelling mistakes in these sentences are underlined.
Write the correct spelling in the boxes.

41 The kitten had a pink <u>noze</u>.

42 The kitten wanted to <u>slepe</u>.

43 The kitten was <u>fluffyer</u> than the puppy.

44 Tooth <u>fairys</u> collect teeth.

45 John said his homework had <u>dissappeared</u>.

Each line has one word that is incorrect.
Write the correct spelling of the word in the box.

46 Dad needed two loafes of bread.

47 The car alahm was loud.

48 Clime the stairs carefully.

49 Im hungry for lunch.

50 Peta didn't bring her raincote.

☞**Answers and explanations on pages 206-208**

NUMERACY TEST 2
Advanced level

1 Bob has these coins.

How much money does Bob have?

A 78 cents   **B** 87 cents   **C** $3.57   **D** $3.75

2 Which clock shows the time as quarter past ten?

A   **B**   **C**   **D**

3 Which shape has the most squares coloured?

A   **B**

C   **D**

4 What shape is at B3 on the grid?

A   **B**

C   **D**

5 Blake has these balloons.
He keeps 5 and gives the rest to Riley.
How many balloons did Blake give to Riley?

☞ **Answers and explanations on pages 208–211**

Excel Revise in a Month Year 2 NAPLAN*-style Tests

Online-
Style Sample
Test

NUMERACY TEST 2
Advanced level

(continued)

6 Write the number three hundred and four. [   ]

7 Which object is most like a cylinder?

A   B   C   D

8 Some students voted for their favourite colour.

Favourite colours

KEY
= 2 students

Red   Blue   Pink   Green   Yellow

How many students voted for blue? [   ]

9 Which triangle will look the same when flipped over the dotted line?

A   B   C   D

10 Ali is making a pattern with pins.
How many pins will go in Box 4?

A 10   B 11
C 12   D 13

Box 1   Box 2   Box 3   Box 4

11 Ben opened a packet of nails. He used half of
the nails. These are the nails that Ben has left.

How many nails were in the full packet? [   ]

☞ **Answers and explanations on pages 208-211**

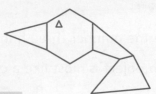

12 Molly made a picture with shapes.
How many triangles did Molly use?

It would be a good idea to check your answers to
questions 1 to 12 before moving on to the other questions.

13 What shape comes next in this pattern?

A ▢ B ● C ◯ D ◇

14 4 + 300 + 70 =

A 437 B 374 C 473 D 743

15 How many faces does this solid have?
A 10 B 9
C 8 D 7
E 6

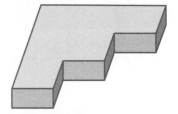

16 This graph shows the number of
pets owned by students.
Which is true? Select all the correct statements.

A There are more fish than cats.

B There are more birds than dogs.

C There are more dogs than fish.

D There are fewer birds than cats.

Pets owned by students

Dog
Cat
Fish
Bird

1 2 3 4 5 6 7 8 9 10 11 12

17 James has some blocks that are all the same size.

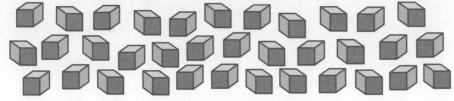

He uses some of the blocks to build this tower.

How many blocks does James use?

☞ **Answers and explanations on pages 208–211**

18 A shape is being turned a quarter of a turn each time in a pattern.

What comes next?

A   B   C   D

19 49 + 37 has the same value as 50 + ☐

20 Dan has 60 eggs. He puts the eggs in cartons like this. Which shows the way Dan could work out how many cartons he needs?

A 60 + 12   B 60 − 12

C 60 × 12   D 60 ÷ 12

21 Place the numbers 2503, 5032, 3205, 2350, 5230 and 3025 in order from lowest to highest.

lowest   highest

☐ ☐ ☐ ☐ ☐ ☐

22 This is a photo of a singing group.
Who is second from the left in the back row?

A Joe   B Mai

C Ray   D Mel

23 What number comes next in this pattern?

5, 8, 11, 14, ☐

24 Adam put his toy cars in 4 rows.
There are 5 cars in each row.

How many cars are there altogether? ☐

It would be a good idea to check your answers to questions 13 to 24 before moving on to the other questions.

☞ Answers and explanations on pages 208-211

25 This table shows the number of days students went to the beach last month.

How many more days did Emma spend at the beach than Marc?

Name	Number of days
Steve	7
Jo	4
Emma	12
Ellen	1
Marc	5

26 Write a number in the box to make this number sentence correct.

17 + [ ] = 30

27 Zac leaves the post office and turns right into Main Street.
He goes along Main Street and turns into the next street on his left.

What street is Zac in now?

A Park St **B** Beach St

C Railway St **D** Wattle St

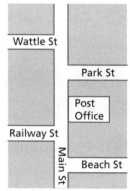

28 Mary makes a pattern with numbers. In her pattern she adds 5 each time.
Which could be Mary's pattern?

A 5, 10, 20, 40, 80, … **B** 5, 11, 17, 23, 29, … **C** 6, 11, 16, 21, 26, … **D** 55, 50, 45, 40, 35, …

29 This money is shared between 3 girls.

The girls all get the same amount of money.
How much money does each girl get?

A $1.45 **B** $1.25 **C** $1.20 **D** 46c

30 1, 8, 15, **?**, 29, 36
What number is missing in this pattern?

A 20 **B** 21 **C** 22 **D** 23

☞**Answers and explanations on pages 208–211**

31 This is a normal dice. If it is rolled again, what **must** the number **it** shows be? Select all correct answers.

A 6

B less than 1

C less than 7

D more than 2

E 1 or more

32 Which shape has one-quarter shaded?

A

B

C

D

33 Jay's birthday is 13 August. Fred's birthday is three weeks after Jay's.

AUGUST						
Sunday	Monday	Tuesday	Wednesday	Thursday	Friday	Saturday
						1
2	3	4	5	6	7	8
9	10	11	12	13	14	15
16	17	18	19	20	21	22
23	24	25	26	27	28	29
30	31					

What is the date of Fred's birthday?

A 26 August

B 30 August

C 2 September

D 3 September

34 Which of these numbers is closest to 60?

A 56

B 59

C 63

D 69

35 Pam has these 4 cards.

What number is it impossible for Pam to make with these cards?

A 642

B 424

C 266

D 446

36 How many ☐ does each ◯ balance?

A 1

B 2

C 3

D 4

☞ Answers and explanations on pages 208–211

WEEK 1

NUMBER AND ALGEBRA (Real Test)
Numbers and place value

Pages 7–8

1 594 **2** A **3** B **4** 63 **5** D **6** C **7** D **8** A **9** 47 **10** 117
11 B **12** 150 **13** A **14** B **15** 630, 603, 360, 306

EXPLANATIONS

1 Five hundred and ninety-four is 5 hundreds, 9 tens and 4 ones. So it is 594.

2 56 is 5 tens and 6 ones.
This is shown by

3 408 is 4 hundreds, 0 tens and 8 ones.
So it is four hundred and eight.

4 Imagine the numbers filled in on the number line.

50 51 52 53 54 **55** 56 57 58 59 **60** 61 62 63

The arrow is pointing to 63.

5 831 is 8 hundreds, 3 tens and 1 one.
So 831 is 800 + 30 + 1.

6 135 has 1 hundred, 3 tens and 5 ones.
219 has 2 hundreds, 1 ten and 9 ones.
348 has 3 hundreds, 4 tens and 8 ones.
372 has 3 hundreds, 7 tens and 2 ones.
So, in order, the numbers are 135, 219, 348 and 372.

7 400 + 50 + 7 is 4 hundreds, 5 tens and 7 ones. So it is 457.

8 98 + 8 = 98 + 2 + 6 = 100 + 6

9 By counting, there are 4 rows of 10 stars and 7 more stars. So there are 4 tens and 7 ones. There are 47 stars.

11 There is 1 hundred, 1 ten and 7 ones.

The number is 117.

11 Write out some numbers around 30.
25, 26, 27, 28, 29, 30, 31, 32, 33, 34, …
Of the choices the number closest to 30 is 28.

12 This calf has number 149.
The next calf will have the number one more than this. It will have number 150.

13 9 + 7 = 16
Try the choices.
10 + 8 = 18
6 + 10 = 16
7 + 9 = 16
8 + 8 = 16
10 + 8 is not the same as 9 + 7.

14 The numbers on the number line are counting by twos.

A B C   D

70 72 74 76 78 **80** 82 84 86 88 **90** 92 94 96

87 is between 86 and 88.
The arrow pointing to 87 is B.

15 Two of the choices have 6 hundreds and the other two have 3 hundreds. So, the two largest numbers are 603 and 630.
Now 603 has 0 tens but 630 has 3 tens.
So 630 is the largest number.
The two smallest numbers are 306 and 360.
Now 306 has 0 tens but 360 has 6 tens.
So 306 is the smallest number.
So, in order from largest to smallest, the numbers are 630, 603, 360 and 306.

NUMBER AND ALGEBRA (Real Test)
Patterns and number sentences

Pages 14–15

1 25 **2** 50 **3** 16 **4** B **5** 15 **6** 5
7 52 **8** B **9** 22 **10** C **11** A **12** 1042
13 D **14** 32 **15** 25 **16** D **17** A **18** 6, 10, 14, 18

EXPLANATIONS

1 17 + 8 = 17 + 3 + 5 = 20 + 5 = 25

2 25, 30, 35, 40, 45, ?
The numbers are counting forward by fives.
The next number is 45 + 5 or 50.

3 32 + 16 = 48 so the number must be 16.
48 = 40 + 8
= 30 + 10 + 8
= 30 + 18
= 30 + 2 + 16
= 32 + 16

4 ◆◇☺■◆◇☺■◆◇☺■◆ …
There are 4 shapes that are repeating.
◆◇☺■

The shape that comes after ◆ is ◇
So the next bead is ◇

5 1, 8, ?, 22, 29

You know that 7 is being added each time.

Now 8 + 7 = 15.

So the missing number is 15.

6 42 − 5 = 37

So the number that goes in the box is 5.

7 27 + 25 = 27 + 3 + 22

$\qquad$ = 30 + 22

$\qquad$ = 52

8 68, 60, 52, ?

The numbers are going down by 8 each time.

52 − 8 = 44

So the next number is 44.

9 56 − 34 = 22

10 There are 3 more cards every time.

11 + 3 = 14

So the next shape will have 14 cards.

11 ?, 31, 35, 39, 43

The numbers are going up by 4 each time.

[31 + 4 = 35, 35 + 4 = 39, 39 + 4 = 43]

So the first number will be 4 less than 31.

31 − 4 = 30 − 3 = 27

The first number will be 27.

12 742, 842, 942, ?

You need to add 100. 942 + 100 = 1042

The next number will be 1042.

13 ✳☐☐◆☐☐☐ ✳☐☐◆☐☐☐ ✳ ...

There are 7 shapes that are repeating.

✳☐☐◆☐☐☐

There is 1 ◆ and 5 ☐

So there are 5 ☐ for every ◆

14 38 + 32 = 70

So the number in the box is 32.

15 43 − 18 = 45 − 20 = 25

16 Count the number of extra sticks needed each time.

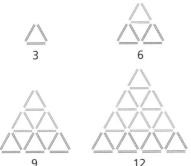

3 $\qquad$ 6

9 $\qquad$ 12

The number of extra sticks needed goes up by 3 each time. So 15 extra sticks will be needed for the fifth shape.

Now 30 + 15 = 45 so 45 sticks will be needed for the fifth shape.

17 43, 49, 55, 61 ?

The numbers go up by 6 each time.

[43 + 6 = 49, 49 + 6 = 55, 55 + 6 = 61]

Now 61 + 6 = 67.

So the next number will be 67.

18 The first number is 6.

4 is being added each time.

6 + 4 = 10, 10 + 4 = 14, 14 + 4 = 18

The pattern is 6, 10, 14, 18.

SPELLING (Real Test)
Hard and soft c and g, and consonant digraphs
Pages 18–19

1 careful 2 huge 3 dangerous 4 Giant 5 cancel
6 juice 7 exercise 8 spicy 9 cicadas 10 bucket
11 elephant 12 sock 13 chicken 14 dragon 15 back
16 fudge 17 going 18 alphabet 19 class 20 concert
21 musical 22 happy 23 said 24 chance
25 microphone 26 introduce 27 fantastic
28 telephone 29 Throw 30 bush 31 Where
32 clock 33 whip 34 photo 35 three

EXPLANATIONS

1 The *c* has a hard sound.

2 The *g* makes a soft sound because *g* is followed by *e*.

3 The *g* is soft because it is followed by *e*.

4 The *g* is soft because it is followed by *i*. *Giant* has a capital *G* because it names a particular species of frog and is therefore a proper noun: *Giant Tree Frog*.

5 *Cancel* has a hard *c* at the beginning and a soft *c* in the middle. The middle *c* is followed by an *e*.

6 The *c* is soft because it is followed by *e*.

7 The *c* is soft because it is followed by *i*.

8 The *c* is soft because it is followed by *y*.

9 The *c* is soft at the beginning of *cicadas*, because it is followed by *i*.

10 *Bucket* has a 'ck' digraph. Digraphs are two letters that combine to make one sound.

11. Use the 'ph' digraph for the *f* sound.

12. Use the 'ck' digraph for the *k* sound.

13. *Chicken* has two digraphs: 'ch' and 'ck'. Note that words such as *school*, *stomach* and *technology* have 'ch' but it is not a digraph. The *h* in these words is silent. The *c* is hard.

14. The *g* makes a hard sound.

15. The 'ck' is a digraph. The two letters 'ck' make one sound k.

16. The three letters 'dge' make a *j* sound. The *d* is silent.

17. The suffix 'ing' is added to *go*. Note the long *o* sound in *go*.

18. The digraph 'ph' make an *f* sound.

19. *Class* has a hard *c*. The *c* is followed by *l*.

20. *Concert* has a hard *c* to start and a soft *c* in the middle. The middle *c* is followed by *e*.

21. *Musical* has a hard *c* to make the middle *k* sound.

22. *Happy* is a common word. Remember to spell it with double *p*.

23. *Said* is a useful word to learn to spell. The short *e* sound is spelt with a vowel digraph 'ai'.

24. The final *c* is soft because the *c* is followed by an *e*.

25. The digraph 'ph' is pronounced *f*.

26. The final sound is a soft *c* followed by *e*.

27. *Fantastic* has a hard *c* at the end of the word.

28. The *f* sound is spelt by the digraph 'ph'.

29. There is no *f* sound in the word *throw*. Make sure you pronounce the word correctly and listen for the 'th' sound. *Throw* starts with a capital letter because it is used at the beginning of the sentence.

30. The final sound is spelt by the digraph 'sh'.

31. The *w* sound is spelt by the digraph 'wh'. *Where* starts with a capital letter because it is used at the beginning of the sentence.

32. The *k* sound is spelt by the digraph 'ck'.

33. The *w* sound is spelt by the digraph 'wh'.

34. The *f* sound is spelt by the digraph 'ph'.

35. There is no *f* sound in the word *three.* Make sure you pronounce the word correctly and listen for the 'th' sound.

GRAMMAR AND PUNCTUATION
(Real Test)
Nouns and noun groups   Pages 22–23

1 A   2 A   3 C   4 B   5 C   6 D   7 C   8 C   9 D
10 C   11 D   12 D   13 B   14 B   15 D   16 D   17 A
18 A   19 C   20 B   21 A   22 D   23 C   24 B   25 B

EXPLANATIONS

1. The noun that makes sense is *insects*.

2. The verb *played* is the clue to choosing the appropriate noun. Only *games* can be played.

3. *Pretty, ugly* and *my* are not nouns. *Fruit* is the only noun that the children could eat.

4. *Funny, sad* and *angry* are adjectives. *Homework* is the only noun that makes sense in the sentence.

5. *Wooden* is the only adjective that makes sense. *New* contradicts the other adjective, *old*. *My* and *your* can only be used at the start of a noun group and not in the middle of it.

6. The sentence needs an adjective that makes sense to describe a *cave*. *Car* and *table* are nouns. Caves can't be described as *tasty*. *Dark* is the only word that makes sense.

7. *Michael* and *Sydney* are proper nouns. They need capital letters. The sentence needs a full stop at the end.

8. *Suri* is the name of a person. *Taronga Zoo* is the name of a place. The sentence needs a full stop at the end.

9. A *Black Prince* is a cicada. The noun group is *A large Black Prince cicada*.

10. *Shell* is the only noun that makes sense. The sentence starts with *It* which refers to the cicada. The answer needs to be something the cicada *has* that is *black and brown*.

11. *Juice* is the only noun that makes sense. Cicadas cannot suck *potatoes, apples* or *trees* from plants.

12. *They* is a pronoun. It refers to cicadas. Cicadas have *wings*.

13. *Delicious* is the only adjective that describes taste. *Yellow, red* and *blue* are adjectives that describe colour.

14. *An* at the beginning of the noun group means that the next word starts with a vowel sound. *Enormous* is the only adjective that starts with a vowel sound. For *huge, big* and *large* to be appropriate, the article *a* is needed.

15. The question mark at the end means that a question word is needed at the beginning of the sentence. *Which* is the only question word. *This, that* and *those* are words that point out rather than ask questions.

16. *Kathy* is talking about the book she owns so she says … *my book*.

17. The plural noun *children* needs a plural possessive word in the noun group, *their spelling test*.

18. The article *a* should be used before a word starting with a consonant sound: *a swimming lesson*.

19. *The* is used with plural nouns: *the children*. *A* and *An* are used with singular nouns.

20 *An* is used before a word starting with a vowel sound: *interesting*.

21–25 All the choices are nouns but only the correct answers make sense in the text. A *family* of magpies lives in the *trees* near my home. The baby *birds* are always hungry. The *parents* bring the babies *food* all day long.

READING (Test Your Skills)
Reports
Page 25

Go to page 212 for a guide to question types.

Magpies
EXPLANATIONS

1 This is a **fact-finding type of question**. The answer is a fact in the text. You read *Magpies are very common in Australia (see line 2)*. A and D are false because they use the word *only*. Magpies live in the bush as well as in cities. B is false because the text says: *All magpies have black and white feathers (see line 3)*.

2 This is a **fact-finding type of question**. The answer is a fact in the text. You read *Magpies mostly peck for food on the ground (see line 13)*.

3 This is a **fact-finding type of question**. The answer is a fact in the text. You read *Magpies nest in trees (see line 11)*.

4 This is a **fact-finding type of question**. The answer is a fact in the text. You read *Magpies eat worms, snails, lizards, frogs, spiders and insects (see lines 12–13)*.

5 This is a **fact-finding type of question**. The answer is a fact in the text. You read *Baby magpies beg loudly and constantly for food (see lines 11–12)*.

6 This is a **fact-finding type of question**. The answer is a fact in the text. You read *male magpies might swoop at people to protect their nests (see lines 10–11)*.

7 This is a **judgement type of question**. You read *Magpies are very common in Australia (see line 1)*. You also read many other facts about magpies. The report is not specifically about baby magpies or travelling in Australia, or about Australian animals in general. It is about one bird, the magpie, which you can judge to be an interesting Australian bird, based on the information given in the report. Another good title for the text would therefore be *An interesting Australian bird*.

READING (Real Test)
Reports
Page 26

Important sites
1 A   2 B   3 A   4 B   5 C   6 D   7 B

EXPLANATIONS

1 This is a **fact-finding type of question**. The answer is a fact in the text. You read *There are Aboriginal sites all over Australia (see line 2)*.

2 This is a **language type of question**. You read *There are Aboriginal sites all over Australia. These are special places (see lines 2–3)*. The word *These* links the words *site* and *place*. So another word for *site* is *place*.

3 This is a **fact-finding type of question**. You read *Many Aboriginals believe that sacred sites are protected by ancestor spirits (see lines 7–9)*.

4 This is a **fact-finding type of question**. You read *Many experts think Birrigai rock shelter is the oldest Aboriginal site in Canberra (see lines 13–14)*.

5 This is a **fact-finding type of question**. You read *Local Aboriginal elders allow visitors onto these sites (see lines 11–12)*.

6 This is a **judgement type of question**. You can judge that the text is most likely directed at children because of the way it is written. The report was not written for girls only or boys only. The report's audience is most likely *children*.

7 This is a **judgement type of question**. You read *There are Aboriginal sites all over Australia (see line 2)*. You also read many other facts about Aboriginal sites. Another good title for the text is *Aboriginal sites*.

READING (Real Test)
Reports: biography
Page 27

School champion
1 B   2 D   3 C   4 C   5 A   6 A   7 4–1–3–2

EXPLANATIONS

1 This is a **fact-finding type of question**. The answer is a fact in the text. You read *She started swimming in races when she was four (see lines 3–4)*.

2 This is an **inferring type of question**. To work out the answer you have to 'read between the lines'. You read *The name of the club [Little Dolphins] suits the way Judy swims (see lines 10–11)*. Judy swims butterfly stroke. In butterfly *you keep your feet together and move them up and down just like a dolphin (see lines 11–13)*. Judy is like a dolphin because of the way she kicks her feet up and down.

3 This is a **fact-finding type of question**. The answer is a fact in the text. You read that the *local swimming club [is] called 'Little Dolphins' (see lines 9–10)*.

4 This is a **fact-finding type of question**. The answer is a fact in the text. You read *Judy has won all the butterfly events at our school swimming carnival for the last four years* (see lines 7–9).

5 This is a **judgement type of question**. The fact that she swims regularly tells readers that Judy is energetic and not lazy. Also, you read that *Judy hopes to compete in the Olympics* (see line 15). She is a member of Nippers and Little Dolphins so you can judge that she is not lonely or timid.

6 This is a **judgement type of question**. You read *She loves competing in swimming events. She also loves just having fun in the pool or in the surf* (see lines 4–5). You also read that *Judy has won all the butterfly events at our school swimming carnival for the last four years* (see lines 7–9). Use this information to work out that the best match is that *if you love something you will most likely be good at it*. When you love doing something you want to do it all the time and the more you do it the better you get at it. There is no evidence in the text to support answers B, C or D.

7 This is a **synthesis type of question**. To work out the answer you have to read the whole text to understand the order of events in Judy's life. The question asks for the boxes to be ordered according to the timing of events. Don't be tricked into numbering the boxes according to the order they are mentioned in the text.

WRITING (Real Test)
Descriptive text 1
Page 32

Tick each correct point.
Read the student's work through once to get an overall view of their response. Then read the text a second time to consider each of the ten assessment criteria below. The same criteria are used to assess the NAPLAN Writing Task. Not all criteria will be evident in any piece of writing. You may choose to focus on one or two areas only when giving feedback to the student.

Audience
☐ Is the text interesting?
☐ Is it relevant for its target audience?
☐ Does the writing make sense?

Text structure
☐ Does the text have an appropriate structure?
☐ Does it include an introduction to orient the reader?
☐ Does the body of the text have enough detail?

Ideas
☐ How many ideas does the writer have?
☐ Are the ideas logical?
☐ Are the ideas well thought through?
☐ Is the writer able to write credibly about the animal?

Character and setting
☐ Could you form a mental picture of the animal?
☐ Is the writer's point of view evident?
☐ Can you tell how the writer feels about the animal?
☐ Can a reader feel empathy with the writer or the animal?
☐ Is there anthropomorphism and is it appropriate?

Vocabulary
☐ Are noun groups (nouns and adjectives) used effectively to describe how the animal looks, sounds and feels?
☐ Is there evidence of technical language?
☐ Are verbs used appropriately to depict the animal's actions and behaviour?
☐ Is verb tense accurate and consistent?

Cohesion
☐ Does the text flow logically?
☐ Is noun–pronoun referencing accurate (e.g. The lion … it)?
☐ Does the writer use synonyms, antonyms and word sets to create interesting or varied lexical chains (e.g. The lion … this fierce beast … a big pussy cat … wild animal)?

Paragraphing
☐ Are paragraphs used to organise ideas logically?
☐ Are paragraphs built around topic sentences?
☐ Does each paragraph have a main idea and supporting detail or elaboration?

Sentence structure
☐ Does the writing include varied sentence structures, if appropriate (simple, compound, complex)?
☐ Are sentence lengths varied for pace or emphasis, if appropriate?

Punctuation
☐ Is the punctuation accurate?
☐ Are there capital letters for sentence beginnings and proper nouns?
☐ Are full stops used accurately and consistently?
☐ Does the student use apostrophes for possession (e.g. the lion's mane)?

Spelling
☐ Does the writer spell simple, common, difficult and challenging words correctly?
☐ Are spelling attempts phonetically correct or readable?

☐ Do the writer's attempts to spell unknown words demonstrate understanding of spelling?

WRITING (Real Test)
Descriptive text 2   Page 33

Tick each correct point.
Read the student's work through once to get an overall view of their response. Then read the text a second time to consider each of the ten assessment criteria below. The same criteria are used to assess the NAPLAN Writing Task. Not all criteria will be evident in any piece of writing. You may choose to focus on one or two areas only when giving feedback to the student.

Audience
☐ Is the text interesting and relevant for a target audience?
☐ Does the writing make sense?
☐ Could you form a mental picture of the place?

Text structure
☐ How is the text structured?
☐ Does it have an introduction to orient the reader?
☐ Does the body of the text have enough detail?
☐ Does the text have a suitable conclusion or summing up?

Ideas
☐ How many ideas does the writer have?
☐ Are the ideas logical?
☐ Are the ideas well thought through?
☐ Is there enough detail?
☐ Is the writer able to write credibly about the place?

Character and setting
☐ Could you form a mental picture of the place?
☐ Could you tell how the writer feels about the place (point of view)?
☐ Is the place real or imaginary?
☐ Is the writing credible?

Vocabulary
☐ Are noun groups (nouns and adjectives) used effectively to describe the place?
☐ Is verb tense accurate and consistent?

Cohesion
☐ Does the text flow logically?
☐ Is noun–pronoun referencing accurate (e.g. The playground … it)?
☐ Does the writer use synonyms, antonyms in reference chains and lexical chains (e.g. My bedroom … a pirate cave)?

Paragraphing
☐ Are paragraphs used to organise ideas logically?
☐ Are paragraphs built around topic sentences?
☐ Does each paragraph have a main idea and supporting detail or elaboration?

Sentence structure
☐ Does the writing include varied sentence structures, if appropriate (simple, compound, complex)?

Punctuation
☐ Is the punctuation accurate?
☐ Are there capital letters for sentence beginnings and proper nouns?
☐ Are full stops used accurately and consistently?
☐ Does the student use apostrophes for possession (e.g. the alien's spaceship)?

Spelling
☐ Does the writer spell simple, common, difficult and challenging words correctly?
☐ Are spelling attempts phonetically correct or readable?
☐ Do the writer's attempts to spell unknown words demonstrate understanding of spelling?

WRITING (Real Test)
Descriptive text 3   Page 34

Tick each correct point.
Read the student's work through once to get an overall view of their response. Then read the text a second time to consider each of the ten assessment criteria below. The same criteria are used to assess the NAPLAN Writing Task. Not all criteria will be evident in any piece of writing. You may choose to focus on one or two areas only when giving feedback to the student.

Audience
☐ Is the text interesting and relevant for its target audience?
☐ Does the writing make sense?

Text structure
☐ Does the text have an appropriate structure?
☐ Does it include an introduction to orient the reader?
☐ Does the body of the text have enough detail?
☐ Does the text have a suitable conclusion or summing up?

Ideas
☐ How many ideas does the writer have?
☐ Are the ideas logical?
☐ Are the ideas well thought through?
☐ Is the writer able to write with authority?

Check Your Answers

Character and setting
- [ ] Could you form a mental picture of the writer's home and family?
- [ ] Is the writer's point of view evident?
- [ ] Could you tell how the writer feels about the topic?

Vocabulary
- [ ] Are noun groups (nouns and adjectives) used effectively?
- [ ] Is verb tense accurate and consistent?

Cohesion
- [ ] Does the text flow logically?
- [ ] Is pronoun referencing used accurately?
- [ ] Does the writer build interesting lexical chains (e.g. My mum … the boss … my sister's taxi driver …)?

Paragraphing
- [ ] Are paragraphs used to organise ideas logically?
- [ ] Are paragraphs built around topic sentences?
- [ ] Does each paragraph have a main idea and supporting detail or elaboration?

Sentence structure
- [ ] Does the writing include a varied sentence structure if appropriate (simple, compound, complex; direct and indirect speech)?

Punctuation
- [ ] Is the punctuation accurate?
- [ ] Are there capital letters for sentence beginnings and proper nouns?
- [ ] Are full stops used accurately and consistently?
- [ ] Does the student correctly use apostrophes for possession (e.g. my mum's job)?

Spelling
- [ ] Does the writer spell simple, common, difficult and challenging words correctly?
- [ ] Are spelling attempts phonetically correct or readable?
- [ ] Do the writer's attempts to spell unknown words demonstrate understanding of spelling?

Marker's suggestions (optional)

WEEK 2

NUMBER AND ALGEBRA (Real Test)
Adding, subtracting, multiplying and dividing Pages 41–42

1 D 2 C 3 B 4 B 5 D 6 5 7 35 8 $5
9 3, 15 10 A 11 56 12 C 13 A 14 6 15 C

EXPLANATIONS

1 By counting, Molly had 9 pencils.
Now $9 - 3 = 6$.
So, if Molly gave 3 pencils to Ken she would have 6 left.

Ken   Molly

2 Will has 3 stacks.
There are 6 blocks in each stack.
The number of blocks is $6 + 6 + 6$ or 6×3.

3 Total books $= 37 + 56$
$= 37 + 3 + 53$
$= 40 + 53$
$= 93$

4 Every pack holds 4 balls.
So one pack would have 4 balls and 2 packs would have 8 balls altogether.
Sam needs 11 balls, so 2 packs are not enough.
3 packs would hold 12 balls.
This would give Sam 1 extra ball.
The smallest number of packs Sam needs is 3.

5 There are 30 trucks.
Each row has 5 trucks.
Jay needs to know how many lots of 5 there are in 30.
This means he needs to find $30 \div 5$.

6 Each box holds 4 pies.
There are 20 pies altogether.
Number of boxes $= 20 \div 4$
$= 5$

7 $18 + 37 = 18 + 2 + 35 = 20 + 35$
So 35 is the number that must be written in the box.

8 $30 must be divided into 6 parts.
Each boy gets $30 \div 6 = 5

9 There are 3 pictures.
Each picture has 5 candles.
Number of candles $= 3 \times 5$ candles
$= 15$ candles

10 3 rows of 8 books is the same as twice as many rows of half as many books.
It is the same as 6 rows of 4 books.

11 83 − 27 = 86 − 30 = 56

So, Bill has 56 more spanners than Jed.

12 There are 3 plates. Each plate has 4 cakes. So, one way of working out the number of cakes is to find 4 × 3.

[Another way is to add three 4s:

4 + 4 + 4.]

13 9 + 7 is the same as 7 + 9.

[9 + 7 = 7 + 9 = 16; 10 + 8 = 18;

8 + 6 = 14; 12 + 10 = 22]

14 Divide the marbles into 3s.

There are 6 lots of
3 marbles.

So 6 boys share
the marbles.

15 There are 2 girls and each has 3 cars. So there are
2 × 3 cars or 6 cars altogether.

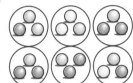

Girl 1   Girl 2   Girl 1   Girl 2   Girl 1   Girl 2

NUMBER AND ALGEBRA (Real Test)
Fractions and money
Pages 48–49

1 B 2 C 3 A 4 B 5 B, D 6 12 7 A 8 D 9 D
10 C 11 B 12 80

EXPLANATIONS

1 Ed has 12 pencils.

He divides them into 2 equal parts.

Half of 12 is 6.

So Ed gave 6 pencils to Nick.

2 Kylie has two $2 coins and one $1 coin.

2 + 2 + 1 = 5

So Kylie has $5.00 in those coins.

She has one 20c coin, one 10c coin and one
5c coin.

20 + 10 + 5 = 35

So Kylie has 35 cents from those coins.

Altogether, Kylie has $5.35.

3 One orange can be cut into 4 quarters.

So, two oranges can be cut into 4 + 4 quarters or
8 quarters.

Max cut 2 oranges.

4 One-eighth is one of eight equal parts.

So, count the number of parts in each shape.

10   8   7   6

So the shape with
one-eighth shaded is

5 Check the choices.

The coins are 20c, $2 and $1.

20c has a lower value than the other two coins so
this is not an answer.

The coins are $2, $1 and 50c.

The $2 has the largest value. The 50c has the
lowest value. So this is an answer.

The coins are 20c, 10c and $2.

The $2 coin has a higher value than the other
coins. So this is not an answer.

The coins are $1, 10c and 5c.

The $1 coin has the highest value. The 5c coin has
the lowest value. So, this is an answer.

The coins in options B and D are in order from
highest value to lowest value.

6 There are 4 quarters in each apple.

So there are 4 + 4 + 4 or 3 × 4 quarters in 3 apples.

Jake would have 12 quarters.

7 Kevin has these coins.

The ruler cost 75 cents.

So Kevin could use these coins to pay for the ruler.

He would have these coins left.

So Kevin would have $1.35 left.

8 One-half is one of two equal parts.
Look at each of the choices.
This has one of two parts shaded, but the parts are not equal. This is not the answer.

This has one of four equal parts shaded. This is not the answer.

This has one of three equal parts shaded. This is not the answer.

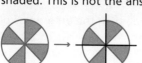

This has 4 of 8 equal parts shaded. Or, out of every 2 parts, 1 is shaded. This is the answer.

9 The scoop holds half a cup. So two scoops would hold one cup.
Toby needs 2 scoops to hold one cup and 1 scoop to hold half a cup so he needs 3 scoops altogether.

10 Sue has one $50 note, two $20 notes, one $10 note and one $5 note.
Now 50 + 20 + 20 + 10 + 5 = 105
So Sue has $105.

11 Jill has 12 balloons.
If Jill gives half the balloons to Luke she will have 6 left.

Jill

Luke

Then if Jill gives half of the balloons that she has left to Alice, she will have 3 balloons left.

Jill   Alice

12 Ellen had one 50c coin and one 5c coin left.
So, these are the coins that Ellen used to buy the banana.

Now 50 + 20 + 5 + 5 = 80.
So the banana cost 80 cents.

SPELLING (Real Test)
Two- and three-letter consonant blends, silent consonants and vowel digraphs
Pages 52–53

1 Climb **2** knuckles **3** scent **4** Who **5** Wednesday
6 could **7** autumn **8** Island **9** knitting **10** knee
11 ghost **12** comb **13** sword **14** know **15** squeal
16 listen **17** scratch **18** steel **19** salmon **20** sank
21 went **22** whole **23** Listen **24** beach **25** knights
26 tight **27** hour **28** shrink **29** wrist **30** boots
31 pool **32** glue **33** should **34** might **35** Think

EXPLANATIONS

1 *Climb* ends in a silent *b*. It has a capital *c* because it starts the sentence.

2 *Knuckles* starts with a silent *k*. It also has the 'ck' digraph.

3 *Scent* means 'smell'. It has a silent *c*. *Scent* is a homophone for *cent* which is money.
Homophones are words that sound the same but have different spellings and meanings.

4 *Who* has a silent *w*. It has a capital letter because it starts the sentence.

5 *Wednesday* has a silent *d*. It has a capital letter because it is the proper noun name of a day of the week.

6 *Could* has a silent *l*.

7 *Autumn* has a silent *n*.

8 *Island* has a silent *s*. *Island* in this sentence starts with a capital *I*. It is a proper noun. It names a specific place: *Kangaroo Island*.

9 *Knitting* starts with a silent *k*.

10 *Knee* starts with a silent *k*.

11 *Ghost* has a silent *h*.

12 *Comb* has a silent *b*.

13 *Sword* has a silent *w*.

14 The *k* is silent. The word *know* is the base of words such as *knowing*, *known* and *knowledge*.

15 The vowel digraph 'ea' makes the long *e* sound.

16 The *t* is silent.

17 When the 'ch' digraph follows a vowel, a *t* is often used between the vowel and the digraph (e.g. *stitch*, *catch*, *hutch*). The *t* is silent.

18 The vowel digraph 'ee' makes a long *e* sound.

19 *Salmon* has a silent *l*.

20 *Sank* has the blend 'nk' found in *pink*, *sunk*, *stank* and *plonk*. There is no *g* in the spelling of these words.

21 *Went* is spelt differently from 'wh' words such as *where*, *why* and *when*. It starts with a *w* and it ends in the 'nt' blend.

22 *Hole* and *whole* are homophones. They sound the same but have different meanings and different spelling; *whole* has the digraph 'wh'. It means the entire thing. *Hole* is used for a gap or space.

23 *Listen* has a silent *t*.

24 *Beach* has the vowel digraph 'ea'. It rhymes with *each*, *peach*, *reach* and *teach*.

25 *Knights* has a silent *k*. *Knights* and *nights* are homophones—they sound the same but have different meanings and different spelling.

26 *Tight* has a silent 'gh'. It rhymes with *sight, right, might, light, night* and *delight*.

27 *Hour* has a silent *h*. Remember how to spell the pronoun *our* and put *h* in front of it.

28 *Shrink* ends in the consonant blend 'nk'.

29 *Wrist* has a silent *w*.

30 *Boots* has the 'oo' vowel digraph.

31 *Pool* has the 'oo' vowel digraph.

32 *Glue* has the 'ue' vowel digraph.

33 *Should* has a silent *l* and the vowel digraph 'ou'.

34 *Might* has a silent 'gh'.

35 *Think* ends in the 'nk' blend and not the 'ck' digraph. It starts with a capital letter because it begins the sentence.

GRAMMAR AND PUNCTUATION (Real Test)

Verbs, commas in lists and commas in direct speech
Pages 56–57

ANSWERS

1 D 2 A 3 B 4 D 5 C 6 A 7 B 8 B 9 B
10 B 11 D 12 B 13 A 14 B 15 D 16 A 17 C
18 C 19 A 20 B 21 A 22 D 23 C 24 C 25 D

EXPLANATIONS

1 *Jumped* is the correct form of the verb to match the noun *frog*; *jumping* and *jump* need helper verbs such as *can jump, is jumping, was jumping* or *will jump. Jumper* is a noun, not a verb.

2 The plural noun *ducks* needs a verb that agrees with it: *were*. It needs to be past tense to match *yesterday*.

3 The singular noun *duck* needs the singular past-tense helping verb *was*.

4 The singular noun *duck* needs a verb that agrees with it in number: *is*. The verb needs to be present tense to match *right now*.

5 The plural noun *ducks* needs a plural helping verb that agrees with it: *are*.

6 *Will go* is used for an event planned for some time in the future, in this sentence *tomorrow*.

7 *Children* is a plural noun and needs the verb *were collecting* to agree with it.

8 *Dad bought rice, cashews, chicken, broccoli and onions for the stir fry*. Commas go between each item in a list but not before the *and*.

9 The correct verb form is *saw. Billy … saw … .*

10 *Suggested* is correct; *asked* is used for a question; *talk* and *speaking* are the wrong tense.

11 *Said* is the correct form of the verb.

12 *Left* is the correct form of the verb.

13 *Go to the library* is a complete sentence because it includes a verb, *go,* and it makes sense. Remember that a sentence must have a verb.

14 The word *is* is a being verb.

15 The verb *am* matches the singular pronoun *I.*

16 The plural noun *children* needs the plural verb *are.*

17 The having verb *has* matches the singular noun *Dunedoo.*

18 *Wendy ran in the race* is a complete sentence. The verb is *ran.* The other suggestions do not include verbs. A sentence needs at least one verb.

19 *Went* is the only past-tense verb.

20–**23** The verb at the beginning of each command needs to make sense.

24 Speech marks go outside the direct speech and any other punctuation marks such as commas or question marks.

25 *Eat* is the correct verb form to complete the verb group *does not eat* in the sentence.

READING (Test Your Skills)
Procedures: recipes
Page 59

Go to **page 212** for a guide to question types.

Hair-growth tonic

EXPLANATIONS

1 This is a **judgement type of question**. The text is a recipe. The clues are the list of ingredients and the steps in the method.

2 This is a **language type of question**. To work out the answer you have to read the text carefully. You read *Discard any lumpy bits (see line 12)*. The meaning of the word *discard* can be worked out from its use in the text. The lumpy bits are discarded after the mixture has been poured *through a strainer (see line 11)*. Combine this information with your own knowledge to work out that *discard* means 'throw away'.

3 This is a **fact-finding type of question**. The answer is a fact in the text. You read one of the ingredients listed in the recipe is *coconut oil (see line 6)*.

4 This is a **fact-finding type of question**. The answer is a fact in the text. You read the *Instructions for use* which say to *Massage into affected area … Only for use on heads (see lines 16–19)*.

5 This is a **language type of question**. To work out the answer you have to read the text carefully. You read Step 2 of the Method which says: *Pour mixture through a strainer (see line 11)*. Step 3 says: *Discard any lumpy bits (see line 12)*. Combine this information with your own knowledge to work out that the job of a strainer is to sort out lumpy bits.

6 This is a **fact-finding type of question**. The answer is a fact in the text. You read *Store Hair-growth Tonic in fridge (see line 15)*.

7 This is an **inferring type of question**. To find the answer you have to 'read between the lines'. You read *Massage into affected areas (bald spots) (see lines 16–17)*. So you can work out that *bald people* should use the tonic. The text also says: *Not suitable for babies (see line 3)*.

READING (Real Test)
Procedures: instructions
Page 60

How to train a pet mouse
1 A 2 C 3 A 4 B 5 A 6 D 7 C

EXPLANATIONS

1 This is an **inferring type of question**. To work out the answer you have to 'read between the lines'. You read the title which is *How to train a pet mouse (see line 1)*, so you can work out that the text is for people with pet mice. Teachers, vets and children could all have pet mice but the audience is all people with pet mice.

2 This is a **fact-finding type of question**. The answer is a fact in the text. You read *Reward your mouse with its favourite food treat … Try treats such as millet, oats or sunflower seeds (see lines 7–8)*. The only option offered is *oats*.

3 This is an **inferring type of question**. To work out the answer you have to 'read between the lines'. You read *Mice are sociable and like to live with other mice. Single mice get bored and lonely (see line 15)*. You can work out from this that *sociable* means 'friendly'.

4 This is a **fact-finding type of question**. The answer is a fact in the text. You read Step 3 in the instructions which says that the mouse *will learn that the clicking sound means a treat (see lines 10–11)*.

5 This is a **fact-finding type of question**. The answer is a fact in the text. You read *Mice are timid so training will take time and patience (see line 2)*.

6 This is an **inferring type of question**. To work out the answer you have to 'read between the lines'. You read that *Single mice get bored and lonely (see line 15)* so you can work out that they are lonely when they don't have other mice to live with.

7 This is a **fact-finding type of question**. The answer is a fact in the text. You read *rub your hands on the mouse bedding so that you smell more mouse-like (see lines 5–6)*.

READING (Real Test)
Procedures: rules
Page 61

Rules for young chimpanzees
1 B 2 B 3 C 4 D 5 A 6 C 7 D

EXPLANATIONS

1 This is a **fact-finding type of question**. The answer is a fact in the text. You read *Listen out for happy, barking sounds in the morning. These sounds signal that food has been found (see lines 4–6)*.

2 This is an **inferring type of question**. To work out the answer you have to 'read between the lines'. You read *Build nests high in trees for night sleeping, safe from hungry leopards (see lines 13–14)*. Combine this information with your own knowledge to work out that leopards eat chimpanzees.

3 This is a **fact-finding type of question**. The answer is a fact in the text. You read *Build nests high in trees for night sleeping (see lines 13–14)*.

4 This is a **fact-finding type of question**. The answer is a fact in the text. You read *Stay out of the way of the alpha male (see line 2)*.

5 This is a **fact-finding type of question**. The answer is a fact in the text. You read *build ground nests, for afternoon naps (see lines 10–11)*.

6 This is a **synthesis type of question**. To work out the answer you have to read the whole text. You read rules to keep chimpanzees safe from the alpha male and leopards. You also read rules covering relations with other chimpanzees and about rest and food. Combine this information to work out that the set of rules is necessary to help young chimps learn how to be safe and happy. A, B and D are each only partly correct. C is the best answer.

7 This is a **language type of question**. To work out the answer you have to read the text carefully. You read that chimps *Eat fruit, leaves, termites, vegetables, eggs, nuts, honey and wild pig, when you can catch one (see lines 7–9)*. Combine this

with your own knowledge that *variety* means a 'number of different kinds' to work out that chimps eat a variety of plant and animal foods.

WRITING (Real Test)
Procedure text 1
Page 62

Tick each correct point.

Read the student's work through once to get an overall view of their response. Then read the text a second time to consider each of the ten assessment criteria below. The same criteria are used to assess the NAPLAN Writing Task. Not all criteria will be evident in any piece of writing. You may choose to focus on one or two areas only when giving feedback to the student.

Audience
- [ ] Is the text interesting and useful for its target audience?
- [ ] Does the recipe make sense?
- [ ] Is it easy to follow?

Text structure
- [ ] Does the recipe have an appropriate structure?
- [ ] Does it include a title or goal to orient the reader?
- [ ] Are the ingredients and method identified?
- [ ] Does the recipe include warnings or special advice?

Ideas
- [ ] Are the ideas entertaining, imaginative and coherent?
- [ ] Are the ideas well thought through?
- [ ] Is there enough detail?
- [ ] Is the recipe creative?
- [ ] Is the writer able to write with authority?

Factual or emotive
- [ ] Is the recipe modelled on real recipes?

Vocabulary
- [ ] Are technical terms used for ingredients, equipment and method?
- [ ] Are noun groups (nouns and adjectives) used effectively?
- [ ] Are noun groups specific enough (e.g. quantities of ingredients)?
- [ ] Are adverbs used to tell how (e.g. carefully)?
- [ ] Are action verbs used for commands?

Cohesion
- [ ] Is the recipe numbered to show sequencing?
- [ ] Is noun–pronoun referencing accurate (e.g. the sugar—it)?

Paragraphing
- [ ] Are paragraphs used to organise aspects of the topic?
- [ ] Are paragraphs effective?

Sentence structure
- [ ] Is the method written as a sequence of commands?
- [ ] Are commands used as warnings?
- [ ] Is there a statement to indicate where and when the recipe might be used?

Punctuation
- [ ] Is sentence punctuation evident and accurate?
- [ ] Are there capital letters for sentence beginnings?
- [ ] Are commas used in lists (e.g. Add carrots, potatoes, pumpkin …)?
- [ ] Are full stops used accurately and consistently?

Spelling
- [ ] Is the spelling accurate?
- [ ] Have attempts been made to spell unknown words?
- [ ] Are the attempts phonetically correct or readable?
- [ ] Do the writer's attempts to spell unknown words demonstrate understanding of spelling?
- [ ] Does the writer spell simple, common, difficult and challenging words correctly?

WRITING (Real Test)
Procedure text 2
Page 63

Tick each correct point.

Read the student's work through once to get an overall view of their response. Then read the text a second time to consider each of the ten assessment criteria below. The same criteria are used to assess the NAPLAN Writing Task. Not all criteria will be evident in any piece of writing. You may choose to focus on one or two areas only when giving feedback to the student.

Audience
- [ ] Does the writer consider what instructions would be relevant to a reader?
- [ ] Do the instructions make sense?
- [ ] Is the text easy to follow?

Text structure
- [ ] Does the text have an appropriate structure?
- [ ] Does it include a title, stated goal or heading to orient the reader?
- [ ] Does it list any equipment necessary?
- [ ] Does it include steps in logical order?

Ideas
- [ ] Are the ideas entertaining, imaginative and coherent?
- [ ] Are the ideas well thought through?
- [ ] Is there enough detail?
- [ ] Is the writer able to write with authority on the topic?

Factual or emotive

☐ Are the instructions modelled on real instructions?

Vocabulary

☐ Are technical terms used appropriately?

☐ Are noun groups (nouns and adjectives) used effectively?

☐ Are adverbs used to tell where, when and how?

☐ Are action verbs used in theme position in commands (e.g. <u>Walk</u> ten steps)?

Cohesion

☐ Are the instructions numbered or bullet-pointed?

☐ Are connectives used effectively?

☐ Is noun–pronoun referencing accurate?

Paragraphing

☐ Are paragraphs relevant and, if so, are they used effectively?

Sentence structure

☐ Are the instructions written as a series of commands?

☐ Are statements appropriately included?

Punctuation

☐ Is sentence punctuation evident and accurate?

☐ Are there capital letters for sentence beginnings?

☐ Are commas used in lists?

☐ Are full stops used accurately and consistently?

Spelling

☐ Is the spelling accurate?

☐ Have attempts been made to spell unknown words?

☐ Are the attempts phonetically correct or readable?

☐ Do the writer's attempts to spell unknown words demonstrate understanding of spelling?

☐ Does the writer spell simple, common, difficult and challenging words correctly?

WRITING (Real Test)
Recount text   Page 66

Tick each correct point.
Read the student's work through once to get an overall view of their response. Then read the text a second time to consider each of the ten assessment criteria below. The same criteria are used to assess the NAPLAN Writing Task. Not all criteria will be evident in any piece of writing. You may choose to focus on one or two areas only when giving feedback to the student.

Audience

☐ Is the text interesting and relevant for its target audience?

☐ Does the recount make sense?

Text structure

☐ Does the text have an appropriate structure?

☐ Does it include an introduction to orient the reader in terms of setting, people and time?

☐ Does the body of the text have enough detail?

☐ Does it have a suitable concluding statement or summing up, if appropriate?

Ideas

☐ Are the ideas sequenced chronologically?

☐ Are the ideas well thought through?

☐ Is the writer able to write with authority about the events?

Character and setting

☐ Are the writer's opinions about the event evident?

Vocabulary

☐ Is there sufficient descriptive detail?

☐ Are noun groups used effectively?

☐ Are verbs used appropriately for actions and activity?

☐ Are past-tense verbs used consistently?

☐ Are pronouns used consistently in a first-person recount?

Cohesion

☐ Does the text flow chronologically?

☐ Are time connectives used to link ideas (e.g. then, after that, meanwhile)?

☐ Are words used to establish time sequence (e.g. last weekend, on Monday)?

☐ Is noun–pronoun referencing accurate?

Paragraphing

☐ Are paragraphs used to organise aspects of the topic?

☐ Are paragraphs built around topic sentences?

Sentence structure

☐ Are a variety of appropriate sentence structures evident?

Punctuation

☐ Is sentence punctuation evident and accurate?

☐ Are there capital letters for sentence beginnings and proper nouns?

☐ Are commas and full stops used accurately and consistently?

Spelling

☐ Is the spelling accurate?

☐ Have attempts been made to spell unknown words?

☐ Are the attempts phonetically correct or readable?

☐ Do the writer's attempts to spell unknown words demonstrate understanding of spelling?

☐ Does the writer spell simple, common, difficult and challenging words correctly?

Marker's suggestions (optional)

WEEK 3

MEASUREMENT AND GEOMETRY
(Real Test)
Measurement and shape
Pages 74–75

1 C   2 D   3 B, D, E   4 B   5 C   6 15
7 4   8 27   9 A   10 B   11 D   12 A

EXPLANATIONS

1
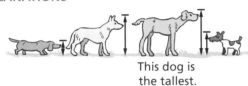

This dog is the tallest.

2   This object is shaped like a can, but is lying on its side.
It is a cylinder.

3   Triangles have exactly 3 sides.

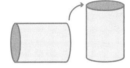

So the shapes in option B, D and E are triangles.

4   The square pyramid has 5 faces.
There are 4 faces that are triangles.

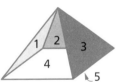

The face at the bottom is a square.

5   Look at the choices.
This is a stopwatch. It is used to measure time.

These are bathroom scales.
They are used to measure mass.

This is a tape measure.
It is used to measure length.

These are kitchen scales.
They are also used to measure mass.

The tape measure would be used to measure length.

6   5 stamps will fit across the card.
3 stamps will fit down the card.
The number of stamps is 5 + 5 + 5 stamps or 3 × 5 stamps.
So 15 stamps will fit on the card.

7   The numbers in the circle are 1, 2, 3 and 4.
The numbers in the triangle are 3, 4, 5 and 6.
The numbers in the square are 2, 3, 6, 7 and 8.
So 3 and 4 are in both the circle and triangle. But 3 is also in the square.

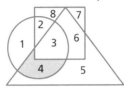

The number in the circle and in the triangle, but not in the square, is 4.

8   The top layer has 3 × 3 or 9 blocks.
There are 3 layers.
So the number of blocks is 9 + 9 + 9 or 3 × 9.
There are 27 blocks in the cube.

9   Rectangles have exactly 4 sides. The angles of a rectangle are right angles.

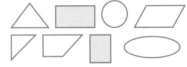

There are 2 rectangles.

10   The bucket holds 20 litres when full. It is a bit more than half full.

It has about 11 litres of milk.

11   A rectangular prism has 12 edges.

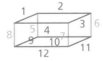

12   Count the squares for each shape.

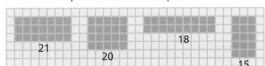

21   20   18   15

The first shape covers the most squares.

MEASUREMENT AND GEOMETRY (Real Test)
Time and mass
Pages 81–82

1 B 2 C 3 D 4 B 5 5:45, 6:45, 5:15, 6:15 6 A
7 A 8 B 9 C 10 D 11 C 12 A

EXPLANATIONS

1 The long hand is pointing to 9. This means it is quarter to the hour. The shorter hand is pointing to just before 5.
So, the time is a quarter to five.

2 18 July was a Wednesday.

July 2012						
SUN	MON	TUE	WED	THU	FRI	SAT
1	2	3	4	5	6	7
8	9	10	11	12	13	14
15	16	17	18	19	20	21
22	23	24	25	26	27	28
29	30	31				

3 Scales are used to measure mass.
The clock measures time.
The thermometer measures temperature.
The tape measure measures length.

Clock   Thermometer   Tape measure   Scales

4 The hour hand is halfway between 8 and 9. So the time is half past eight.

5 The time on this clock is a quarter to six or 45 minutes after 5 o'clock. It is 5:45.

The time on this clock is a quarter to seven or 45 minutes after 6 o'clock. It is 6:45.

The time on this clock is a quarter past five or 15 minutes after 5 o'clock. It is 5:15.

The time on this clock is a quarter past six or 15 minutes after 6 o'clock. It is 6:15.

6 December, January and February are the summer months in Australia.
March, April and May are autumn.
June, July and August are winter.
September, October and November are the spring months.
So when Jo gets married it will be spring.

7 One hour is 60 minutes. Half an hour is 30 minutes. A quarter of an hour is 15 minutes.

8 The date of the third Saturday is 20 September.

September						
SUN	MON	TUE	WED	THU	FRI	SAT
	1	2	3	4	5	6
7	8	9	10	11	12	13
14	15	16	17	18	19	20
21	22	23	24	25	26	27
28	29	30				

9 Look at the choices.
February has 28 days or 29 days in a leap year.
April and November both have 30 days.
The month that has 31 days is October.

10 The first balance shows that ⬭ has a greater mass than ⬮
The second balance shows that ⬛ has a greater mass than ⬭
So, in order from lowest mass to highest mass, the objects are ⬮ ⬭ ⬛

11 From 9 o'clock until 12 o'clock is 3 hours. From 12 o'clock to 4 o'clock is 4 hours.
Now 3 + 4 = 7.
So it is 7 hours from 9 o'clock in the morning until 4 o'clock in the afternoon.
Ben will be at work for 7 hours.

12 Three weeks before 25 December is 4 December.

December						
SUN	MON	TUE	WED	THU	FRI	SAT
				1	2	3
4	5	6	7	8	9	10
11	12	13	14	15	16	17
18	19	20	21	22	23	24
25	26	27	28	29	30	31

SPELLING (Real Test)
Long vowels, 'qu', common contractions and vowel/consonant blends
Pages 85–86

1 cake 2 hope 3 made 4 make 5 Use 6 prize
7 home 8 bite 9 time 10 tube 11 kite 12 gate
13 smile 14 doesn't 15 quarrel 16 don't 17 rope
18 Saturday 19 stone 20 hate 21 side 22 Save
23 stale 24 chose 25 cows 26 relay 27 quit
28 quack 29 queen 30 quick 31 earthquake
32 quiet 33 don't 34 It's 35 You're

EXPLANATIONS

1 The silent **e** on the end of the word, after the single consonant, makes the **a** take a long vowel sound.

2 The silent *e* on the end of the word, after the single consonant, makes the *o* take a long vowel sound.

3 The silent *e* on the end of the word, after the single consonant, makes the *a* take a long vowel sound.

4 The silent *e* on the end of the word, after the single consonant, makes the *a* take a long vowel sound.

5 The silent *e* on the end of the word, after the single consonant, makes the *u* take a long vowel sound. *Use* has a capital *U* because it starts the sentence.

6 The silent *e* on the end of the word, after the single consonant, makes the *i* take a long vowel sound.

7 The silent *e* on the end of the word, after the single consonant, makes the *o* take a long vowel sound.

8 The silent *e* on the end of the word, after the single consonant, makes the *i* take a long vowel sound.

9 The silent *e* on the end of the word, after the single consonant, makes the *i* take a long vowel sound.

10 The silent *e* on the end of the word, after the single consonant, makes the *u* take a long vowel sound.

11 The silent *e* on the end of the word, after the single consonant, makes the *i* take a long vowel sound.

12 The silent *e* on the end of the word, after the single consonant, makes the *a* take a long vowel sound. *Gate* rhymes with *hate, mate, state, fate, rate* and *late*.

13 The silent *e* on the end of the word, after the single consonant, makes the *i* take a long vowel sound.

14 A contraction is where two words combine and shorten (contract) to form one word. The letter that has been left out is replaced with an apostrophe (*does + not = doesn't*).

15 The letter *q* is usually followed by a *u*. Together the 'qu' says 'kw'.

16 The contraction of *do not* is *don't* where the second *o* is replaced with an apostrophe.

17 The silent *e* at the end of *rope* gives the *o* a long *o* sound.

18 Days of the week are proper nouns so Saturday begins with a capital *S*.

19 The silent *e* on the end of the word, after the single consonant, makes the *o* take a long vowel sound.

20 The silent *e* on the end of the word, after the single consonant, makes the *a* take a long vowel sound.

21 The silent *e* on the end of the word, after the single consonant, makes the *i* take a long vowel sound. *Side* rhymes with *ride, hide, slide* and *glide*.

22 The silent *e* on the end of the word, after the single consonant, makes the *a* take a long vowel sound. *Save* has a capital *S* because it begins the sentence.

23 The silent *e* on the end of the word, after the single consonant, makes the *a* take a long vowel sound.

24 The silent *e* on the end of the word, after the single consonant, makes the *o* take a long vowel sound. *Chose* rhymes with *rose, hose, nose* and *pose*.

25 *Cows* is spelt using the vowel/consonant blend 'ow'. In a blend you can hear a sound made by each letter. *Cow* rhymes with *how, now* and *pow*.

26 *Relay* ends in the vowel/consonant blend 'ay' which is also found in *Sunday, pay, day, ray, hay, stray* and *May*.

27 The 'kw' sound is spelt with 'qu'.

28 The 'kw' sound is spelt with 'qu'. *Quack* rhymes with *stack, rack, back, crack* and *hack*.

29 The 'kw' sound is spelt with 'qu'.

30 The 'kw' sound is spelt with 'qu'. *Quick* rhymes with *thick, stick, slick, chick, sick* and *pick*.

31 The 'kw' sound is spelt with 'qu'. *Earthquake* is a compound word: *earth + quake*.

32 The 'kw' sound is spelt with 'qu'. Note the *e* before *t* in *quiet*. Say the word and listen for the 'qu–i–e–t' sounds.

33 *Do not* has been contracted to *don't*. The letter left out of the word *not* is *o*. Its place is marked by an apostrophe.

34 *It is* has been contracted. An apostrophe marks the place of the missing letter *i*. Note that *it's* always means *it is*.

35 *You are* has been contracted to form *you're*. An apostrophe marks the place of the missing letter *a*. When writing contractions, be careful to place the apostrophe where the missing letter or letters belong.

GRAMMAR AND PUNCTUATION (Real Test)
Types of sentences, joining   Pages 89–91
sentences and sentence punctuation

1 C   2 B   3 C   4 C   5 D   6 D   7 D   8 C   9 A   10 A
11 A   12 C   13 B   14 A C   15 A D   16 A   17 B
18 B   19 C   20 A   21 D   22 A   23 C   24 B   25 C

EXPLANATIONS

1. *Rina lives with her stepfather* is the only sentence. A sentence must have a verb. The other suggestions are noun groups and not sentences.

2. *Lina was early for school so she helped the teacher.* The conjunction *so* joins the two clauses logically so the sentence makes sense. The other connecting words, *but*, *then* and *because*, do not make sense in the sentence.

3. *Where does your grandfather live?* This is a question with an appropriate question mark. Questions ask for an answer. A, B and D are statements that have been incorrectly punctuated.

4. *Did you invite your parents to the concert? Did* is a question word. This sentence is a question. It needs a question mark.

5. *"Look out, Nan!"* is an exclamation and needs an exclamation mark. Short warnings are often exclamations. Warnings are often shouted or said loudly.

6. *Sachin is becoming a good cricket player because he practises every day.* The two clauses need a connecting word (because) that makes sense. The other connecting words, *so*, *then* and *but*, do not make sense in this sentence.

7. *Mark shouted, "Careful!"* An exclamation mark is needed for a shouted warning.

8. *Where is your brother?* This is a correctly punctuated question. It starts with the question word *Where*.

9. *Where is Kenny* is incorrectly punctuated. The sentence needs a question mark. The other three sentences are correctly punctuated.

10. *Aadrika* is a name. It is a proper noun and needs a capital letter.

11. *Sydney* is a place name. It is a proper noun and needs a capital letter.

12. *Tim had soccer practice yesterday. Today he does gymnastics.* There are two sentences. Each sentence has a verb: *had* and *does* are the verbs.

13. *It is raining today. I hope it will be sunny tomorrow.* There are two sentences. Each sentence has at least one verb: *is*, *hope* and *will be* are the verbs.

14. Speech marks go around what is being said: *"Will you help me practise goal kicking?" asked Jessica.*

15. Speech marks go around what is being said: *"Stop! Don't cross the road yet," shouted Keith.*

16. An exclamation mark is used after a word that is said loudly or with emphasis: *"Yuk!" shrieked Julia. "That tasted terrible."*

17. The conjunction *because* connects the clauses so that the sentence makes sense.

18. A cause and effect conjunction, *because,* is needed so that the sentence makes sense.

19. *Although* is needed to link the clauses so that the sentence makes sense.

20. *Until* is a connecting word that links events in time. It can be used at the beginning of a sentence: *Until it stopped raining, the dogs had to stay indoors. Until* could also be used in the middle of the sentence without changing the meaning: *The dogs had to stay indoors until it stopped raining.*

21. *Kate ran to school so she'd have time to play. So* is a connecting word. It links clauses through cause and effect.

22. *Carl ran to school because he wanted to race Frankie. Because* is used to connect the events in a way that makes sense.

23. *Matilda ran until she ran out of breath. Until* is a connecting word that means 'until that time'.

24. *Jim ran to the corner and then he walked the rest of the way.* The conjunction *and* is used to link two equal clauses by adding information.

25. The vital information in the two sentences is underlined here: <u>*Yusuf's cat*</u> *is very* <u>*tiny*</u>*. It is called* <u>*Alpa*</u> *which is a* <u>*Hindu*</u> *word meaning* <u>*'little'*</u>*.* The only example which includes all the information is: *Yusuf's tiny cat is called Alpa which means 'little' in Hindu.*

READING (Test Your Skills)
Narratives   Page 93

Go to **page 212** for a guide to question types.

The spoilt prince

EXPLANATIONS

1. This is a **fact-finding type of question**. The answer is a fact in the text. You read *… in a kingdom far, far away lived … Johan* (see lines 2–3).

2. This is a **fact-finding type of question**. The answer is a fact in the text. You read that the prince *was lazy and rude* (see line 5) and that he *was mean to everyone* (see line 6).

3. Answers will vary. This is a **synthesis type of question**. To work out the answer you have to read the whole text. You read that Prince Johan

was *mean to everyone, even his parents (see line 6).* You also read that his parents *went on holidays to New Zealand as often as they could, without Johan (see line 15).* You need to answer this question in a way that makes sense in the context of the story. You might suggest that because the prince wasn't a nice person his parents wanted him to get married and move out of the castle. You could also say that maybe his parents hoped that the prince might become a nicer person if he had a nice wife. If you are familiar with fairytales you will know that princes and princesses often get married so your answer might be that the story is a fairytale. Your answer can't be wrong if it makes sense in the context of the story.

4. This is a **language type of question**. To work out the answer you have to read the text carefully. You read the beginning words *Once upon a time (see line 2)* and the ending words *happily ever after (see line 14)* which indicate that the text is a narrative in the form of a fairytale. Combine this information with your own knowledge of fairytales to work out that the purpose is to tell a story to entertain.

5. This is a **judgement type of question**. You read *The princesses didn't want to marry a mean and rude prince (see line 12).* Combine this information with your own knowledge to work out that the main reason the princesses didn't want to marry the prince was because he wasn't a nice person.

6. This is a **language type of question**. You read *He demanded that the cook make him special cakes (see lines 5–6).* You can tell by the way *demanded* is used in the text that it doesn't mean *begged for* or *hoped for* or *needed.* The prince is mean so he would have *insisted on* the cakes being made for him.

7. This is a **language type of question**. You read that the prince *lived happily ever after (see line 14).* These are the only words that describe the prince's feelings: he was *happy.* The other options do not describe his feelings, only actions.

READING (Real Test)
Narratives
Page 94

A conversation with Grandma
1 C   2 D   3 D   4 B   5 A   6 B   7 D

EXPLANATIONS

1. This is a **fact-finding type of question**. The answer is a fact in the text. You read Zumu says: *"I was born in a farming village in China" (see line 4).*

2. This is a **fact-finding type of question**. The answer is a fact in the text. You read the title of the text is *A conversation with Grandma (see line 1).* You

also read *Cynthia and her grandmother were talking (see line 2).*

3. This is a **synthesis type of question**. To work out the answer you have to read the whole text. When you read the whole text you can understand that Cynthia is a determined person. She does not give up easily. When Zumu says she will not take Cynthia to China, Cynthia announces she will go anyway. This is determination.

4. This is a **fact-finding type of question**. The answer is a fact in the text. You read *"Will you take me to see where you were born?" (see line 8).*

5. This is an **inferring type of question**. To work out the answer you have to 'read between the lines'. You read Cynthia *slumped her shoulders. She pretended she might cry. She wanted Zumu to give in and agree to take her to China (see lines 14–15).* When people talk to one another they use facial expression and body language to help make their meaning clear. Cynthia purposely slumped her shoulders and pretended that she might cry so that Zumu would see that she was upset. Cynthia used body language to try to convince Zumu to take her to China.

6. This is a **judgement type of question**. Zumu's interactions with Cynthia tell readers that Zumu is very patient. She does not get angry with Cynthia. She seems kindly.

7. This is a **fact-finding type of question**. You read that at the end of the conversation Cynthia declares, *"I will go to China one day" (see line 17).*

READING (Real Test)
Narratives
Page 95

Stuck
1 C   2 B   3 C   4 C   5 D   6 A   7 B

EXPLANATIONS

1. This is a **fact-finding type of question**. The answer is a fact in the text. You read Jenny calls Pongo, *'Puss' (see line 2). Puss* is often used as a nickname for a cat. It is short for 'pussy cat'. You also read that Jenny *told her mother that the cat was stuck in a tree (see lines 13–14).*

2. This is a **synthesis type of question**. To work out the answer you have to read the whole text. You read *Pongo had climbed a tree and Jenny wanted him to come down (see lines 3–4).* You also read *She went inside and told her mother that the cat was stuck in a tree (see lines 12–14).* You can work out that Jenny's problem is that she thinks the cat is stuck in a tree. The cat is not stuck in the tree. It comes down from the tree when it feels like it.

3 This is a **fact-finding type of question**. The answer is a fact in the text. You read that *chicken* [is] *Pongo's favourite food (see line 7)*.

4 This is a **fact-finding type of question**. The answer is a fact in the text. You read that Jenny *went inside and told her mother (see lines 12–13)*.

5 This is an **inferring type of question**. To work out the answer you have to 'read between the lines'. You read that at the end of the story Jenny says to Pongo *"You are such a tricker!" (see line 17)*. This is affectionate language so you can work out that Jenny was happy the cat had come down from the tree.

6 This is a **synthesis type of question**. To work out the answer you have to read the whole text. You read that Jenny says to Pongo *"You are such a tricker!" (see line 17)*. You can work out that the most suitable title would be *Tricky Pongo* because that is really what the text is all about. Jenny's cat Pongo is *a tricker*.

7 This is a **language type of question**. You read *Jenny was worried that Pongo didn't know how to get back down (see lines 5–6)* and *Now Jenny was really getting worried (see line 12)*. *Concerned* and *worried* are synonyms. Synonyms are words with similar meanings. The sentence would mean the same thing if it said: *Now Jenny was really getting* <u>concerned</u>.

WRITING (Real Test)
Narrative text 1
Page 98

Tick each correct point.
Read the student's work through once to get an overall view of their response. Then read the text a second time to consider each of the ten assessment criteria below. The same criteria are used to assess the NAPLAN Writing Task. Not all criteria will be evident in any piece of writing. You may choose to focus on one or two areas only when giving feedback to the student.

Audience
- ☐ Is the text interesting and entertaining?
- ☐ Does the action in the plot draw the reader in?
- ☐ Does the narrative make sense?

Text structure
- ☐ Does the text have an appropriate structure?
- ☐ Does the plot build to a climax?
- ☐ Is the resolution satisfying for a reader?

Ideas
- ☐ Is the story true to fantasy or science fiction genre?
- ☐ Are the ideas logical, original and imaginative?
- ☐ Are the ideas well thought through?

Character and setting
- ☐ Could you form a mental picture of the characters and setting?
- ☐ Is any character's point of view evident?
- ☐ Could a reader feel empathy with any of the characters?
- ☐ Is the setting established?

Vocabulary
- ☐ Is there sufficient descriptive detail?
- ☐ Are noun groups (nouns and adjectives) used effectively?
- ☐ Are verbs used appropriately to depict the characters' actions and behaviour?
- ☐ Is verb tense accurate and consistent?
- ☐ Are adverbs used appropriately?
- ☐ Does the writer use alliteration or onomatopoeia, if appropriate?

Cohesion
- ☐ Is the use of third-person narrator consistent throughout the text (e.g. Kim and Terry—they)?
- ☐ Does the text flow logically?
- ☐ Are connectives used to link ideas?
- ☐ Does the writer use synonyms, antonyms and word sets to create interesting lexical chains (e.g. the shimmering silver ball—the object—a magical thing)?

Paragraphing
- ☐ Are paragraphs used to organise sections of the story?
- ☐ Are paragraphs built around topic sentences?

Sentence structure
- ☐ Are a variety of appropriate sentence structures evident (simple, compound, complex)?
- ☐ Do characters talk to one another (direct or reported speech)?
- ☐ Are sentence lengths varied for pace and emphasis?

Punctuation
- ☐ Is sentence punctuation accurate?
- ☐ Are there capital letters for sentence beginnings and proper nouns, such as the names of characters?
- ☐ Are commas and full stops used accurately and consistently?

Spelling
- ☐ Is the spelling accurate?
- ☐ Have attempts been made to spell unknown words?
- ☐ Are the attempts phonetically correct or readable?
- ☐ Do the writer's attempts to spell unknown words demonstrate understanding of spelling?
- ☐ Does the writer spell simple, common, difficult and challenging words correctly?

WRITING (Real Test)
Narrative text 2
Page 99

Tick each correct point.

Read the student's work through once to get an overall view of their response. Then read the text a second time to consider each of the ten assessment criteria below. The same criteria are used to assess the NAPLAN Writing Task. Not all criteria will be evident in any piece of writing. You may choose to focus on one or two areas only when giving feedback to the student.

Audience
☐ Is the text interesting and entertaining?
☐ Does the action in the plot draw the reader in?
☐ Does the story make sense?

Text structure
☐ Does the text have an appropriate structure?
☐ Is there an orientation, complication, series of events and resolution?
☐ Is the resolution satisfying for a reader?

Ideas
☐ Is the story true to adventure genre?
☐ Are the ideas logical, original and imaginative?
☐ Are the ideas well thought through?
☐ Is there enough detail?
☐ Is the writer able to write with authority?

Character and setting
☐ Could you form a mental picture of the characters and setting?
☐ Are the characters well rounded?
☐ Are the points of view of characters evident?
☐ Could a reader feel empathy for the characters?
☐ Is the setting credible and well described?

Vocabulary
☐ Are noun groups (nouns and adjectives) used effectively?
☐ Are verbs used appropriately to depict the characters' actions and behaviour?
☐ Is verb tense accurate and consistent?
☐ Are adverbs used appropriately?
☐ Does the writer make use of figurative language (simile, alliteration, onomatopoeia)?

Cohesion
☐ Is the use of first- or third-person narrator consistent throughout the text?
☐ Are connectives used to link ideas?
☐ Does the writer use synonyms, antonyms and word sets to create interesting lexical chains?

Paragraphing
☐ Are paragraphs used to organise sections of the story?
☐ Are paragraphs built around topic sentences?

Sentence structure
☐ Is a variety of appropriate sentence structures evident (simple, compound, complex; direct and reported speech)?
☐ Does the text include statements, commands and exclamations, as appropriate, including in conversations between characters?
☐ Are sentence lengths varied for pace and emphasis if appropriate?

Punctuation
☐ Is sentence punctuation evident and accurate?
☐ Are there capital letters for sentence beginnings and proper nouns, such as the names of characters?
☐ Are commas and full stops used accurately and consistently?

Spelling
☐ Is the spelling accurate?
☐ Have attempts been made to spell unknown words?
☐ Are the attempts phonetically correct or readable?
☐ Do the writer's attempts to spell unknown words demonstrate understanding of spelling?
☐ Does the writer spell simple, common, difficult and challenging words correctly?

WRITING (Real Test)
Narrative text 3
Page 100

Tick each correct point.

Read the student's work through once to get an overall view of their response. Then read the text a second time to consider each of the ten assessment criteria below. The same criteria are used to assess the NAPLAN Writing Task. Not all criteria will be evident in any piece of writing. You may choose to focus on one or two areas only when giving feedback to the student.

Audience
☐ Is the text interesting and entertaining?
☐ Does the conflict between the characters draw the reader in?

Text structure
☐ Is there an orientation, complication, series of events and resolution?
☐ Is the resolution satisfying for a reader?

Ideas
☐ Are the ideas logical, original and imaginative?
☐ Is the original tale changed effectively?
☐ Are the ideas well thought through?
☐ Is there enough detail?

Character and setting

- ☐ Could you form a mental picture of the characters and setting?
- ☐ Are the characters true to the chosen tale?
- ☐ Are the points of view of characters evident?

Vocabulary

- ☐ Is there sufficient descriptive detail?
- ☐ Are noun groups (nouns and adjectives) used effectively?
- ☐ Are verbs used appropriately to depict the characters' manner of speaking (e.g. said, whispered, sniggered)?
- ☐ Is verb tense accurate and consistent?
- ☐ Does the writer use figurative language (simile, alliteration, onomatopoeia)?

Cohesion

- ☐ Are connectives used to link ideas?
- ☐ Does the text make sense?

Paragraphing

- ☐ Are paragraphs used effectively?

Sentence structure

- ☐ Does the text include statements, commands and exclamations, as appropriate, including in conversations between characters?
- ☐ Does the writer vary sentence length for pace and emphasis where appropriate?

Punctuation

- ☐ Is sentence punctuation evident and accurate for statements, questions and exclamations?
- ☐ Are there capital letters for sentence beginnings and proper nouns, such as the names of characters?
- ☐ Are speech marks, commas and full stops used accurately and consistently?

Spelling

- ☐ Is the spelling accurate?
- ☐ Have attempts been made to spell unknown words?
- ☐ Are the attempts phonetically correct or readable?
- ☐ Do the writer's attempts to spell unknown words demonstrate understanding of spelling?
- ☐ Does the writer spell simple, common, difficult and challenging words correctly?

Marker's suggestions (optional)

WEEK 4

MEASUREMENT AND GEOMETRY (Real Test)
Pages 107–108
Location and transformation

1 C 2 C, E, F 3 B 4 D 5 A
6 B 7 D1 8 D 9 A 10 A

EXPLANATIONS

1 Between the cow paddock and the shed is the cattle yard.

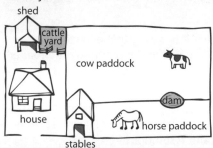

2 Imagine each shape flipped over the dotted line.

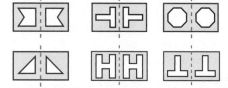

The shapes that look the same when flipped over the dotted line are those in options C, E and F.

 and

3 The shape that is at F2 is ✿

4 The shape is turned through a half turn.

5 The counter moves 3 squares to the right.

6

If this shape is flipped over the dotted line it looks like this.

Folding a piece of paper and cutting out a shape works like a flip.

Lucy's paper will be

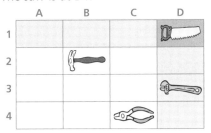

7 The saw is at D1.

	A	B	C	D
1				saw
2		hammer		
3				wrench
4			pliers	

8 The arrow is turned a quarter of a turn.

9 Billy's shape has 2 white squares between the shaded square and the square with a dot.

This is Billy's shape.

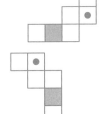

It has been turned a quarter of a turn in an anticlockwise direction.

10 Nat is second from the left.

left   right

STATISTICS AND PROBABILITY
(Real Test)
Chance and data   Pages 114–115

1 3   **2** B   **3** B   **4** B/D   **5** C
6 C   **7** 26   **8** 10   **9** A   **10** 12

EXPLANATIONS

1

Favourite movie	
Movie	Number of votes
Good Times	7
Old Dogs	**10**
Red and Blue	8
Kangaroos	**13**

13 students voted for *Kangaroos*.

10 students voted for *Old Dogs*.

Now 13 − 10 = 3.

So 3 more students voted for *Kangaroos* than voted for *Old Dogs*.

2 There are 10 jelly beans on the dish.

Only one of the jelly beans is green.

So, the chance of taking a green jelly bean could be described as unlikely.

3 The key tells us that each clock picture means one hour. So 5 clocks will mean 5 hours.

The day that has 5 clocks is Tuesday.

So Mr Lee spent 5 hours at work on Tuesday.

4 From the graph you can see that there were 12 white cars, 7 red cars, 6 blue, 9 silver and 4 black cars.

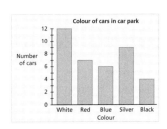

Now look at the choices.

There were more black cars than silver cars. This is not correct. There were 5 more silver cars than black ones.

There are more red cars than black cars. This is correct. There were 3 more red cars than black ones.

There are more blue cars than white cars. This is not correct. There were 6 more white cars than blue ones.

There are more silver cars than blue cars. This is correct. There were 3 more silver cars than blue ones.

The correct statements are: 'There are more red cars than black cars.' and 'There are more silver cars than blue cars.'

5. Tally marks are put into groups of 5. There is one group of 5 tally marks for Mia. So 5 students voted for Mia.

6. The sector for 3 is the largest on the spinner. So the spinner is most likely to stop on 3.

7.
Class	Boys	Girls
2K	13	14
2P	15	11
2Y	12	12

In 2P there are 15 boys and 11 girls.
Now 15 + 11 = 26.
So there are 26 children in 2P.

8. The key tells us that each picture means 2 cherries. So, counting by twos, Jill ate 10 cherries.

9. The smallest number on each dice is 1.
Now 1 + 1 = 2.
So the smallest total is 2.
It is impossible to get 1.
[5 could be 2 + 3; 9 could be 4 + 5; 11 could be 5 + 6.]

10. Sid counted 8 birds and Eli counted 4.

Name	Sid	Dana	Ruby	Nat	Eli	Sam
Birds	8	5	2	9	4	6

Now 8 + 4 = 12.
So, altogether Sid and Eli counted 12 birds.

SPELLING (Real Test)
Singular and plural nouns, prefixes and suffixes
Pages 118–119

1 potatoes 2 tomatoes 3 cherries 4 women 5 feet
6 babies 7 mangos or mangoes 8 sheep 9 benches
10 teeth 11 dingoes 12 geese 13 mice 14 races
15 helpless 16 loaves 17 respectful 18 whales
19 uncomfortable 20 undone 21 unfinished
22 unfold 23 careful 24 helping 25 careless
26 hopeless 27 gardener 28 runner 29 cyclist
30 florist 31 dentist 32 baker 33 doctor
34 plumber 35 teacher

EXPLANATIONS

1. When a noun ends in **o** (after a consonant) you usually add 'es' to form the plural.

2. When a noun ends in **o** (after a consonant) you usually add 'es' to form the plural.

3. When a noun ends in **y** you usually change the **y** to **i** before adding 'es' to form the plural.

4. *Women* is the plural of *woman*.

5. *Feet* is the plural of *foot*.

6. When a noun ends in **y** you usually change the **y** to **i** before adding 'es' to form the plural.

7. When a noun ends in **o** (after a consonant) you usually add 'es' to form the plural. *Mangos* is also accepted because it is commonly used.

8. *Sheep* is a noun that stays the same for both singular and plural.

9. Nouns ending in 'ch' form the plural by adding 'es'.

10. *Teeth* is plural for *tooth*.

11. When a noun ends in **o** (after a consonant) you usually add 'es' to form the plural.

12. *Geese* is plural for *goose*.

13. *Mice* is plural for *mouse*.

14. Adding **s** makes the word plural.

15. The suffix 'less' means 'without'.

16. Many words that end in **f** change the **f** to **v** to form the plural, e.g. *calf—calves, elf—elves, knife—knives*. Note the vowel digraph 'oa' makes a long **o** sound. Other words with this spelling pattern include *soap, toast, road* and *boat*.

17. The suffix 'ful' means 'full of'. Note that only one **l** is used in the suffix.

18. The 'wh' is a consonant digraph where two letters make one sound **w**. The **a** says its name, making the long **a** sound. Adding **s** makes the word plural.

19. The prefix 'un' is added to the beginning of the word *comfortable* to make its meaning opposite.

20. The prefix 'un' is added to the beginning of the word *done* to make its meaning opposite.

21. The suffix 'ed' must be added to the end of the word.

22. The prefix 'un' is added to the beginning of the word *fold* to make its meaning opposite. There is no double **n**.

23. When the suffix 'ful' meaning 'full' is added to a word, it usually only has one **l**.

24. There is no need to double the final consonant (**p**) before adding 'ing' to *help*.

25. The suffix 'less' means 'without'.

26. The suffix 'less' means 'without'.

27. Spell the word *garden* and remember that a person working in a garden is a *gardener*.

28. The suffix 'er' is used to spell *runner*.

29 Remember that occupations can end in 'ist' but not 'est'. A *cyclist* is a person who cycles on a bicycle.

30 Remember that occupations can end in 'ist' but not 'est'. A *florist* works with flowers.

23 A *dentist* works with people's teeth.

32 A *baker* is a person who bakes goods such as bread.

33 A *doctor* helps people who are sick.

34 A *plumber* works with pipes, taps, toilets, roofs and gutters—fixtures that carry water and waste.

35 Remember that *teacher* ends in an 'er' by thinking about the smaller word, 'her', at the end of the word.

GRAMMAR AND PUNCTUATION (Real Test)
Personal pronouns, HOW adverbs and adjectives that compare
Pages 122–123

1 D   2 A   3 B   4 B   5 C   6 C   7 D   8 me
9 him   10 They   11 I   12 B   13 big   14 bigger
15 biggest   16 B   17 B   18 C   19 A   20 A
21 B   22 D   23 B   24 C   25 B

EXPLANATIONS

1 You need a word that tells HOW the goanna walked. The adverb is *softly*.

2 You need a word that tells HOW the beetle munched. The adverb is *noisily*.

3 You need a word that tells HOW the children should smile. The adverb is *nicely*.

4 You need a word that tells HOW to hit the nail. The adverb is *carefully*.

5 *It* is the pronoun used to refer to *the book*.

6 *Them* is the pronoun used to refer to *these shoes*.

7 *Gently* is a HOW adverb. It tells HOW to pat a kitten.

8 *Me* is the pronoun that matches the pronoun *I*. *I* and *me* are first-person pronouns.

9 *Him* is the pronoun that refers to *Liam* in the sentence. Pronouns replace nouns in texts so that the nouns do not have to be repeated. Using pronouns makes texts flow smoothly.

10 *They* is the pronoun that refers to *Koalas*.

11 *I* is the correct pronoun to match the narrator, *Zac*, who is talking about himself.

12 *Better* is the adjective that is used to compare two things, *cats* and *dogs*.

13 Use the adjective *big* to describe the elephant: *That elephant is big.*

14 *Bigger* compares two things: *the red balloon* with *the green balloon*.

15 *Biggest* compares three or more things when one thing is the *biggest of them all*.

16 The adjectives *good—better—best* compare by degrees. When two things are compared, use *better*.

17 *Well* is the adverb. It tells HOW the sister ran. *Good, great* and *wonderful* are adjectives and cannot be used to describe the verb *ran*.

18 An adverb is needed to tell HOW the snake lived: *quietly*.

19 An adverb is needed to tell HOW the books should be stacked *on* the shelf: *carefully*.

20 When comparing three or more things and the adjective is less than three syllables in length, it needs to end in 'est': *fastest*.

21 An adverb is needed to tell HOW the kookaburra sang: *loudly*. *Silently* is an adverb but it would not make sense in the sentence.

22 *You* is the pronoun needed to match *you* in the first sentence.

23 The pronoun *her* is needed to refer to *Lara*.

24 The adverb *swiftly* tells HOW the magpies flew.

25 It is impossible to be 'deader' or 'deadest'. Some adjectives can't compare (e.g. dead, full, empty, closed, open). It would be incorrect to say the 'deader battery' or the 'deadest battery' in the sentence: *Mum said the battery was dead.*

READING (Test Your Skills)
Persuasive texts: argument
Page 125

Go to   page 212   for a guide to question types.

Be kind to possums

EXPLANATIONS

1 This is a **language type of question**. To work out the answer you have to read the text carefully. You read *Brush-tailed possums are common in Australia (see line 2)*. Combine your reading of the text with your own knowledge that *common* means 'everyday' or 'widespread'. From this you can work out that in the text *common* means there are many possums.

2 This is a **judgement type of question**. You read that possums *prefer to live in hollow trees (see line 3)*. Possums can live in roofs, possum houses or zoos but the best place for a possum is in a hollow tree.

3 This is a **fact-finding type of question**. The answer is a fact in the text. You read *Possums are territorial, which means they have an area that they call their own. They do not let new possums come into their area* (see lines 6–7).

4 This is a **fact-finding type of question**. The answer is a fact in the text. You read *[T]he best thing to do is to build a possum-house in a tree in your own backyard* (see lines 10–12).

5 This is a **fact-finding type of question**. The answer is a fact in the text. You read *Possums usually die when people move them out of their own territory. They starve. I think that is very sad* (see lines 8–9).

6 This is a **fact-finding type of question**. The answer is a fact in the text. You read *Once the possum is out of your roof and in its new house you can cover over any holes in your roof. Then it won't be able to get back inside your roof* (see lines 13–16).

7 This is a **synthesis type of question**. To work out the answer you have to read the whole text to understand that it is a persuasive text. It presents the writer's opinion. The writer's purpose is to give opinions about possums and persuade others to agree.

READING (Real Test)
Persuasive texts: argument
Page 126

Circuses are NOT good for animals
1 B 2 B 3 B 4 C 5 A 6 B 7 A
EXPLANATIONS

1 This is a **fact-finding type of question**. The answer is a fact in the text. You read *I don't like circuses that use animals* (see line 2).

2 This is a **fact-finding type of question**. The answer is a fact in the text. You read *Lions, tigers and elephants don't belong in circuses … They belong in the wild* (see lines 3–6).

3 This is a **fact-finding type of question**. The answer is a fact in the text. You read *Circuses should just have human performers … I love these kinds of circuses* (see lines 10–12).

4 This is a **fact-finding type of question**. The answer is a fact in the text. You read *In … the Flying Fruit Fly Circus … the humans do the tricks and perform* (see lines 11–12).

5 This is a **fact-finding type of question**. The answer is a fact in the text. You read *My favourite act is the flying trapeze* (see line 13).

6 This is a **language type of question**. To work out the answer you have to read the text carefully. You read *Animal circuses are cruel* (see line 15). You

can tell the meaning of *cruel* by the way it is used in the text and the way the writer feels about animal circuses. The writer presents all the reasons why animals should not be used in circuses. From this you can work out that *cruel* means 'unkind'.

7 This is a **synthesis type of question**. To work out the answer you have to read the whole text. You read *I don't like circuses that use animals* (see line 2). The writer begins with an opinion and continues to give opinions throughout the text. From this you can work out that the writer's purpose is *to give an opinion about circuses*.

READING (Real Test)
Persuasive texts: advertising
Page 127

Be a winner
1 B 2 B 3 D 4 A 5 C 6 C 7 B
EXPLANATIONS

1 This is a **fact-finding type of question**. The answer is a fact in the text. You read *All you need to do is eat an apple a day* (see line 10).

2 This is a **language type of question**. To work out the answer you have to read the text carefully. You read *So kids—what are you waiting for?* (see lines 23–24). From this you can work out that the audience for the advertisement is children and so the *you* is children.

3 This is a **language type of question**. To work out the answer you have to read the text carefully. The text says that readers can *WIN at sports* (see line 13) and *WIN all those computer games* (see lines 16–17). Don't be tricked by the adjective *winning* because the ad also says that *kids* can gain a *winning smile* (see line 15) and a *winning personality* (see line 19). The advertisement might also confuse because it says that kids can *BE A WINNER with Apple Power* (see lines 1–2)—this doesn't mean they win Apple Power. The answer is that eating apples will help you win at sports and at computer games.

4 This is a **judgement type of question**. You read *crisp, crunchy, juicy, shiny, green [or] red* (see lines 3–8). These words are adjectives. They are used to make apples sound delicious so that you will want to eat them.

5 This is a **fact-finding type of question**. The answer is a fact in the text. You read *All you need to do is eat an apple a day and the benefits will be … more friends* (see lines 10–18).

6 This is a **fact-finding type of question**. The answer is a fact in the text. You read *Apples have sustainable*

packaging—*eat the skin or recycle it: No waste (see lines 21–22).* Answer A is only partially correct.

7 This is a **synthesis type of question**. To work out the answer you have to read the whole text. The text is trying to make children want to eat more apples by pointing out all the advantages to children of eating apples. The text does not prove apples are good for you or that apples make you happier, although it does make these claims.

WRITING (Real Test)
Persuasive text 1
Page 130

Tick each correct point.
Read the student's work through once to get an overall view of their response. Then read the text a second time to consider each of the ten assessment criteria below. The same criteria are used to assess the NAPLAN Writing Task. Not all criteria will be evident in any piece of writing. You may choose to focus on one or two areas only when giving feedback to the student.

Audience
- ☐ Does the text engage the reader?
- ☐ Are the writer's values evident?

Text structure
- ☐ Is there an introduction to define the topic or outline the writer's point of view?
- ☐ Are there reasons and elaboration?
- ☐ Does the conclusion draw together the arguments?
- ☐ Is there a recommendation or a call to action?

Ideas
- ☐ Are the ideas well thought through?
- ☐ Does the writer show understanding of wider implications (local community, global) or only personal implications?
- ☐ Are ideas original?
- ☐ Is there depth of thinking?

Persuasive devices
- ☐ Does the writer persuade though reason and logic?
- ☐ Does the writer make an emotional appeal?
- ☐ Is the argument supported by facts?
- ☐ Does the text have high modality?
- ☐ Are auxiliary verbs and modal adverbs used (e.g. must, should, absolutely, definitely)?

Vocabulary
- ☐ Are technical terms used?
- ☐ Are noun groups used effectively to label issues and content?

Cohesion
- ☐ Are reference chains consistent (e.g. children—they—them)?
- ☐ Are arguments linked logically using connectives (e.g. therefore, because, so)?
- ☐ Is there repetition for emphasis?

Paragraphing
- ☐ Are paragraphs sequenced and logical?
- ☐ Is each paragraph based on a main idea with supporting detail?

Sentence structure
- ☐ Are sentences grammatically correct and meaningful?
- ☐ Does the writer use a range of appropriate sentence types?
- ☐ Does the writer vary sentence length for emphasis?

Punctuation
- ☐ Is punctuation accurate (e.g. full stops, commas, exclamation marks, contractions, speech marks)?

Spelling
- ☐ Is the spelling accurate?
- ☐ Have attempts been made to spell unknown words?
- ☐ Are the attempts phonetically correct or readable?
- ☐ Do the writer's attempts to spell unknown words demonstrate understanding of spelling?
- ☐ Does the writer spell simple, common, difficult and challenging words correctly?

WRITING (Real Test)
Persuasive text 2
Page 131

Tick each correct point.
Read the student's work through once to get an overall view of their response. Then read the text a second time to consider each of the ten assessment criteria below. The same criteria are used to assess the NAPLAN Writing Task. Not all criteria will be evident in any piece of writing. You may choose to focus on one or two areas only when giving feedback to the student.

Audience
- ☐ Does the text engage an audience?
- ☐ Does it draw the reader in?
- ☐ Are the writer's values evident?

Text structure
- ☐ Is there an introduction to define the topic or outline the writer's point of view?
- ☐ Are there reasons and elaboration?
- ☐ Is one point of view presented or a number of viewpoints?
- ☐ Does the conclusion draw together the arguments?

Check Your Answers

Ideas
- [ ] Are the ideas well thought through?
- [ ] Are ideas logical?
- [ ] Has the writer thought deeply about the topic or only superficially?

Persuasive devices
- [ ] Does the writer persuade though reason and logic?
- [ ] Does the writer make an emotional appeal?
- [ ] Are the arguments supported by facts?
- [ ] Does the text include high modality statements?
- [ ] Are auxiliary verbs and modal adverbs used (e.g. must, should, absolutely, definitely)?

Vocabulary
- [ ] Are technical terms used?
- [ ] Are noun groups used effectively to label issues and content?
- [ ] Are a range of thinking verbs used to express opinions (e.g. think, believe, recognise, hope)?

Cohesion
- [ ] Are reference chains consistent (e.g. food outlets—they—them)?
- [ ] Are arguments linked logically using connectives (e.g. therefore, because, so)?
- [ ] Is there repetition for emphasis or reinforcement?

Paragraphing
- [ ] Are paragraphs sequenced logically?
- [ ] Is each paragraph based on a main idea with supporting detail?

Sentence structure
- [ ] Are sentences grammatically correct and meaningful?
- [ ] Does the writer use a range of appropriate sentence types?
- [ ] Does the writer vary sentence length for pace and emphasis if appropriate?

Punctuation
- [ ] Is punctuation accurate for sentence beginnings and endings, contractions and exclamations?

Spelling
- [ ] Is the spelling accurate?
- [ ] Have attempts been made to spell unknown words?
- [ ] Are the attempts phonetically correct or readable?
- [ ] Do the writer's attempts to spell unknown words demonstrate understanding of spelling?
- [ ] Does the writer spell simple, common, difficult and challenging words correctly?

Tick each correct point.
Read the student's work through once to get an overall view of their response. Then read the text a second time to consider each of the ten assessment criteria below. The same criteria are used to assess the NAPLAN Writing Task. Not all criteria will be evident in any piece of writing. You may choose to focus on one or two areas only when giving feedback to the student.

Audience
- [ ] Does the text engage an audience?
- [ ] Does it draw the reader in?

Text structure
- [ ] Is there a heading?
- [ ] What claims are made?
- [ ] Are there reasons and elaboration?
- [ ] Is there a call to action?

Ideas
- [ ] Are the ideas well thought through?
- [ ] Does the writing show originality or creativity?
- [ ] Does the text reflect an understanding of real-life advertisements?

Persuasive devices
- [ ] Does the writer persuade though logic, emotions, exaggeration?
- [ ] Does the writer address the reader directly (you)?
- [ ] Does the writer make an emotional appeal?
- [ ] Are illustrations and layout used to persuade?
- [ ] Does the text include high modality statements?
- [ ] Are auxiliary verbs and modal adverbs used (e.g. must, should, absolutely, definitely)?

Vocabulary
- [ ] Are technical terms used?
- [ ] Are noun groups used effectively to label goods or services?
- [ ] Are a range of adjectives used (e.g. fantastic, wonderful, cheap)?

Cohesion
- [ ] Are reference chains consistent (e.g. this product—it)?
- [ ] Are arguments linked logically using connectives (e.g. therefore, because, so)?
- [ ] Is there repetition for emphasis or reinforcement?

Paragraphing
- [ ] If paragraphs are appropriate, are they sequenced logically?
- [ ] Is each paragraph based on a main idea with supporting detail?

Sentence structure

☐ Are sentences grammatically correct and meaningful?

☐ Does the writer use a range of appropriate sentence types?

Punctuation

☐ Is punctuation accurate for sentence beginnings and endings, contractions and exclamations?

Spelling

☐ Is the spelling accurate?

☐ Have attempts been made to spell unknown words?

☐ Are the attempts phonetically correct or readable?

☐ Do the writer's attempts to spell unknown words demonstrate understanding of spelling?

☐ Does the writer spell simple, common, difficult and challenging words correctly?

Marker's suggestions (optional)

SAMPLE TEST PAPERS
SAMPLE TEST 1

LITERACY—WRITING   Page 134

Tick each correct point.

Read the student's work through once to get an overall view of their response. Then read the text a second time to consider each of the ten assessment criteria below. The same criteria are used to assess the NAPLAN Writing Task. Not all criteria will be evident in any piece of writing. You may choose to focus on one or two areas only when giving feedback to the student.

Audience

☐ Does the story make sense?

☐ Is it entertaining?

☐ Does it engage the reader?

Text structure

☐ Does the text have an appropriate structure?

☐ Does it include an orientation to character and setting?

☐ Is the plot well developed?

☐ Does it have a suitable resolution?

Ideas

☐ Are the ideas well thought through?

☐ Is there enough detail?

☐ Is the writer able to write with authority on the events?

Character and setting

☐ Are characters described well?

☐ Could readers develop empathy with the characters?

☐ Is anthropomorphism effective?

☐ Is the setting established?

Vocabulary

☐ Is there sufficient descriptive detail?

☐ Are noun groups (nouns and adjectives) used effectively?

☐ Are verbs used appropriately for actions and activity?

☐ Does the writer use simile, alliteration or onomatopoeia?

☐ Are pronouns used consistently for a first-person narrative?

Cohesion

☐ Does the text flow chronologically or logically?

☐ Are time connectives used to link ideas (e.g. then, after that, meanwhile)?

☐ Is noun–pronoun referencing accurate?

Paragraphing

☐ Are paragraphs used to organise ideas?

☐ Are paragraphs built around topic sentences?

Sentence structure

☐ Are a variety of appropriate sentence structures evident (simple, compound, complex; direct and indirect speech)?

☐ Are sentence lengths varied for pace and interest?

Punctuation

☐ Is sentence punctuation evident and accurate?

☐ Are there capital letters for sentence beginnings and proper nouns?

☐ Are commas and full stops used accurately and consistently?

Spelling

☐ Is the spelling accurate?

☐ Have attempts been made to spell unknown words?

☐ Are the attempts phonetically correct or readable?

☐ Do the writer's attempts to spell unknown words demonstrate understanding of spelling?

☐ Does the writer spell simple, common, difficult and challenging words correctly?

Marker's suggestions (optional)

LITERACY—READING   Pages 135–141

Go to **page 212** for a guide to question types.

Nana's cat
1 B 2 B 3 D 4 A 5 A

EXPLANATIONS

1 This is a **fact-finding type of question**. The answer is a fact in the text. You read *My nana calls him Des (see line 10)*.

2 This is an **inferring type of question**. To work out the answer you have to 'read between the lines'. The clue to the answer is in the illustration of a pram. As the poem tells you that Nana pushes the cat in a pushchair you can conclude a pushchair is a pram.

3 This is an **inferring type of question**. To work out the answer you have to 'read between the lines'. You read *My nana's cat just lives to eat (see line 7)*. From this you can infer that the cat loves food.

4 This is a **fact-finding type of question**. The answer is a fact in the text. You read *He sleeps beside her bed (see line 16)*.

5 This is a **fact-finding type of question**. The answer is a fact in the text. You read *Des lies upon her knees. His tummy fits upon her lap. The rest hangs in the breeze (see lines 12–14)*. The illustration that shows this correctly is A. The cat's tummy is across Nana's lap. The cat's legs are hanging down *in the breeze*.

Ride a bike
6 A 7 C 8 D 9 A 10 B 11 B
12 Answers will vary.

EXPLANATIONS

6 This is a **language type of question**. To work out the answer you have to read the text carefully. Paragraph one uses the term *bike riding (see lines 2–3)*. Paragraphs two, three and four refer to *cycling (see lines 5, 9 and 16)*. *Bike riding* and *cycling* mean the same thing.

7 This is an **inferring type of question**. To work out the answer you have to 'read between the lines'. You read the title of the text is *Ride a bike*. The first sentence in the text says: *More people should ride bikes instead of using cars (see line 2)*. So, you can work out that the writer wants more people to ride bikes.

8 This is a **fact-finding type of question**. The answer is a fact in the text. You read *He [Papi] has a basket on the back of his bike to carry his groceries. Sometimes he cycles with his little dog in the basket (see lines 14–16)*. So Papi carries groceries and a dog.

9 This is a **fact-finding type of question**. The answer is a fact in the text. You read *My Papi rides a tricycle. It has three wheels (see line 13)*.

10 This is a **fact-finding type of question**. The answer is a fact in the text. You read *He [Papi] says he can't balance on a two-wheeled bicycle any more (see lines 13–14)*.

11 This is a **fact-finding type of question**. The answer is a fact in the text. You read *He [Papi] rides his tricycle to the shops (see line 14)*.

12 This is a **language type of question**. To work out the answer you have to read the text carefully. You read *It's not an electric cycle so he has to use pedal power to get anywhere. He says that keeps him fit (see lines 16–17)*. Bicycles have pedals. People push the pedals to power the bikes rather than use electricity, petrol or diesel fuel. This is why cycling keeps people fit.

Eating for health
13 C 14 A, B 15 B 16 B 17 D

EXPLANATIONS

13 This is a **fact-finding type of question**. The answer is a fact in the text. You read *dairy foods … provide calcium for bones and teeth (see lines 10–13)*.

14 This is a **fact-finding type of question**. The answer is a fact in the text. You read *wholegrain cereals … provide energy, as well as fibre for digestion (see lines 3–6)*.

15 This is a **fact-finding type of question**. The answer is a fact in the text. You read *lean meat … provide protein (see lines 3–5)*.

16 This is a **fact-finding type of question**. The answer is a fact in the text. You read *fruit and vegetables … provide … vitamins and minerals (see lines 3–6)*.

17 This is a **fact-finding type of question**. The answer is a fact in the text. You read that *oats are a wholegrain cereal (see lines 3–4)*.

Join Earth Hour
18 C 19 A 20 A 21 B 22 D 23 A

EXPLANATIONS

18 This is a **fact-finding type of question**. The answer is a fact in the text. You read *Earth Hour started in Sydney, Australia (see line 4)*.

19 This is a **synthesis type of question**. To work out the answer you have to read the whole text. The writer begins by saying: *I think that Earth Hour is a really good way … (see line 2)*. The words *I think* indicate the writer is giving an opinion. The body of the text gives reasons for the opinion.

20 This is a **synthesis type of question**. To work out the answer you have to read the whole text. You read *Earth Hour is a really good way to let people know that little things they do can make a big difference to the planet (see lines 2–3)*. The writer then suggests many ways people can save energy and repeats the words *help the planet*. You read *People should help the planet every hour of every day (see lines 9–10)* and *so many simple things people can do every day to help the planet (see lines 13–14)*. From this you can work out that the writer wants to encourage people to help the planet.

21 This is a **judgement type of question**. You read *I am going to be part of Earth Hour again next year (see lines 15–16)*. The whole text is encouraging people to help the planet by saving energy. Combine this information with your own knowledge of people to work out that the writer cares about the environment.

22 This is an **inferring type of question**. To work out the answer you have to 'read between the lines'. You read *During Earth Hour people are asked to switch off their lights to save their planet. 'Switching off' also includes turning off televisions (see lines 5–7)*. You also read in paragraph 3 ways to save energy. Options A, B and C are ways to save energy. D uses energy.

23 This is a **judgement type of question**. Evaluate each suggested title in conjunction with your reading of the whole text. You read *Earth Hour is a really good way to let people know that little things they do can make a big difference to the planet (see lines 2–3)*. The message of the whole text is about getting people to *Help planet Earth*.

How to choose the right pet
24 A, E, F   25 B   26 C   27 C   28 D   29 A
EXPLANATIONS

24 This is a **fact-finding type of question**. The answer is a fact in the text. You read that pets need *shelter from the sun, rain or cold (see line 9)*.

25 This is a **fact-finding type of question**. The answer is a fact in the text. You read that grooming means *washing, combing, clipping its fur (see line 12)*. 'Picking up its droppings' is not included as part of grooming.

26 This is a **fact-finding type of question**. The answer is a fact in the text. You read *barking dogs can annoy neighbours (see line 15)*.

27 This is a **language type of question**. You need to know what each item is for so that you can choose the item needed by a bird. Or, if you don't know what an aviary is, you can work out that a pet bird will not need a leash, kennel or comb.

28 This is a **fact-finding type of question**. The answer is a fact in the text. You read *vaccinations, medicines, worming* in brackets after *medical bills* because they are examples of medical bills *(see line 17)*.

29 This is a **synthesis type of question**. To work out the answer you have to read the whole text. You first read the title which is *How to choose the right pet (see line 1)*. By then reading the rest of the text you can tell that its purpose is to help people choose the right pet.

Simple Fried Rice
30 B   31 C   32 D   33 A   34 B   35 A, E, D
EXPLANATIONS

30 This is a **fact-finding type of question**. The answer is a fact in the text. You read *Heat the peanut oil in a wok or large frypan (see lines 12–13)*.

31 This is a **language type of question**. You read *1 onion, finely chopped (see line 5)*. Use your knowledge of word meanings to work out that *finely* means 'thinly'. You can also work out the correct answer by eliminating the options that seem wrong. In this case it is unlikely a recipe would say to chop onion 'really', 'slowly' or 'carefully'.

32 This is a **fact-finding type of question**. The answer is a fact in the text. You read *Peanut oil* is used first in the *Method*. The text says: *Heat the peanut oil … (see line 12)*.

33 This is a **fact-finding type of question**. The answer is a fact in the text. You read *150 g cooked chicken (see line 8)*.

34 This is a **fact-finding type of question**. The answer is a fact in the text. You read the last step in the *Method* which says: *Stir until everything is hot (see lines 19–20)*. It is ready when it is hot.

35 This is a **judgement type of question**. The text says the recipe is easy to cook. You can judge for yourself whether or not it looks tasty. It has vegetables so you can judge that it seems healthy. B is incorrect as it's only the onions that take 2 minutes to cook. C is incorrect because nothing in the text tells you the recipe is popular.

Lost and found

36 B **37** D **38** A **39** B

EXPLANATIONS

36 This is a **fact-finding type of question**. The answer is a fact in the text. You read *They had chased it [the dog] and now they were definitely lost (see lines 4–5)*. The first paragraph includes the sequence of events that caused the children to become lost. The children chased after their dog. They didn't get lost because Holly chased a dog or because it was getting dark at the park.

37 This is a **fact-finding type of question**. The answer is a fact in the text. You read *The children's mother said, "I knew Holly would bring you home." (see line 18)*.

38 This is a **fact-finding type of question**. The answer is a fact in the text. You read that the children walked *into the front yard of their own home, where their mother was waiting (see lines 16–17)*.

39 This is an **inferring type of question**. To work out the answer you have to 'read between the lines'. You read *The children called out excitedly …The children hugged her. She licked them joyfully (see lines 12–14)*. You can work out that the dog would have felt the children's happiness and relief and would have licked them because they were happy to see her.

LITERACY— CONVENTIONS OF LANGUAGE
Pages 142–145

GRAMMAR AND PUNCTUATION

1 B **2** D **3** D **4** C **5** C **6** C **7** C **8** A
9 Damon, Rina, Wednesday **10** A **11** C **12** D
13 C **14** C **15** Jesper has gym on Wednesday. **16** A
17 B **18** B **19** B **20** B **21** A a, B an, C an, D a
22 B **23** B **24** D **25** B

SPELLING

26 school **27** gave **28** mail **29** camels **30** birthday
31 locked **32** thanked **33** three **34** bucket
35 might **36** photo **37** blue **38** went **39** cook
40 made **41** When **42** great **43** thanked
44 tomorrow **45** riding **46** scratch **47** quickly
48 Wednesday **49** couldn't **50** everywhere

EXPLANATIONS

1 The plural noun *dogs* needs a plural verb, *were*. (One *dog* would need the singular verb *was*.)

2 *Y*esterday tells you to use a past-tense verb because the event happened in the past. The singular pronoun *I* needs a singular verb: *was*.

3 Nouns are names for people, places, animals and things. The noun is *museum*. It is a common noun.

4 Adjectives are words that describe. *Muddy* describes the path.

5 Words that tell how often end in **ly**. *Quickly* tells how the children walked.

6 *Today is the first day of April.* A capital letter is needed at the beginning of the sentence and for the proper noun *April*. A full stop is needed at the end of the sentence.

7 The correct answer is *Robert is a fast reader*. The article *a* is used before a word that starts with a consonant sound (fast). The articles are incorrect in the other suggestions. They should say *a new school bag, a great runner, an excellent cook*.

8 The verb *plays* is present tense. The activity is ongoing. It happens *each Saturday*.

9 Damon and Rina are names of people and Wednesday is the name of a day of the week, so they are all proper nouns.

10 A past-tense verb is needed for an event that has happened: *rode*.

11 *Will eat* is used for something that will happen in the future, *later*.

12 An exclamation mark is needed for a shouted warning, *"Look out!"*

13 *So* is the conjunction that joins the two clauses to make sense. The other options do not make sense.

14 *Mum* can replace the female pronoun *her* in this sentence.

15 A sentence needs to make sense.

16 A HOW adverb is needed to tell HOW the paint is stored: *safely*.

17 *Where are the keys?* is a question. It begins with a question word: *where*. It is punctuated correctly.

18 Commas are needed between items in a list but not usually before 'and'. *Ted bought apples, oranges, bananas and a pineapple.*

19 *Them* is a pronoun. It refers to *those books*.

20 *Well* is an adverb. It tells HOW he swam.

21 *A* is used before words that start with a consonant sound. *An* is used before words that start with a vowel sound.

22 The adjective *better* is used to compare two things: in this case the two apples.

23 *Quietly* is an adverb that tells HOW she ran.

24 *"I love spelling tests," said Ryan.* Speech marks go outside what is actually said.

25. *So* is the conjunction that joins the two clauses to make sense. The other options do not make sense.

26. *School* has a consonant digraph 'ch'; the two letters make one sound.

27. *Gave* has the long *a* vowel sound and a silent *e*. Words that rhyme with *gave* include *cave, shave, pave, crave* and *behave*.

28. *Mail* has the 'ai' digraph. It is also a homophone for *male*. Remember that homophones are words that sound the same but have different meanings and spelling.

29. *Camels* begins with a hard *c*.

30. Say *birthday* carefully and listen for the 'th'

31. *Locked* is a past-tense verb with the suffix 'ed'.

32. *Thanked* is a past-tense verb with the suffix 'ed'.

33. *Three* is a number word. It starts with the consonant digraph 'th.' Pronounce the word carefully to hear the 'th' sound. The word *free* means without cost (e.g. Entry to the park is free). *Free* can also mean 'free to move around; not locked in a cage or prison'. Also, if someone says they are *free* it usually means they are not busy at that moment. The word *free* does not make sense in the sentence.

34. *Bucket* has the consonant digraph 'ck.'

35. *Might* has a silent 'gh'. 'gh' is not pronounced before a *t*. Other examples are *light, fight, tight, sight* and *right*.

36. The word *photo* has a consonant digraph 'ph' which is pronounced *f*.

37. The word *blue* has a vowel digraph 'ue'. *Blue* is a homophone for *blew*. Homophones are words which sound the same but have different meanings and spelling.

38. The word *went* does not have a consonant digraph 'wh'.

39. The word *cook* has a 'oo' vowel digraph, also found in *chook, took, look, stood* and *hood*.

40. The word *made* has a long *a* vowel sound and a silent *e*. *Made* and *maid* are homophones. Remember that homophones are words that sound the same but have different meanings and spelling.

41. The word *when* starts with the 'wh' consonant digraph. Remember that the smaller word *hen* comes after the *w*. *When* has a capital letter here because it starts the sentence.

42. The adjective *great* has a vowel digraph 'ea' pronounced as a long *a* sound. Remember the smaller word *eat* at the end of the word *great*.

43. The word *thanked* ends in the suffix 'ed'.

44. The word *tomorrow* starts with the small word *to*.

45. When adding the suffix 'ing' to *ride* you need to drop the final *e*.

46. *Scratch* has a silent *t*.

47. *Quickly* has the digraph 'ck'. Two consonants make a single sound.

48. *Wednesday* has a silent *d*.

49. *Couldn't* is a contraction. The apostrophe marks the place of the missing letter *o*.

50. *Everywhere* is tricky. Remember the *e*.

NUMERACY   Pages 146–151

1 B 2 40 3 12 cm 4 A 5 D 6 Angus, Billy, Con, Max
7 A 8 928 9 B 10 D 11 5 12 8 13 C 14 A, C, E
15 C 16 809, 835, 840, 853 17 A 18 D 19 C 20 A,
D 21 C 22 A 23 4 24 C 25 65 26 B 27 60
28 March, April, May, August 29 33, 23, 13, 3 30 A
31 103 32 B 33 D 34 5, 20 35 D 36 A

EXPLANATIONS

1. The longer hand is pointing to 9. This means it is a quarter to the hour. The hour hand is pointing to just before 6 so it is a quarter to six.

2. 15, 20, 25, 30, 35, ?
The numbers are counting by 5s.
35 + 5 = 40
So the next number is 40.

3. The tip of the pencil is at the 12 cm mark on the ruler. The other end is at 0. So the pencil is 12 cm long.

4. Each cat picture means 1 cat. So 2 pictures will mean 2 cats.
There are 2 cat pictures for Dave so Dave will have 2 cats.

Number of cats

Key
🐱 = 1 cat

Ali   Dave   Penny   Sophie

5. 762 = 7 hundreds, 6 tens and 2 ones.
So 762 = 700 + 60 + 2.

6 Angus is the tallest. Then comes Billy. Next is Con and then Max.

Angus Billy Con Max

7 There are 5 rows of stamps. There are 6 stamps in each row. Sally could work out the total number of stamps by adding 6 + 6 + 6 + 6 + 6 or by multiplying 5 × 6.

8 Nine hundred and twenty-eight has 9 hundreds, 2 tens and 8 ones. It is 928.

9 Imagine the card flipped over the dotted line.

After the flip the card looked like this:

10 Triangles have 3 sides.

Tess drew 4 triangles.

11 28 + 7 = 28 + 2 + 5 = 30 + 5

12 Divide the plants into 2 equal parts. Meg put 8 plants in the garden.

13 A cone has a circle at one end and comes to a point at the other end. This is a cone.

14 The bathroom scales, kitchen scales and balance scales are all used to measure mass.

15 Count the cubes in each shape.

 9   8

10  7

The object made from 10 cubes is made from the most cubes.

16 All the numbers have 8 hundreds. So compare the tens. The numbers have 3 tens, 5 tens, 0 tens and 4 tens. The smallest number has 0 tens and the next smallest has 3 tens. The largest number has 5 tens. So, in order from lowest to highest, the numbers are 809, 835, 840 and 853.

17 15 March is a Thursday.

March						
Sunday	Monday	Tuesday	Wednesday	Thursday	Friday	Saturday
				1	2	3
4	5	6	7	8	9	10
11	12	13	14	15	16	17
18	19	20	21	22	23	24
25	26	27	28	29	30	31

18 The arrow is being turned through a quarter turn in an anticlockwise direction.

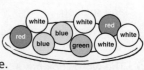

19 There are no yellow marbles in the dish. So, it is impossible to get a yellow marble.

20 Count the faces on each object.

5 faces   6 faces   6 faces   5 faces

The objects that have exactly 5 faces are the square-based pyramid and the triangular prism.

21 Mia has a $2 coin and a $1 coin. Together they make $3. She also has a 50c coin, two 20c coins and a 10c coin. Together they make another dollar. That makes $4 altogether. There are two 5c coins. They add up to 10c. So Mia has $4.10.

22 The counter goes up 2 squares and right 3 squares.

23 $2 \times 6 = 12$
Now $3 \times 4 = 12$.
So the missing number is 4.

24 There are 5 plates and each has 3 cakes. So the number of cakes needed altogether is 5 lots of 3 cakes.

25 Number of pencils $= 23 + 42$
$= 65$

26 One-quarter means one of four equal parts. The shape with one-quarter shaded is

27 There are 3 piles of 20 coins.
Number of coins $= 20 + 20 + 20$
$= 60$

28 In order, the months of the year are January, February, March, April, May, June, July, August, September, October, November and December. So March is the first of the given months, followed by April, May and August.

29 53, 43, …
The numbers are going down by 10 each time.
So the next number is $43 - 10 = 33$.
The number after that is $33 - 10 = 23$.
Then $23 - 10 = 13$.
and finally $13 - 10 = 3$.
The numbers to write in the boxes are 33, 23, 13 and 3.

30 Alice won 3 stars.
Now $3 + 4 = 7$.
Tom won 7 stars.
So Tom won 4 more stars than Alice.

Name	Number of stars
Alice	☆☆☆
Manu	☆☆☆☆☆
Susan	☆☆☆☆☆☆☆
Rosie	☆☆☆☆☆☆
Tom	☆☆☆☆☆☆☆

31 $68 + 35 = 68 + 2 + 33$
$= 70 + 33$
$= 103$

32 I might be going to the park.

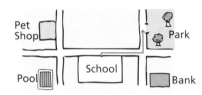

33 There is a group of 5 tally marks plus 3 more tally marks for red. As $5 + 3 = 8$, there are 8 red cars.

Colour of cars	
Colour	Tally
White	~~||||~~ ~~||||~~	
Red	~~||||~~ |||
Blue	||||
Silver	~~||||~~ ||
Black	~~||||~~
Other	|||

34 There are 5 groups of 4 stars.

$5 \times 4 = 20$

35 The spinner that has the largest space for 2 is most likely to stop on 2.

36 The marbles are divided into 4 shares.
Each boy will get 7 marbles.

SAMPLE TEST 2

LITERACY—WRITING   Page 152

Tick each correct point.
Read the student's work through once to get an overall view of their response. Then read the text a second time to consider each of the ten assessment criteria below. The same criteria are used to assess the NAPLAN Writing Task. Not all criteria will be evident in any piece of writing. You may choose to focus on one or two areas only when giving feedback to the student.

Audience
- ☐ Does the text engage an audience?
- ☐ Does it draw the reader in?
- ☐ Are the writer's values evident?

Text structure
- ☐ Is there an introduction to define the topic or outline the writer's stance?
- ☐ Are there reasons and elaboration?
- ☐ Does the conclusion draw together the arguments?
- ☐ Is there a recommendation or a call to action?

Ideas
- ☐ Are the ideas well thought through?
- ☐ Does the writer show understanding of wider implications or only personal implications?
- ☐ Are ideas logical?
- ☐ Has the writer thought deeply about the topic or only superficially?

Persuasive devices
- ☐ Does the writer persuade through reason and logic?
- ☐ Which words present the writer's point of view?
- ☐ Are opinions presented as facts?
- ☐ Does the writer make an emotional appeal?
- ☐ Are the arguments supported by facts?
- ☐ Does the text include high modality statements?
- ☐ Are auxiliary verbs and modal adverbs used (e.g. must, should, absolutely, definitely)?

Vocabulary
- ☐ Are technical terms used?
- ☐ Are noun groups used effectively to label issues and content?

- ☐ Is a range of thinking verbs used to express opinions (e.g. think, believe, recognise, hope)?

Cohesion
- ☐ Are reference chains consistent (e.g. school—it)?
- ☐ Are arguments linked logically using connectives (e.g. therefore, because, so)?
- ☐ Is there repetition for emphasis or reinforcement?

Paragraphing
- ☐ Are paragraphs sequenced logically?
- ☐ Is each paragraph based on a main idea with supporting detail?

Sentence structure
- ☐ Are sentences grammatically correct and meaningful?
- ☐ Does the writer use a range of appropriate sentence types?
- ☐ Does the writer vary sentence length for emphasis if appropriate?

Punctuation
- ☐ Is punctuation accurate for sentence beginnings and endings, commas, contractions, exclamations, and proper nouns?

Spelling
- ☐ Is the spelling accurate?
- ☐ Have attempts been made to spell unknown words?
- ☐ Are the attempts phonetically correct or readable?
- ☐ Do the writer's attempts to spell unknown words demonstrate understanding of spelling?
- ☐ Does the student spell simple, common, difficult and challenging words correctly?

Marker's suggestions (optional)

LITERACY—READING   Pages 153–159

Go to **page 212** for a guide to question types.

Bullying
1 D   2 B   3 B   4 A   5 D

EXPLANATIONS

1 This is a **fact-finding type of question**. The answer is a fact in the text. You read *Bullies can hurt you physically by hitting, pushing or tripping you* (see lines 3–4).

2 This is an **inferring type of question**. To work out the answer you have to 'read between the lines'. You read *They* [bullies] *might say nasty things to you or they might say hurtful things about you to others* (see lines 6–8). You can work out that this includes 'calling you names'.

3 This is a **fact-finding type of question**. The answer is a fact in the text. You read *Bullying can also happen through technology … This is called cyberbullying* (see lines 12–14).

4 This is a **fact-finding type of question**. The answer is a fact in the text. You read *If you are being bullied, you need to tell someone* (see line 16).

5 This is a **fact-finding type of question**. The answer is a fact in the text. You read *This means not letting you join in with games or other activities. If it happens often it is bullying* (see lines 9–10).

How to make a worm farm
6 B, E, F   7 C   8 C   9 B   10 B   11 C

EXPLANATIONS

6 This is a **fact-finding type of question**. The answer is a fact in the text. You read *Feed your worms kitchen waste … No oranges, lemons or raw onions* (see line 19).

7 This is a **fact-finding type of question**. The answer is a fact in the text. You read *Mix worm wee with water for use in your garden* (see line 21).

8 This is a **fact-finding type of question**. The answer is a fact in the text. You read *Place a brick in the bottom box so that if worms do fall through, they won't drown* (see lines 15–16).

9 This is a **fact-finding type of question**. The answer is a fact in the text. You read *Add worms that you have bought from a nursery* (see lines 12–13).

10 This is a **fact-finding type of question**. The answer is a fact in the text. You read *Add shredded newspaper, soaked in water, for worm bedding* (see lines 11–12).

11 This is a **fact-finding type of question**. The answer is a fact in the text. You read *Keep your worm farm in the shade* (see line 18).

The Greater Bilby
12 D   13 C   14 C   15 B   16 D   17 B, D

EXPLANATIONS

12 This is a **fact-finding type of question**. The answer is a fact in the text. You read *foxes and feral cats attack and eat bilbies* (see line 6).

13 This is a **language type of question**. To work out the answer you have to read the text carefully. You read *Bilbies eat seeds, fruit, bulbs, termites and other insects, as well as spiders* (see lines 10–11). Combine this information with your own knowledge of word meanings to work out that bilbies eat plants and animals.

14 This is an **inferring type of question**. To work out the answer you have to 'read between the lines'. You read *Female bilbies have backwards-facing pouches. This is so dirt doesn't get in the pouch when they are digging and harm the bilby babies* (see lines 14–16). You can work out that the newborn bilbies live in the pouch.

15 This is a **fact-finding type of question**. The answer is a fact in the text. You read *feral rabbits eat the same foods as bilbies* (see line 5).

16 This is a **fact-finding type of question**. The answer is a fact in the text. You read *Its inner ears are pink and so are its feet* (see line 8).

17 This is a **fact-finding type of question**. The answer is a fact in the text. You read *Bilbies dig deep burrows to keep safe from predators and to keep cool on hot desert days* (see lines 12–13).

Class discussion
18 B   19 A   20 A   21 B   22 C   23 D

EXPLANATIONS

18 This is a **fact-finding type of question**. The answer is a fact in the text. You read *Lily: I loved the painting by Ian Abdulla, 'Swimming before school'* (see lines 7–9).

19 This is a **fact-finding type of question**. The answer is a fact in the text. You read *Selina: I liked it because I could walk around it* (see lines 20–21).

20 This is an **inferring type of question**. To work out the answer you have to 'read between the lines'. You read that Ralph says … *where can the bats go if there are no trees?* (see lines 27–28). You can work out that he means that bats need to use the clothes lines because they have to hang somewhere.

21 This is a **language type of question**. To work out the answer you have to read the text carefully. You read *My mum says fruit bats are really important for forests. Bats spread plant seeds and pollen* (see lines 28–31). *How* is the question word that is important. By reading the text you can find the answer that bats help forests by spreading *plant seeds and pollen*.

22 This is a **fact-finding type of question**. The answer is a fact in the text. You read that Julia said *I liked the wooden disks that were the bats' droppings* (see lines 33–34).

23 This is a **synthesis type of question**. To work out the answer you have to read the whole text. You read discussion about people not liking bats *in their garden* but that *bats are really important for forests* (see lines 26–30). You read the sculpture was also *about Aboriginal culture* (see lines 37–38).

From this discussion you can recognise that the sculpture represents the artist's view that all people and animals need to share the environment.

African child

24 B 25 A 26 A 27 D 28 B 29 D

EXPLANATIONS

24 This is a **fact-finding type of question**. The answer is a fact in the text. You read *Mariama was worried about the boys. They were so skinny and so sick (see lines 12–13)*.

25 This is a **fact-finding type of question**. The answer is a fact in the text. You read *She needed to hurry. She had to fetch the water and take it home before she could go to school (see lines 2–4)*.

26 This is an **inferring type of question**. To work out the answer you have to 'read between the lines'. You read the clue as to why the well was dry at the end of paragraph 1: *… there had been little food for months, since the drought (see line 8)*. From this you can work out that the drought dried up the water in the well.

27 This is a **fact-finding type of question**. The answer is a fact in the text. You read *They had been drinking dirty water and they had diarrhoea (see line 10)*.

28 This is an **inferring type of question**. To work out the answer you have to 'read between the lines'. You read there *had been little food for months, since the drought (see line 8)*. You can work out from this that Mariama was hungry because there wasn't enough food.

29 This is a **fact-finding type of question**. The answer is a fact in the text. You read *her friend was taken by a lion (see line 16)*.

Children spend too much time on computers

30 C 31 D 32 A 33 B 34 B 35 D

EXPLANATIONS

30 This is a **language type of question**. To work out the answer you have to read the text carefully. You read *it's important to balance computer use with other activities (see lines 16–17)*. This means that you can spend time on the computer as long as you spend time off the computer as well, doing things like sport.

31 This is a **fact-finding type of question**. The answer is a fact in the text. You read *I think computers are good for children (see line 9)*.

32 This is a **fact-finding type of question**. The answer is a fact in the text. You read *You have to sit correctly so you don't hurt your back (see lines 22–23)*.

33 This is an **inferring type of question**. To work out the answer you have to 'read between the lines'. You read *You need to think about being safe online (see lines 24–25)*. You also read *Don't post personal information online (see lines 28–29)*. *Personal information* means things like addresses and phone numbers. So you can work out from this that being safe online means not telling strangers where you live.

34 This is a **fact-finding type of question**. The answer is a fact in the text. You read that children should spend time *having fun outdoors (see lines 18–19)*.

35 This is a **language type of question**. To work out the answer you have to read the text carefully. You read *You need to think about being safe online: don't chat with people you don't know or who your family doesn't know. Don't post things like photos online. Don't post personal information online (see lines 24–29)*. This list of online safety risks includes <u>all</u> the options <u>except</u> straining your back. From this you can work out that straining your back is <u>not</u> an online safety risk.

Our edible school garden

36 A 37 C 38 B 39 D

EXPLANATIONS

36 This is a **fact-finding type of question**. The answer is a fact in the text. You read *We are learning about environmental stewardship. This means taking care of the earth (see lines 8–9)*.

37 This is a **fact-finding type of question**. The answer is a fact in the text. You read *The money will help us buy organic fertilisers, worms, seeds and weed mats (see line 12)*.

38 This is a **fact-finding type of question**. The answer is a fact in the text. You read *We enjoy eating the foods we grow ourselves (see line 7)*.

39 This is a **fact-finding type of question**. The answer is a fact in the text. You read *Organic gardeners don't use any chemicals (see line 14)*.

LITERACY—CONVENTIONS OF LANGUAGE
Pages 160–163

GRAMMAR AND PUNCTUATION

1 C 2 A 3 B 4 D 5 D 6 B 7 C 8 B 9 A 10 B
11 C 12 B 13 D 14 D 15 B 16 B 17 B 18 C
19 C 20 B 21 A 22 C 23 B 24 A 25 D

SPELLING

26 was   27 squashed   28 quit   29 emergency
30 dangerous   31 twice   32 police   33 choice
34 dance   35 clock   36 teachers   37 ponies
38 helpless   39 ginger   40 white   41 nose
42 sleep   43 fluffier   44 fairies   45 disappeared
46 loaves   47 alarm   48 Climb   49 I'm   50 raincoat

EXPLANATIONS

1 Adjectives are words that describe. *Yellow* describes the dress.

2 *Ellie loves bananas* is the only option with a verb: *loves*. A complete sentence must have a verb.

3 *Because* connects the reason *he was hungry* to the event *George ate all the cherries*.

4 Nouns are names for people, places, animals and things. The noun is *apples*. It is a plural noun.

5 *An* is used when a noun starts with a vowel sound: *an insect*.

6 *Tom invited Lisa, Ben, Jai and Sachar to his party.* Commas are used between items in a list, but not before *and*.

7 The correct answer is the past-tense verb *swam*. For the other answers to be correct, helper verbs are needed (e.g. will swim, did swim, is swimming, has swum).

8 The present-tense verb *drawing* shows that the action is ongoing and not fixed in the past.

9 *Because* is used to connect ideas through reason or cause and effect.

10 *After* is used to connect events in a time sequence. *We'll visit Gran <u>after</u> we wash the car.*
None of the other connectives make sense.

11 *Although* connects events logically in the sentence. The connective has to make sense.

12 *They* is a pronoun that refers to two people: *Jenny and Leanne*.

13 *Well* is an adverb. Adverbs can modify verbs such as *played* by telling HOW.

14 Words that tell how often end in **ly**. *Carefully* tells how to hold the baby.

15 *The children* can replace the plural pronoun *They* in this sentence.

16 *Those* is the correct answer. *These* implies something close to the speaker. *Those* is used for something further away.

17 When comparing two things, the one-syllable adjective *short* takes the form ending in 'er', *shorter*.

18 *One* is used to replace *puppy*. *One* is a reference word in this sentence.

19 The only sentence which includes all the important information is: *The noisy baby magpies squawk for food all day.*

20 *Should have* is correct. *Of* is a preposition. It can't be used in a verb group with *should*.

21 *Full* is an absolute adjective. It cannot compare. Something is either full, half full or nearly full. It cannot be 'fuller' or 'more full'.

22 *Him* is a pronoun that can replace the male proper noun *Jack*.

23 The contraction *we'll* stands for *we will*. The apostrophe marks the place of missing letters **w** and **i**.

24 It is only the speech marks that differ in each sentence. The correct punctuation is: *"Where's my hat?" asked Fillipo.* Speech marks belong outside and around what was said and the question mark.

25 The correct answer is *"Stop!" shouted the police officer.* Speech marks belong outside and around what was said and the exclamation mark.

26 *Was* is a common word that needs to be learned by sight rather than trying to sound it out.

27 *Squashed* has a 'qu' which makes the 'kw' sound. Note that it also has the 'sh' digraph.

28 *Quit* has a 'qu' which makes the 'kw' sound.

29 *Emergency* makes a soft **g** sound because the **g** is followed by **e**. It has the soft **c** sound because the **c** is followed by **y**.

30 *Dangerous* has a soft **g** because the **g** is followed by **e**.

31 *Twice* has a soft **c** because **c** is followed by **e**.

32 *Police* has a soft **c** because **c** is followed by **e**.

33 *Choice* has a soft **c** in the middle because the **c** is followed by **e**. Note that *choice* starts with the digraph 'ch'.

34 *Dance* has a soft **c** because the **c** is followed by **e**.

35 *Clock* ends in the consonant digraph 'ck'. It starts with a hard **c**.

36 *Teacher* ends in the suffix 'er'. Add **s** to make the word plural: *teachers*.

37 The singular word *pony* changes **y** to **i** to add 'es' for the plural, *ponies*.

38 *Helpless* has the suffix 'less', which means 'without.'

39 Each **g** in *ginger* is soft because **g** is followed by **i** or **e**.

40 *White* has the consonant digraph 'wh' and a long **i** sound because of the silent **e** at the end of the word.

41 *Nose* has a long **o** vowel sound caused by the silent **e** at the end of the word. The **s** makes a sound like **z**.

42 *Sleep* has the vowel digraph 'ee' which makes a long **e** sound. The same 'ee' spelling can be found in *sheep, peep, deep, cheep* and *seep*.

43 *Fluffier* is an adjective that compares two things. To add the suffix 'er' to *fluffy* you first need to change the **y** to **i**.

44 *Fairies* is a plural noun. The singular word *fairy* changes **y** to **i** before adding 'es' to form the plural, *fairies*.

45 *Disappeared* has the prefix 'dis' before the word *appear*. 'Dis' is a prefix that makes words opposite in meaning. *Disappeared* has a suffix 'ed' to tell you it happened in the past.

46 The singular *loaf* changes **f** to **v** to form the plural, *loaves*.

47 *Alarm* has the vowel-consonant pair 'ar'.

48 *Climb* has a silent **b**.

49 *I'm* is a contraction for *I am*. The apostrophe takes the place of the missing letter **a**.

50 *Raincoat* has the vowel digraphs 'oa' and 'ai'. *Raincoat* is a compound word. A compound word is a word made up of two other words. Other examples of compound words include *football, playground, classroom* and *sunshine*.

NUMERACY   Pages 164–169

1 D   2 B   3 B   4 A   5 7   6 304   7 A   8 8   9 C
10 D   11 12   12 2   13 C   14 B   15 A   16 C, D   17 20
18 B   19 36   20 D   21 2350, 2503, 3025, 3205, 5032, 5230
22 A   23 17   24 20   25 7   26 13   27 D   28 C   29 A
30 C   31 C, E   32 D   33 D   34 B   35 C   36 C

EXPLANATIONS

1 Bob has a $2 coin and a $1 coin. This is a total of $3.
He has a 50c coin, a 20c coin and a 5c coin.
50 + 20 + 5 = 75
So Bob has $3.75.

2 At a quarter past ten, the big hand will point to 3 as that is a quarter past the hour. The small hand will be a quarter of the way past 10.

3 Count the coloured squares.
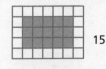
15

16

12

13

The shape that has the most squares coloured is

4

The shape at B3 is

5 By counting there are 12 balloons.
Blake keeps 5 balloons.
Now 12 − 5 = 7.
So Blake gave 7 balloons to Riley.

6 Three hundred and four has 3 hundreds, 0 tens and 4 ones.
It is the number 304.

7 The object most like a cylinder is the can of tuna.

cylinder   cone   rectangular prism   triangular prism

8 Each picture means 2 students.

Favourite colours

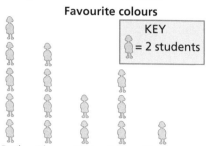

KEY
= 2 students

Red   Blue   Pink   Green   Yellow

Blue has 4 pictures. Counting by twos that means 8 students.

9 Imagine each triangle flipped over the dotted line.

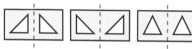

The triangle that will look the same is

10 Count the number of pins in each box.

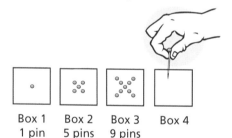

Box 1   Box 2   Box 3   Box 4
1 pin   5 pins   9 pins

Each box has 4 extra pins.
Now 9 + 4 = 13.
So 13 pins will go in Box 4.

Box 4

11 By counting, Ben has 6 nails left. He must have had another 6 in the packet.

6 + 6 = 12 so the packet had 12 nails.

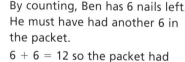

12 Triangles have exactly 3 sides. Molly used 2 triangles.

13 There are four different shapes that are repeating in the pattern.

The shape that comes after the diamond is the large circle.
So the next shape will be the large circle.

14 4 + 300 + 70 = 300 + 70 + 4
There are 3 hundreds, 7 tens and 4 ones.
So the answer is 374.

15 The solid has 10 faces.
There are 8 faces around the sides plus the top face and the bottom face.

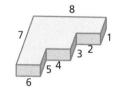

16 The longer the bar the more animals there are.

Pets owned by students

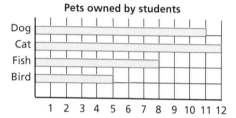

So there are more cats than fish.
There are more dogs than birds.
There are more dogs than fish.
There are more cats than birds.
The true statements are that there are more dogs than fish and there are fewer birds than cats.

17 The tower is 5 rows high.
There are 4 blocks in every row.
The number of blocks is 5 × 4 = 20.

18 The shape is being turned a quarter of a turn each time.

The next shape will be

19 49 + 37 = 49 + 1 + 36 = 50 + 36

20 Each carton holds 12 eggs.
So Dan needs to know how many lots of 12 there are in 60.
So Dan needs 60 ÷ 12.

21 First look at the first digits.
2503 and 2350 both have 2 thousands so they are the two smallest numbers.
Then look at the second digits of those numbers.
2503 has 5 hundreds while 2350 has 3 hundreds. So 2350 is the smallest number and 2503 is the second smallest number.

Of the other numbers, two have 3 thousands and two have 5 thousands.

So the next two numbers are 3205 and 3025 in some order. 3205 has 2 hundreds while 3025 has no hundreds. 3025 is the smaller of those two numbers.

The two largest numbers are 5032 and 5230. The largest of those is 5230 because it has two hundreds and 5032 has none.

So, in order from lowest to highest, the numbers are 2350, 2503, 3025, 3205, 5032, 5230.

22 Alex, Joe, Mai and Rose are in the back row. Alex is on the left and Rose on the right.

The person who is second from the left is Joe.

23 5, 8, 11, 14, ?
The numbers are going up by 3 each time.
As 14 + 3 = 17 the next number must be 17.

24 There are 4 rows.
There are 5 cars in each row.
So the number of cars altogether is
5 + 5 + 5 + 5 or 4 × 5 which is 20.

25 Emma spent 12 days at the beach.
Marc spent 5 days at the beach.

Name	Number of days
Steve	7
Jo	4
Emma	12
Ellen	1
Marc	5

Now 12 − 5 = 7.
So, Emma spent 7 more days at the beach than Marc.

26 17 + 13 = 30
The number must be 13.

27 Zac is now in Wattle Street.

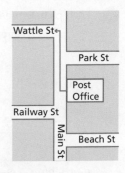

28 Try each pattern by adding 5 each time.
- 5, 10, 20, 40, 80, …
  5 + 5 = 10 but 10 + 5 = 15 not 20.
  This is not the pattern.
- 5, 11, 17, 23, 29, …
  5 + 5 = 10 not 11 so this is not the pattern.
- 6, 11, 16, 21, 26, …
  6 + 5 = 11
  11 + 5 = 16
  16 + 5 = 21
  21 + 5 = 26
  This is the pattern.
- 55, 50, 45, 40, 35, …
  The numbers go down by 5 not up, so this is not the pattern.
- The pattern is 6, 11, 16, 21, 26, …

29 There are 3 $1 coins, 6 20c coins and 3 5c coins. So each girl will get one $1 coin, two 20c coins and one 5c coin.

Each girl will get $1.45.

30 1, 8, 15, ?, 29, 36
The numbers are going up by 7 each time.
1 + 7 = 8 and 8 + 7 = 15
15 + 7 = 22 and 22 + 7 = 29
The missing number is 22.

31 The number on the dice could be 1, 2, 3, 4, 5 or 6.

So, it must be less than 7 and it must be 1 or more.

(It cannot be less than 1. It **might** be 6, and it **could** be more than 2; but those are not outcomes that **must** occur.)

32 One-quarter is one of four equal parts. Try each choice.

This has one of four parts shaded but the parts are not equal. This is not the shape.

This has one of five parts shaded so it is not the shape.

This has two of four equal parts shaded. This is not the shape.

This has two of eight equal parts or one of four equal parts. This is the shape.

33 One week after 13 August is 20 August and a week after that is 27 August.

AUGUST						
Sunday	Monday	Tuesday	Wednesday	Thursday	Friday	Saturday
						1
2	3	4	5	6	7	8
9	10	11	12	13	14	15
16	17	18	19	20	21	22
23	24	25	26	27	28	29
30	31	1	2	3		

The month after August is September. If you fill in the dates for the first few days of September you can see that three weeks after 13 August is 3 September.

34 … 56, 57, 58, 59, 60, 61, 62, 63, 64, …
Of the choices, the number closest to 60 is 59.

35 Two cards show 4, one shows 6 and one shows 2. The number 266 is impossible because there is only one 6.

36 Take ◯ from each balance.

So ◯ balances 3 ▢

To the teacher or parent

Read the word clearly to the student. Then read the sentence with the word in it to the student. Then read the word again.

Give the student time to write an answer. If the student is not sure of the spelling tell them to make their best attempt but that it is okay to skip a word if they cannot attempt a guess.

Spelling words for Real Test Week 1

Word	Example
1. careful	Be careful with the kitten.
2. huge	The emu's egg is huge.
3. dangerous	It's dangerous to ride a bike without a helmet.
4. giant	The Giant Tree Frog lives in treetops.
5. cancel	We need to cancel the trip.
6. juice	Make some carrot juice.
7. exercise	Regular exercise is important.
8. spicy	This curry is too spicy.
9. cicadas	Male cicadas sing.
10. bucket	Jack and Jill carried the bucket.
11. elephant	The elephant was bigger than me.
12. sock	Pick up the dirty sock.
13. chicken	Do you like your chicken dinner?
14. dragon	My story is about a fire-breathing dragon.
15. back	Mum will drive me back to school after soccer.
16. fudge	I asked Dad to make chocolate fudge.
17. going	I am going to see the dentist tomorrow.
18. alphabet	There are twenty-six letters in the alphabet.

Spelling words for Real Test Week 2

Word	Example
1. climb	"Climb down from the tree," called Dad.
2. knuckles	The gorilla's knuckles scraped on the ground.
3. scent	The dog followed the scent of the cat.
4. who	Who wants to play chess?
5. Wednesday	I get my new reading glasses on Wednesday.
6. could	I wish I could go to Jenna's after school.
7. autumn	Some trees lose their leaves in autumn.
8. island	I borrowed a book about Kangaroo Island.
9. knitting	Ya-ya is knitting the baby a jumper.
10. knee	Grandpa said his knee is sore.
11. ghost	I dressed up as a ghost for Halloween.
12. comb	Please use a comb to tidy your hair.
13. sword	King Arthur is said to have pulled a sword from a stone.
14. know	Do you know what time the movie starts?
15. squeal	I heard the brakes on the car squeal.
16. listen	You must listen to the instructions.
17. scratch	Be gentle or the cat will scratch you.
18. steel	Recycle steel cans.

SPELLING WORDS FOR REAL TESTS

To the teacher or parent

Read the word clearly to the student. Then read the sentence with the word in it to the student. Then read the word again.

Give the student time to write an answer. If the student is not sure of the spelling tell them to make their best attempt but that it is okay to skip a word if they cannot attempt a guess.

Spelling words for Real Test Week 3

Word	Example
1. cake	Lee and I cooked a cake for Mum's birthday.
2. hope	We hope to see you soon.
3. made	I only made one mistake in the test.
4. make	Let's make a fruit salad.
5. use	Use your brain in the test.
6. prize	Ben won a prize for spelling.
7. home	I walked home from school.
8. bite	Be kind to animals or they might bite you.
9. time	It's time for bed.
10. tube	Put the lid on the tube of toothpaste.
11. kite	Dad and I flew the kite today.
12. gate	Please shut the gate.
13. smile	You have a lovely smile.
14. doesn't	Our teacher doesn't like us to talk during a test.
15. quarrel	Sometimes I quarrel with my sister.
16. don't	I don't like to eat squishy bananas.
17. rope	Hold the rope as you climb.
18. Saturday	I will do gym this Saturday.

Spelling words for Real Test Week 4

Word	Example
1. potatoes	Li chopped the potatoes for dinner.
2. tomatoes	Maya put lots of tomatoes in the salad.
3. cherries	I love cherries.
4. women	Ten women attended the meeting.
5. feet	Both of my feet hurt after the race.
6. babies	All the babies cried at the same time.
7. mangoes	The fruit shop sells nice mangoes.
8. sheep	Five sheep ran to the fence.
9. benches	Boys and girls sat on separate benches.
10. teeth	The dentist looked at my teeth today.
11. dingoes	The dingoes ran around the bush at dusk.
12. geese	The geese waddled next to the creek.
13. mice	The mice ate all the cheese.
14. races	I went in a number of races at the sports carnival.
15. helpless	The duckling was helpless against the current.
16. loaves	We bought two loaves of bread for the picnic.
17. respectful	Dad said to be respectful of people's opinions.
18. whales	The pod of whales swam along the coast.

Excel Revise in a Month Year 2 NAPLAN*-style Tests

SPELLING WORDS FOR SAMPLE TESTS

To the teacher or parent

Read the word clearly to the student. Then read the sentence with the word in it to the student. Then read the word again.

Give the student time to write an answer. If the student is not sure of the spelling tell them to make their best attempt but that it is okay to skip a word if they cannot attempt a guess.

Spelling words for Sample Test 1

Word	Example
26. school	Jack missed school on Monday.
27. gave	We gave the tomatoes to Peter.
28. mail	Jordan collected the mail from the letterbox.
29. camels	Early explorers rode camels in the desert.
30. birthday	Mina's birthday is in May.
31. locked	The door was locked.
32. thanked	The teacher thanked the parents for visiting.
33. three	Gemma made three mistakes in the spelling test.
34. bucket	The children collected water in a bucket.
35. might	We might go swimming later.
36. photo	Sara had a photo of her grandparents.
37. blue	The sky is a lovely blue today.
38. went	Mum and Greg went into the kitchen.
39. cook	Greg wanted to cook spaghetti for dinner.
40. made	Greg made a lot of noise.

Spelling words for Sample Test 2

Word	Example
26. was	Leo asked when the movie was going to start.
27. squashed	The banana got squashed in my bag.
28. quit	Dad quit the football team when he hurt his knee.
29. emergency	Call 000 in an emergency.
30. dangerous	It's dangerous to climb on the roof.
31. twice	Helen ran around the oval twice.
32. police	We saw police horses in the parade.
33. choice	The class had a choice of tee-ball or cricket.
34. dance	Jake is learning to dance hip-hop.
35. clock	The clock showed the wrong time.
36. teachers	The teachers had a meeting before school.
37. ponies	The Shetland ponies were small and cute.
38. helpless	The smallest kitten looked so helpless.
39. ginger	The kitten was ginger in colour.
40. white	The kitten had white feet.

Notes